Trilingual by Six

Trilingual by Six

THE SANE WAY TO RAISE INTELLIGENT, TALENTED CHILDREN

• • •

Lennis Dippel MD

→ dajcie pro
hiszpański,
→ hiszpańskie! przedszkole
→ polskie szkole
→ polska Pani z
Korny
→ Polskie Mamie:
playdate, Peanut.

ISBN-13: 9780692587713
ISBN-10: 0692587713
Library of Congress Control Number: 2015920049
Lennis Dippel, San Antonio, TX

Table of Contents

CHAPTER 1

Multilingualism for Ordinary Kids

● ● ●

Two things professional educators don't really want you to know:

1. If your children aren't multilingual by age 6, they probably never will be.
2. If your children are taught to read at age 4, some happier child who didn't learn until age 7 will probably surpass them by about the 4th grade.

This just might mean that much of the preschool education we buy is a waste of good money. Maybe it also means that high school and college language courses are a colossal waste of time. (Do you remember it that way?) It tells you that when you see those pricey language-learning products at your local bookstore, maybe you should just keep right on walking. Most importantly, it means that if you want your infant or toddler to be fluent in Spanish, French, or Chinese one day...you'd better not dilly-dally around!

In Papua New Guinea—where the Stone Age is at least a living memory, if not a present-day reality, and the literacy rate is only about 65%—it's common to find tribal villagers who speak five or more languages fluently. In fact, multilingualism may still be more common than literacy in that country. In the United States, on the other hand, where we spend billions of dollars annually on foreign-language education, it's pretty uncommon for mainstream public-school students to actually become fluent in even a second language. For any parent willing to consider raising multilingual children, this raises a set of perplexing questions. It might also open up some very exciting possibilities.

How do the villagers do it? Why can't we? Do they know some ancient secret that we've forgotten? Are false assumptions permeating our educational system, our scientific theories, and our social structure? Having watched my own children become fluent in multiple languages in an ordinary American setting, the answers to these questions seem embarrassingly obvious. Shortly after her first birthday, my oldest daughter became multilingual as if by accident, without my permission, without even consulting me first.

Could be you're already following me here. It's not what we don't know; it's what we *think* we *do* know that holds us back—our false assumptions. Before I show you how to raise trilingual children, I'll need to deconstruct those for you. Maybe you've heard this one already: What do you call someone who speaks three languages? Trilingual. What do you call someone who speaks two languages? Bilingual. What do you call someone who speaks one language? American. In the most linguistically diverse nation the planet has ever seen, most of us who grew up in the United States speak just a single language. In some circles, we may find ourselves the brunt of a lot of jokes. Perhaps they leave us feeling a little insecure. Maybe we really are less intelligent than people in other countries. Maybe we're just spoiled and lazy.

As far as I'm concerned, it's none of those. It's just that our approach to learning additional languages is, quite frankly, all wrong. I'd like to think that we could tweak our educational system just a little. The United States could be just as multilingual as many other countries, but old habits die hard, and frozen bureaucracies move only at a glacial pace. I'm not sure that anything new will happen within a convenient time frame for you and your children. Thus, if you want to give your children this educational advantage, you might have to take matters into your own hands. You would have a high chance of success; it really isn't terribly difficult to raise trilingual children. Don't let anyone tell you otherwise.

However, it is important to start as early in life as you possibly can. That's actually controversial, but as far as I'm concerned, you shouldn't allow yourself to believe otherwise. Historically, American children who attempt to learn a new language in high school, in a classroom setting, the way we've always done it, have a success rate lower than 1%. Everything else you might like your children to learn in life will probably wait until the school years, but languages will not.

The most famous linguist the world has ever known is a guy by the name of Noam Chomsky. Supposedly, only Jesus Christ has been quoted more often. Several decades ago, he theorized the existence of a "language acquisition device" that virtually every human brain has during the early years of life. Though not all scientists accept the theory, it has remained a very popular explanation for why children learn languages so well. Basically, it's a survival instinct. From a very early point in life, children have always needed to communicate with other humans just to stay alive. Since newborns never get to choose where they will be born, their brains are equipped with all the tools necessary to learn any language spoken on the planet. Inside the brain, all human languages are viewed as having some fundamental common form, and learning to speak any one of them is just a matter of fine-tuning what we are born already knowing. Language is like an iceberg, and the fraction of it we acquire after birth is just the tip of the tip. Thus, babies and small children do not "learn" to speak a language; they just tweak their innate ability. Experience has shown that this language acquisition device can fine-tune the brain to use more than just one language if a child's surroundings warrant it. Most small children in the world grow up needing to communicate in at least two languages, and they manage to do so without much trouble at all.

But the language acquisition device doesn't stay active forever. Under ordinary circumstances, most children acquire the fundamental linguistic abilities they need by the time they are about 3 years old. While they may still need a larger vocabulary and smoother pronunciation, by this age, they have learned the basic patterns of whichever languages they will need. At this point, children no longer need the language acquisition device, and it somehow fades into oblivion. Maybe it does not suddenly disappear, but it gradually fades. The "critical period" for language learning draws to an end.

Scientists who do not accept Chomsky's theory are quick to point out that older children, even adults, are perfectly capable of learning new languages. In fact, some say they learn them faster, though I have to wonder if that claim might be a little misleading. Take the case of a Harvard freshman studying Spanish pitted against an average 2-year-old learning the same language. After 2 years, who will be speaking the language better? Why, the Harvard man, of course. Now, fast-forward 20 years. At that point, who will be speaking the language better? Most likely the toddler will have the edge. You get the basic idea. Even if children have no special instinctive language-learning ability, they have more time, more opportunity, fewer other "subjects" to study, fewer responsibilities, no romantic liaisons, no career stressors.

Adults who attempt a new language have a very poor long-term success rate. Teenagers, we've seen, are no better. In the hands of reasonably motivated parents, children probably have a success rate well over 90%. The reasons behind that difference are not necessarily important to us. If you want your children to learn languages (and learn them permanently), start early. Use the language acquisition device to your advantage. If Dr. Chomsky is correct, it's a fundamental human instinct. If he's wrong, do it anyway.

World-famous scientists with off-the-chart IQ scores like to attend international conferences where they fight like cats and dogs about these matters. Are Dr. Chomsky's theories fact or flop? Is there a critical period in life for language learning or not? Is human language an instinct or something we all just learn by imitation? For me, a father who just wants to raise multilingual children, my conclusion is, "It doesn't matter." Look beyond the trees to the forest, because getting bogged down in theoretical arguments will not make anyone a more successful trilingual parent. I've already satisfied myself that young children are superior language learners, and I think I can convince you of that too. Whether they learn them instinctively or not, whether they have a built-in language acquisition device or they don't, whether the first 3 years of life are a critical period or not, just doesn't make all that much difference. With only a little experience in raising your own multilingual children, I believe you'll come to the same conclusions. Nevertheless, because it's a useful way to conceptualize the childhood language-learning process, I give Dr. Chomsky's theory the benefit of the doubt and present it as truth. If you're a scientist, and that sort of thing annoys you, let me cross my fingers behind my back and apologize before I move on.

In terms of practical application, the science on actually raising multilingual children is incredibly sketchy. Most of what exists examines kids over the age of 3, and nearly all of it examines only bilingual children. Almost none of it has anything to say about trilingual children, so a fair amount of educated guessing is necessary. To the greatest extent possible, I've tried to base my comments on the available science, but that's not always an option. Sometimes you have to fall back on common sense. Other times, you just need a vivid imagination! When it comes to many real-world specifics, I have resorted to that—just dreaming stuff up. There is no real alternative at this point in our technical understanding. When I suggest something that I just dreamed up, I'll call your attention to that, so you can take it with a grain of salt if you like. And I'd like to point out that if you wait until science can be more helpful, your children will probably be over 100 years old.

But maybe you're not terribly scientifically inclined. Maybe you're more like a young adult renting a first apartment with a kitchen. One weekend you decide it might be fun to bake your first loaf of bread. You don't want to be a gourmet chef; just a simple recipe will do. You're not terribly interested in all the utility company infrastructure that brings electrical power to your apartment, you don't really care about the engineering that went into the design of your new oven, and you're not overly concerned about the phylogenetic classification of the grain you use in your bread. You just want to follow some simple directions, slap some butter on the finished product, and enjoy a little self-satisfaction. If it's just a recipe you want here, I'll try to give it to you. In fact, the last chapter of this book contains such a recipe. Maybe you'll need a bit of a cooking lesson beforehand, but, if not, just follow the recipe, and you should be fine. Maybe you're pretty busy, and maybe too much information would only slow you down. Feel free to skim anything you don't find helpful, but be advised, you might miss a bad joke or two if you're not giving this your full, undivided attention. (A joke, you see, is an invitation to think outside the box, and I'll ask you to do that, more than a little.)

Across the world, the recent trend has been to teach typical school subjects like math and reading to younger and younger children. About that, I'll have enough to say to make you lapse into a coma. In some instances, maybe this strategy has worked, but in others, it has failed. As we'll see, school subjects are far from instinctive and must be taught in what might fairly be described as a boring way, at least as far as little kids are concerned. Spoken languages, on the other hand, are fun and natural for little ones, unless we as adults go out of our way to make them boring or unless we delay their introduction. After puberty, languages are taught in the same dry, boring way as math and science. As often as not, our schools begin teaching new languages around that time, when they cease to be fun and easy, and I think that's a colossal mistake. It would be better to focus on languages early on and redouble our efforts to teach the traditional school subjects more diligently in the later years. In fact, across the globe, many top-performing educational systems in the most highly literate and multilingual countries do exactly that, as we'll see. But fortunately (or unfortunately, depending upon how you view it), the best language-learning years seem to be the ones well before the start of formal schooling. So schools in their traditional sense can hardly be blamed for this missed opportunity. To illustrate, there are measurable differences in proficiency between children who begin learning a language at birth and children who begin learning at about 10 months of age. Virtually no school system is designed to seize this very early opportunity. Going back even farther, into the 3rd trimester of life in the womb, which is definitely not soundproof, fetuses are listening to their mothers' conversations.[1] By the time they are born, they can already distinguish their mothers' voices from other voices. Within a few weeks, they can distinguish their mothers' languages from other languages.

If you happen to reside somewhere other than the United States, I have to apologize just a little. I've tried my best to make this book relevant, no matter where you happen to be parenting, but obviously, I know my own home system better than I know others. I think you'll find much that is helpful as you read, and I think you'll be able to apply it to your own unique situation in your own country. As I've implied, language is quite political, and circumstances vary greatly from place to place. Nevertheless, the world is rapidly becoming a more globally minded community, and daily life in each country is growing more uniform. Modern life is modern life, no matter where you are, and that will only progress, I think. Whether your setting is urban or rural, developed or primitive, you can formulate a trilingual plan for your children there.

Let me show you how.

CHAPTER 2
Unsolicited Philosophical Advice

• • •

As they say, anything worth doing, is worth doing wrong the first time. If you choose a trilingual journey for your children, be prepared for some uncertainty at the beginning, and realize that you'll probably make some mistakes. There's really no point in waiting until you have as much information as possible. You just have to take that first little step off the edge of the platform and learn to dive on your way to the water. Even if you took the time to read every single publication on raising multilingual children, you'd still be left with some really huge questions, and you'd lose a lot of valuable time. Truth is, the science on this subject has just not yet advanced to the level of practical applicability, and world-renowned researchers still disagree on even the most fundamental points. Many of them flatly admit they just don't have very many answers for parents. Life's biggest decisions are always based on insufficient information, aren't they? No need for this to be an exception.

The basic technique I want to show you here is certainly not the only way to raise multilingual children, but I happen to think it's the best. Some experts will tell you that there are perhaps thousands of ways to go about it. They might be right, but learning a little about all of them could be really confusing when it comes time to formulate your own family action plan. However, if you prefer broad, superficial overviews and you think you can figure out the vexing details on your own, any one of the other books on this topic will be right up your alley. I happen to think that anyone who begins a new endeavor needs clarity and simplicity in the beginning. Too many choices can create a real distraction. As you gain comfort with raising multilingual children, you'll figure out what works for you and what doesn't. At that point, you might want to deviate from my prescribed plan—maybe even scrap it altogether. That'll be more than OK; I'd be honored just to take credit for prodding you a little beyond your comfort zone.

Please understand that there is a difference between being a genius and being multilingual. In cultures where multilingualism is a bit of a rarity, people sometimes view it with awe. It really doesn't deserve that pedestal. By most accounts, over half of the world's population speaks at least two languages; many of these polyglots are illiterate, living in quite primitive conditions, often in abject poverty. Some will go through life never seeing the inside of a classroom or learning to read an ordinary newspaper.

Similarly, you'll need to understand that fluency and literacy are not the same thing. Where young children are concerned, there is a huge difference between speaking a language and reading or writing it. Their amazing talents are really limited to the speaking side, but here they are absolute superstars. Capitalize on that, focus on fluency, and be more patient with everything else. Learning to speak a language is time critical, but learning to read and write it is not.

Children are playful creatures, and play is more than just fun for them. Quite simply, it's the way they learn. On your trilingual journey, respect that. Don't deprive them of their primary learning tool. Unless you've already lost your magical childhood rambunctiousness, playful, everyday settings create the best environment in which to learn a new language. This might also apply to every other form of childhood learning, but it is particularly true for languages. Don't make it a chore for them; don't kill their curiosity and natural enthusiasm. Tap into their chaotic energy, and don't impose a harshly boring drillmaster regimen on them. It's possible for children to learn more language by making mud pies in the garden than by having their noses shoved into lifeless fill-in-the-blank workbooks.

As you develop realistic expectations, maintain the long view, as you'll be running a marathon, not a 100-yard dash. Don't expect perfection from the start, and don't start anything you do not intend to finish. When your children are older, don't stop the process, and don't relinquish your responsibility, or you might see your labors become undone, because, while children are superior language learners, they are also superior language forgetters. At the same time, begin looking for ways that your local school system might do some of the taskwork for you, but keep in mind that the primary responsibility for a trilingual upbringing will always be yours.

Most likely, your children will find plenty of other difficulties in life. Think of extra languages as vaccines against the afflictions and troubles they will encounter many decades down the road. Adults who speak multiple languages have an ability that cannot be taken away or squandered, something to fall back on after an exceptionally bad decision or a major disappointment. There will be times of failure, self-doubt, and other harsh realities in a sometimes unfair world. Multilingualism can always be a reason to look in the mirror and feel proud.

And always try to give your little ones a childhood they will remember fondly. Don't push too hard. Particularly where languages are concerned, it's totally unnecessary. Let their teeming energy and natural curiosity take the lead. To a frustratingly great degree, your children will develop their own talents, their own aptitudes, and (gasp) their own dislikes. Whatever future roads your little ones decide to travel down, multiple languages will complement them, enrich them. You might not persuade obstinate kids to become professional athletes, doctors, lawyers, or Indian chiefs, but they can gradually become multilingual without even realizing that they're doing it, provided, of course, that they're enjoying themselves in the process. That set of skills will enhance their lives in whatever they decide to do, long after they stop worshiping you.

In a sense, it will be your job to worry less. One of the secrets to being a successful trilingual parent is to be a little on the lazy side—sometimes. Be prepared to recruit outside help and rely on this help to get your children where you want them to be, linguistically speaking. If you provide too much direction to your helpers and become like a helicopter, you'll only make the process less fun for everyone, and your results will be no better. You'll deprive your language tutors of much of the joy they'll realize in seeing the absolutely amazing results of their labor. Share the credit with your helpers, and remember to show gratitude.

Many highly talented multilingual parents fail to pass this important skill on to their children because they try to do most of the work themselves. The work is fun, but it takes a lot of time, which most multilingual parents never seem to have enough of. In that respect, they are no different than monolingual parents. I'll go out on a limb here and say that I think monolingual parents are better qualified to raise multilingual children because they do not fail to recognize their own limitations, and they have no choice but to seek outside help.

Whether you're monolingual or multilingual, however, makes no difference: As a parent, let your personal interactions with your children prepare them to do as well in school as their natural abilities will allow. Most experts will tell you that these interactions are best conducted in your own first language, your native tongue. Maybe the best thing you can do to advance your children's education is to find the time to conduct lengthy, elaborate conversations, covering whatever topics your family finds most interesting. Think of the dinner table as the most important preschool your children will ever attend, and make family conversations as leisurely and lengthy as possible. Let your children decide what you'll talk about, and don't dominate the conversation. Listen intently and let your responses reflect the fact that you are doing so. The more elaborate and grammatically complex your responses, the more elaborate and grammatically complex your children's primary language abilities will one day become. Your children will need the opportunity to practice their most sophisticated speech with you, so listen at least as much as you talk.

Also, using your strongest language, read aloud to your children. Choose age-appropriate storybooks that they find fascinating, and allow them to interrupt the narrative with questions. Answer those as best you can. To the greatest extent possible, make this a nightly routine. If your children want to hear the same story 30 nights in a row, then let them, with as much enthusiasm as you can muster.

As you conclude this nightly ritual, give your children a round of big hugs, and make sure they know how much you love them. After you lay the book on the nightstand, if you have a spouse, give another big hug. You're likely to need your spouse's full support on your trilingual journey. Language acquisition, like any other form of childhood learning, is best accomplished in the presence of warm human emotions.

CHAPTER 3

Preschool in Perspective

● ● ●

AND NOW, MAYBE YOU'RE WISHING I'd just stop with all the sentimentality, cut to the chase, and show you what to do. Well, sorry, but before we get down to nuts and bolts, I need to soften your brain with some marginally relevant stuff about the whole preschool educational world. Maybe I inflict this upon you in hopes that a little information will help you keep everything in perspective. Or maybe I just think the typical preschool setting is a grand conspiracy to keep your children monolingual! There's a good chance that, if you choose to raise your children trilingually, you'll have an approach to preschool education that's different from that of your friends and neighbors. Since you care very deeply about education, being an outlier could be a little unsettling, and I think you'll need some facts to reassure you. You'll need to understand why your friends and neighbors choose to educate their preschoolers the way they do, and why you'll travel down a slightly different (and ultimately more rewarding) path.

Imagine that you live in a typical American suburb. Maybe that won't take much imagination. On your left lives a single mom, a really hard working person with a demanding but extremely successful career. Since she has to travel quite a bit, she has a live-in nanny from Mexico who cares for her 2-year-old girl. Whenever she's home, she spends a lot of time with her daughter, but she seems rather overprotective, in your opinion. She has great aspirations for her daughter, who is already on the waiting list of the most prestigious preschool in the city and is undergoing all the IQ testing necessary for admission there. The girl plays only with brain-building toys, listens to classical music exclusively, already owns a violin, and goes to the local tutoring center twice a week for kindergarten-prep courses. If you didn't know better, you'd swear the mom was secretly preparing the outline for her daughter's valedictorian speech when she graduates from Yale in 20 years.

Your next-door neighbors on the other side are very different. They have no intention of enrolling their four children in preschool. They view it as unnecessary, even harmful. In fact, they plan to homeschool from the very start. They're thinking about moving to a farm, where they can grow their own food, build a cabin, and reduce their dependency on civilization.

Over your back fence is an immigrant couple. Last year, the father accepted a junior faculty position at a local college in the Department of Engineering. His wife barely speaks English and does not work outside the home. They have a boy in 3rd grade who's already studying 3 hours a night and, it seems, doing very well in school. There's also a younger sister in her 2nd year of preschool. She speaks English much more fluently than the rest of the family, and her parents regret that they didn't send the son to preschool too. But the father was just a graduate student in those days, and they really couldn't afford it. Because the son's English was pretty limited when he started kindergarten, the couple had to support him in every way they could until his English improved enough for him to understand his teacher.

Despite coming from very different families with very different approaches to preschool education, all these neighborhood children will probably do quite well in school. Are there any secret formulas, any commonalities? How much preschool do you think your own children will need before the first day of kindergarten?

If you begin a trilingual program very early, odds are quite high that your children will be chattering away in all 3 languages before they're old enough to start preschool at age 3 or so. I predict you'll enjoy that, and I feel this early success will influence your attitudes toward preschool. Here's why it matters: If you choose to send your children to several years of a typical full-time preschool that's conducted in the same language you speak in your home (as most will be), your children probably will not be trilingual at age 6. I'm not saying it can't be done; I'm just saying it would be pretty difficult. There are only so many hours in the day, and becoming trilingual must be given its share of them. So how will you make sure your trilingual children are ready for kindergarten—without neglecting their additional languages and reverting them back to monolinguals? It's something you'll have to decide—after I give you a bit of information, of course.

Preschool is a relatively recent phenomenon. Your grandmother likely didn't go to one—in fact, the term was almost unknown in her day. There were a few nursery schools and childcare centers, which mostly just offered babysitting, but not very many American children went to them. Since most experts of the time didn't feel that 3- and 4-year-olds were ready to learn academic school subjects, nobody tried very hard to teach them reading, writing, or math. Children typically stayed at home until 1st grade—or at least until kindergarten—and dove straight into school subjects without any serious preparation.

A change began in the mid-1960s. Amid an intense wave of social upheaval, President Lyndon Johnson's administration created the Head Start Program, a small experiment to help children in poverty that quickly grew. Its primary purpose was to help "disadvantaged" preschoolers, defined as those living in poverty or with a parent who either did not complete high school or received public welfare assistance. Though the program included social services, free meals, and psychological counseling, it mainly focused on using daycare environments to prepare little children for school. The idea was that early exposure to academic subjects would help disadvantaged children succeed in the classroom. Maybe this would help close the achievement gap between rich and poor students, create a more just and equal society, and reduce crime and high school dropout rates.

The very term "Head Start" had an unsettling effect on middle- and upper-income parents. If disadvantaged children were receiving a head start on academic school subjects, wouldn't their children benefit from the same thing? There was a spillover effect as nursery schools in the private sector began offering instruction in future school subjects. Demand grew for this new type of "preschool," and more and more of them opened their doors. Gradually, what had been a small percentage of American children attending nursery school grew into a sizable majority attending preschool.

As the Head Start Program gained momentum, the federal government became unable to meet public demand. It turned to the state legislatures, offering them financial assistance to develop their own versions of Head Start. Washington, DC provided some basic guidelines, but each state developed its own model relatively independently, based on its resources and voter preferences. Each state acquired supplemental funding from a complex maze of income streams beyond the federal government: taxes, private endowments, partnerships with private preschool centers, and even religious institutions.

Though originally intended for children between the ages of 3 and 5, the Head Start Programs also began to serve younger children. In the 1990s, there was an attempt to expand Head Start to include all disadvantaged children between birth and 3 years old. Originating from a private foundation, this Zero to Three movement caught the attention of President Clinton's administration.

Scientists had recently discovered that infants' brains contain billions more nerve cells and trillions more synaptic connections than the brains of older children. These nerve cells inexplicably die as children age, and there was intense interest in finding ways to stimulate the brains of infants and toddlers to prevent this loss. It was hoped that earlier educational intervention could make all children more intelligent. However, pediatric neuroscience did not yet have any answers: no one knew how to prevent "brain loss." To this day, normal children continue to lose billions of brain cells by their third birthdays. Most scientists consider it a normal process of maturation, but quite a lot of research is still going on. Perhaps we might all be smarter in the distant future, but unfortunately for your children—and probably for your children's grandchildren—no form of brain stimulation will come along anytime soon to help children retain these neurons that are destined to die.

As this cruel reality of normal brain development settled in, the Zero to Three movement fell by the wayside, and Head Start benefits were not generally extended to younger children. Nevertheless, the possibility of making their babies smarter through brain stimulation continued to fascinate many parents. Preschools began trying to teach academic school subjects to younger and younger children. The toy industry began to offer lots of products designed to make babies smarter, somehow—toys, audio games, flash cards, classical music. Unfortunately, none of these products have been shown to be any better than the toys your grandmother might've played with: wooden blocks, jigsaw puzzles, dolls, teddy bears, and crayons.

In the last decade or so, the No Child Left Behind Act has advanced the trend of teaching academics to younger and younger children. This federal legislation grew partly from a realization that achievement gaps between advantaged and disadvantaged children were not closing. Disadvantaged children were continuing to drop out of school at an unacceptable rate. Also, American students were not performing particularly well compared with students elsewhere in the world.[2] As some of these international test scores were falling into the bottom quartile, the No Child Left Behind Act implemented a series of federally mandated standardized tests designed to gauge the performance of individual school systems across the country. Basically, the act closely linked the amount of federal tax revenue that a local school system would receive to how well its students performed on these standardized tests—an incentive for chronically cash-strapped school systems to do a better job of teaching their students...or at least of teaching them how to ace the standardized tests.

More recently, a newer international student achievement test has continued to damage our national educational self-esteem. Every year, approximately half a million 15-year-old students from industrialized nations across the world take the PISA (Programme for International Student Assessment) test, which is designed to let policy makers know how their students rank in math, science, and reading when compared with other countries. While we in the United States have not been at the bottom of this particular world ranking, our standings have been consistently lackluster. Being a competitive country, we'd like to think of ourselves in superlative terms, so these PISA test results have not necessarily confirmed our preferred self-image. Furthermore, in an era of fierce global competition, we hope to remain economically relevant on the world playing field, and merely average test scores may not guarantee us the long-term international status we sometimes take for granted.

In response, some states and local school districts have developed "pre-K" programs, publicly funded preschools for 3- and 4-year-olds. They seek to prepare little children for kindergarten and thereafter—and to improve their standardized test scores in the process. A few states, most notably Oklahoma and Georgia, have gone as far as to make their pre-K programs available to all children, not just those from disadvantaged backgrounds. Of course, mainstream parents don't want their children "left behind" either, and private preschools have gotten in on the act, redoubling their efforts to teach 3- and 4-year-olds academic subjects. Topping it all off, private tutoring centers such as Sylvan Center and Kumon Academy now offer kindergarten-prep courses. These are intended to give young children a leg up on the cut-throat competition in the dog-eat-dog kindergarten world through very early supplemental exposure to reading and math. Many parents now expect their children to be reading chapter books and doing long division even before the first day of kindergarten.

If you live in the United States, you've probably heard the phrase "Kindergarten is the new 1st grade." Maybe now you understand the phenomenon a little better. In fact, it might be fair to say that *preschool* is the new 1st grade. Maybe the federal government has pushed this, but some of the responsibility lies with the marketplace, and the parents.

A less influential force in this movement has been the consensus opinion of our professionals, and that's probably unfortunate. Most experts in the field of early childhood development, education, and psychology feel that the attempt to teach very young children the same way we might teach 3rd graders is a bad idea. As we have willingly bought in to a feverish race to the top, our experts are telling us that preschool should not, in fact, be "academic-based."

"Academic-based" or "didactic" refers to any teaching method that uses traditional classroom techniques with rows of desks, workbooks, memorization drills, repetitive exercises, flashcards, and other items of that basic type. What most experts in early childhood education, development, and psychology recommend is a "play-based" curriculum, one that does not necessarily require preschool children to sit still. Under such a model, children explore, experiment with the environment, and learn by doing. The play-based method emphasizes curiosity, creativity, and enjoyment of learning. Though most experts acknowledge that very young children can indeed learn to read and do basic math, many argue that forcing them into activities that they are not quite ready for can do psychological and emotional harm in the long run. The general consensus among professionals is that any advantage that children gain from early academic-style math and reading is temporary—children who begin to learn these subjects when they are a little older catch up and even surpass the early learners.

On the advice of these early childhood experts, some preschools have abandoned the academic-style curriculum in favor of a play-based one. Though there is now increased pressure to rigorously prepare children for kindergarten, there is also a recognition that doing so by traditional methods might cause more harm than good. For this reason, a lot of modern preschools tend to walk a line between academic- and play-based learning. I'm not sure this hybridization helps parents make a decision. It's probably fair to say that highly ambitious and competitive parents favor the academic environment for their preschoolers, while parents who are more concerned about social and emotional development favor the play-based model. Most of us would like to have our cake and eat it too here, and I think that's what the preschool marketplace often tries to sell us—a hybrid.

Modern parents get confusing messages about preschool. We want our children to "race to the top." If we can, we'll give them a "head start," and we certainly don't want them "left behind." We wouldn't want their brains to shrink unnecessarily, but we don't want to leave them with any emotional or psychological problems either. At this point, I think some examination of the available science of early childhood education would be helpful. That way you won't have to rely upon politicians, marketing departments, or idiosyncratic neighbors when it's time for you to plan for preschool.

It's now been about 50 years since Head Start changed the landscape of modern education. In the early years, there were some promising research-study results. A small handful of investigative projects were able to demonstrate some benefits in later school performance among disadvantaged children who had early exposure to math and reading. These early projects included not only daycare with educational programs but also free meals, psychological counseling, home assessments, and family crisis intervention whenever necessary. One well-known program was the HighScope Perry Project. A private foundation funded it, and it studied a relatively small group of 3- and 4-year-olds living in poverty. The children in the project received 2 years of this comprehensive intervention. Participating researchers found some long-term benefits: lowered school dropout rate and reduced incarcerations later in life, as well as better earnings and employment as adults. Though these children initially did somewhat better on IQ testing up to a year after completion of the program, this effect faded until there was no difference between them and children who did not receive the educational intervention. However, at one point at least, in the 8th grade, the children in the study did perform somewhat better on a standardized achievement test.

A little later, another study began: the Abecedarian Project. It involved full-time individualized intervention in the lives of the children who participated. They all came from disadvantaged environments and ranged in age from a few months up to 5 years. As in the HighScope Perry Project, the interventions were comprehensive, including not only preschool education but also free health care, dietary supplements, social support for the family, and tutoring for children who ran into trouble during the school years. The study showed this intervention to have some educational and cognitive benefits extending into adulthood. These at-risk children did better in school, were less likely to become enrolled in special education or drop out of high school, and were more likely to attend college. Girls were less likely to become pregnant as teenagers. As in the HighScope Perry Project, researchers observed no effect on long-term IQ, but the children in the study did do better in school.

These are the two research projects used most often as evidence that preschool does have a positive impact upon the educational and socioeconomic lives of disadvantaged children. It's worth pointing out, though, that the typical Head Start Program in almost any community in the country involves less comprehensive intervention than the HighScope Perry or the Abecedarian Project. At the national level, there's just not enough government funding to provide that degree of support to all disadvantaged children.

Not totally surprising, then, research data coming from the actual Head Start Program itself has been less encouraging. In 2010, the Department of Health and Human Services released its "Head Start Impact Study." This investigation found that, by the 3rd grade, children who had participated in the Head Start Program were not doing any better in school than disadvantaged children who had been to no preschool at all.[3] At the start of kindergarten, they seemed to have a slightly better understanding of school subjects, but this advantage quickly faded out. Generally speaking, data coming from the individual state pre-K programs have shown the same fade-out effect for school performance, though some states have been able to demonstrate reduced rates of students dropping out of school, repeating grades, or being arrested for criminal activity.[4] (This fade-out phenomenon is common in early childhood learning of many kinds, as we'll see. An exception, I hope to show you, is early language acquisition.)

Preschool is a multibillion-dollar industry, so you can probably imagine the political impact of these studies. Opponents of a publicly funded preschool system cite them as a reason to abandon our current tax-supported practices. Supporters of public preschool maintain that mismanagement and inadequate funding cause the problems. Still others say that the problem with Head Start has been its academic style of teaching and that the results would be better if the program developed a purely play-based curriculum.[5] Elsewhere in the world, other countries face the same challenge. Preschools have a very difficult time closing achievement gaps for disadvantaged children, and the initial favorable results seem to fade out in the early grade-school years.[6]

Admittedly, if you bought a copy of this book, there's a good chance you are not raising disadvantaged children. Actually, I feel a little bit uneasy even using the term, but I've found it necessary because so much of the research data makes a distinction between disadvantaged and mainstream children. Anyway, let's look at what available research can tell us about preschool for children who are *not* disadvantaged. As we've just seen, all school systems and all of us who parent in the United States feel at least some pressure to improve our early childhood education. I have mentioned that our PISA scores are less than spectacular, and it would appear that our students are not learning as much as children in other countries.

With respect to preschool for mainstream children, hosts of experts claim that preschool is less beneficial for children from ordinary homes than it is for disadvantaged children.[7] Not too long ago, a research study from California demonstrated that kindergarteners from the general population who attended preschool were about *1 month* ahead in early math and *2 months* ahead in pre-reading at the beginning of the year, when they were compared with their classmates who had not attended preschool.[8] This particular study, like many others, did not evaluate for longer-term advantage or fade-out. However, another research study evaluating a large sample of preschool children from all walks of life across the country showed that children who went to preschool had some academic advantage early on, but by the end of 3rd grade, they were doing no better than children who did not attend preschool. The children who attended preschool, unfortunately, actually had more emotional and behavioral problems that did not fade out.[9] A separate analysis showed that children who attended preschool had an advantage that lasted 1 to 2 years. After that, they really were not doing better than children who had not attended preschool.[10]

With the data just presented, it's not always possible to know whether we are talking about academic- or play-based preschool, simply because the research studies weren't necessarily designed to make that distinction. However, some research conducted several decades ago showed that children who attended academic-based preschool were doing a little better in reading, but not in math at the start of kindergarten. The authors did not assess for fade-out. This slight improvement in reading was associated with more negative behaviors and lowered school motivation compared with children who had been to a play-based preschool.[11] Because of observations like this, most, if not all early childhood professional organizations favor the play-based model of preschool. Probably the most influential of these is the National Association for the Education of Young Children (NAEYC) in Washington, DC. NAEYC thoroughly favors the play-based model of teaching for preschool children, and does not fail to point out the emotional and behavioral drawbacks of using an academic model of instruction at this age.

However, the relatively carefree, low-stress, play-based model of preschool will not necessarily have rowdy 6-year-olds reading chapter books or doing long division at the start of kindergarten. Thus, highly ambitious parents may be tempted to ignore the warnings of the experts and choose a very academic style of learning. In some corners of the country (New York City comes to mind), preschool is taken very seriously—by the parents, at least. There, it's not so much about early childhood development and learning as it is about prepping the children to take the very competitive entrance tests required by most elite private schools.[12] These children could have their entire educational future irrevocably altered if they fail to do well on this test. It just might be the difference between going to Harvard or a state university one day.

Tuition can top $40,000 annually at these elite preschools, where ambitious toddlers have their little hearts set on Ivy League acceptance letters. There are usually waiting lists, so prepping for entry into this world often begins well before age 3. Many preschools themselves require extensive aptitude testing before they will accept a child. No doubt, a fair number of the children who attend these preschools will eventually be accepted into highly prestigious universities. As you might imagine, the percentage of these children who develop emotional and behavioral problems is just not the sort of thing that makes the news, so it's anybody's guess. Several years ago, a Manhattan mom sued her daughter's preschool for allegedly wrecking her chances at an Ivy League scholarship. The mom noted that the place was "just one big play room."[13] The play-based model clearly doesn't appeal to everyone.

So do elite private preschools give their students a permanent long-term educational advantage? It depends on whom you ask. Some experts say yes, some say no, which probably reflects the fact that there isn't much scientific data to be found on the question. In 1989, Dr. Larsen and Dr. Robinson evaluated a small group of children with an average IQ score of 130, with inconclusive results.[14] Most of their parents were graduate students or university professors. One group of these children attended a university-based preschool, and the other group attended none. They found no difference in IQ between those who attended the preschool and those who didn't, but the boys who attended this preschool did a little better on a standardized test in 3rd grade than the boys who didn't. There was no difference between the two groups of girls, however. I think it's very fair to say that it remains anybody's guess how advantageous the elite preschools really are. With aptitude testing required for admission, they probably do their best to accept only the brightest toddlers. Certainly, many of those children come from privileged backgrounds and have parents with phenomenally high IQs, so it's tough to know how much of their ultimate success comes from preschool, and how much is from genetics.

Research has shown that many children, both advantaged and disadvantaged, can be taught to read by age 4, often even earlier than that.[15] But the long-term advantage of such a head start is far from clear. It can be achieved with a combination of academic-style learning, home teaching, and attendance at tutoring centers. Early childhood professionals and elite preschools seem to heavily favor the Montessori system, which combines both academic- and play-based instructional methods with plenty of individualized attention. Some Montessori preschools begin introducing reading at age 3.[16] However, there is no strong or consistent evidence that any type of preschool (regardless of pedagogic approach, daily schedule, or other setting) influences long-term outcomes.[17] In fact, Montessori schools have not been shown to be any better than others in terms of long-term achievement.[18] One research study found disadvantaged children who attended a Montessori preschool to be reading better than disadvantaged children who had attended another type of preschool at age 5, but by age 12, the difference had faded out.[19] Similarly, it has been reported that children who are at the top of their kindergarten class (presumably due in part to earlier exposure to reading and math) have only about a 40% chance of being at the top of their class at the end of 3rd grade.[20] It seems a head start is not always a permanent advantage.

While you're pondering that, let's address the question of the ideal amount and duration of preschool. As I pointed out earlier, 3 years of all-day, ordinary monolingual preschool might be a little unrealistic if you also want your children to be trilingual. Thus, it's important for you to be able to make some well-informed decisions as you plan your family's early education. If you want your children to succeed in kindergarten and beyond in addition to becoming trilingual, how do you achieve both goals? Are there any trade-offs?

Answering those questions lies in deciding how much preschool you think is enough for kindergarten readiness. And possibly, how much might be too much. As you may know, many preschools offer all-day as well as half-day programs, and the starting age is usually up to you. In 2007, a research study evaluated differences between all-day and half-day preschool. Though it did not evaluate for fade-out, the study found that middle- and upper-class children did worse in math and reading if they attended all-day preschool as opposed to half-day sessions. Not too surprisingly, the all-day children also had more behavior problems. Disadvantaged children in this study made more short-term progress in reading and math when they attended the all-day variety, with only small increases in behavior problems.[21]

And how many years of preschool do your children need to be ready for kindergarten? It appears that the most valuable time for preschool occurs immediately before the start of kindergarten, with considerable skill loss occurring if there is a significant time lapse between the final month of preschool and the first day of kindergarten. In 2010, Dr. Leak and his colleagues showed that children who started preschool between the ages of 4 and 4½ got almost as much benefit as children who started quite a bit earlier.[22] The research also found that children who only attended preschool for 6 to 12 months before the start of kindergarten derived almost as much immediate benefit as those who attended longer. In all groups, the preschool advantage lasted only 1 to 2 years. After that, children who did not attend preschool were basically indistinguishable from those who did.

In 2013, Dr. Yoshikawa and his fellow investigators found similar results: Attending preschool for more than a year did have some additional immediate benefit, but only a little.[23] Also in 2013, Dr. Protzko and his group showed that children who attended preschool for a longer amount of time did not do any better in terms of IQ testing than children who attended for shorter periods.[24] Still another group of investigators led by Dr. Loeb in 2007 concluded that, where cognitive gains at the start of kindergarten were concerned, the best age to start preschool was between the ages of 2 and 3, but these earlier starts were associated with significantly more behavioral and emotional problems, particularly among middle-income and wealthy children.[25] Starting preschool before the age of 2 resulted in less school benefit as well as an even higher incidence of emotional problems. The study did not assess whether any of these observed cognitive benefits faded out in the grade-school years.

Based on all this information, I think I can state that sending your children to half-day preschool for half a year immediately before the start of kindergarten would be a very efficient way of achieving kindergarten readiness for most children from ordinary backgrounds. Disadvantaged children might possibly benefit from more, though the conclusions are mixed. Upper-class children hoping to gain access to the elite private school world might need to adhere to the prescribed pathway, which will likely involve a more long-term attendance at a preschool designed to prepare them for it. I wish I could say that the elite preschool culture places a high value on early childhood multilingualism, but I really don't think it does.

The "trouble" with multilingualism where the elite preschool world is concerned has to do with the required entrance exams and IQ tests. Though the phenomenon is temporary, very young multilinguals often have smaller vocabularies in each of their languages when compared with their monolingual counterparts. While their combined vocabularies are often quite a bit larger, they are subjected to monolingual exams that do not take this into account. As a result, these unfortunate children can receive slightly lower test scores. For the overwhelming majority of children, that will not make any difference at all, particularly in the long term, but if the elite private school scene is your thing, investigate this thoroughly before you commit to any trilingual program. I'm a public school guy, philosophically speaking, and I think any temporary trade-off in early monolingual test performance is well worth making, but other parents will feel very differently. I guess it goes without saying that I think these entrance exams are flawed, myopic, perhaps even discriminatory, but they are what they are.

Alternately, maybe you just don't want to send your kids to preschool. Are any experts willing to back you up? Well, despite the fact that the Head Start Program has so far been unable to demonstrate any long-term scholastic benefit for disadvantaged children, the HighScope Perry and Abecedarian projects showed that the potential does exist, and most experts do recommend preschool for disadvantaged youngsters. A study from the RAND Corporation, a Washington think tank, concluded that there is little evidence that preschool benefits kids who are not from disadvantaged backgrounds.[26] I mentioned earlier the 2004 work of Dr. Bridges and her team showing that children who attend preschool are only about 2 months ahead in prereading and 1 month ahead in early math at the start of kindergarten. You can decide for yourself how significant you think that advantage would be. Dr. David Elkind, in his landmark book, *Miseducation*, notes that nursery school is not essential for healthy development.[27] Some experts say that, at the start of kindergarten, children who have been to preschool and those who have not tend to look about the same.[28]

Whether or not you choose to send your children to preschool, you can do some simple things to help prepare them for the first day of kindergarten. Probably the single most important habit you should get into is reading to them every night for at least 15 minutes. This habit has the recommendation of quite a number of child development and education associations, most importantly the National Association for the Education of Young Children and the American Academy of Pediatrics. They recommend choosing books that children find interesting, typically with lots of pictures. The best books may be the ones your children ask you to read over and over again. This may bore you to tears, but it will allow your children to fully digest the meaning of the story. Books that introduce letter concepts as well as letter sounds are good, as these promote pre-reading skills. I would cite Dr. Seuss's *The ABC Book*, though there are many, many choices. I happen to favor Dr. Seuss because he writes books that I can actually enjoy myself. He was a funny guy.

Many childhood development experts claim that school success ultimately depends upon a child's spoken language skills.[29] It has been shown that, by as early as 30 months, babies who do not hear as much human speech begin to fall behind in their vocabulary sizes, and they fall further and further behind as they approach school age. Thus, experts recommend that parents speak with their children as often as they possibly can, using rich and grammatically complex language. Parents should also engage their small children in dialogues rather than simply giving orders or commands. It actually helps them develop speech if they have frequent opportunities to engage in two-way conversations. By the start of kindergarten, children who have not had this frequent opportunity to participate in two-way dialogue are typically a year behind in their speech development, and they tend to struggle more in school. Very importantly, it has been shown that their vocabulary at 36 months predicts the reading and spelling skills from kindergarten through at least the 3rd grade—and probably well beyond that. No doubt, children who hear more human speech, and who participate in more two-way dialogue, have bigger vocabularies. So it is important to engage your children in conversation as much as you possibly can. As we will see, you should probably do this in your *first* language, if you're multilingual.

To be sure, we will visit this topic again, but please do not fail to notice that much future speech ability has already been determined by about age 3. Just keep that in mind for later—there is *every* reason to believe that this phenomenon applies not only to children's first language but also to their second and third languages! Vocabulary size in the second and third languages at 3 years of age probably determines speaking, reading, and even writing ability for many years to come—perhaps for a lifetime.

At this point, I'm wondering (and maybe you are too), did the Zero to Three movement we just discussed miss the boat by leading us to focus on academics and brain-building toys when we should have been focusing on other skills, such as language and socialization, instead? Surely, those billions of brain cells that die before the age of 3 have *some* purpose. Since preschool children who learn reading and math do not necessarily have an advantage over children who learn such skills later, these brain cells must have some *other* purpose. Actually, when I first started to wonder about this, I decided to write this book.

Anyway, we've now had 50 years to learn from these modern educational trends, which are definitely not confined to the United States. The rest of the world is also trying to figure out the best way to educate its children, so let's have a look at what other countries are doing. We'll take a quick world preschool tour, visiting the countries that have highly successful education systems. Maybe that will tell us something helpful.

The German system is worth a brief look. In the 1970s, Germany embarked on a plan to push early academic-style education. Kindergartens were turned into centers for cognitive achievement and didactic learning. But later, a study found that by age 10, the children who had spent more time playing excelled over the others; they were reading at a more advanced level and doing more sophisticated math while being better adjusted socially and emotionally. After that, German kindergartens and preschools returned to a play-based format. Nowadays few schools attempt to introduce academic subjects before about age 7. More recently, a German researcher conducted a study of children who attended one of two types of public preschools. In one, reading was introduced in the preschool years. In the other, children did not receive any instruction in reading until age 7. The findings showed, very interestingly, that the children who did not start learning to read until age 7 eventually caught up to the children who learned to read earlier. After that, the late learners *surpassed* the early learners and read better.[30]

These days, one can't discuss successful education systems without at least mentioning Finland. If I were a preschooler, I would want to be there. Early childhood education receives top priority in the country, to the point that teaching jobs are very competitive, and only the very best applicants are selected. Most who become teachers remain in the profession for their entire working lives. A mother receives subsidies that allow her not to work until her child is 3 years old. After that, preschools are free for children from poor families and almost free for those from wealthy backgrounds. All preschools are play-based, with almost no introduction of academic subjects like reading or math until age 7. Instead, they emphasize social responsibility and development of a child's individual strengths and talents. All children spend around 3 hours per day playing outdoors, even during the frigid winters.[31]

As Finnish children begin grade school, they continue to have lots of outdoor time, with at least 75 minutes per day of recess. Their school days are short—only about 5 hours—and they receive very little homework. They are strongly encouraged to develop extracurricular hobbies, and the school system fosters these. Schools do not place gifted and talented children into special programs but instead expect them to help struggling classmates with their studies. Throughout their entire school careers, Finnish students take only one standardized test: the PISA test at age 15.[32] Considering their relatively stress-free school curriculum and emphasis upon leisure time, what would you guess their international ranking on this PISA test would be?

The best in the world.

Until recently, that is. During the last few years, the South Korean school system has moved to the top. Some of the other Asian countries have moved up as well. Actually, on the most recent PISA test, Shanghai, China, was at the very top, but its results have been called into question because Shanghai is China's wealthiest city and is not necessarily reflective of the educational system of the country as a whole.

The difference between the Finnish and South Korean educational systems is like night and day. Since the end of the Korean War in the 1950s, South Korea's economy has grown 23-fold, due in large part to some very hard work and sacrifice. Most parents work long hours, so most children go to preschool, where they begin to imitate their parents' patterns of self-denial. Some parents spend as much as 70% of their monthly income on their children's education, and many children study as much as 20 hours per day.

Though public preschool is available for all, approximately 2/3 of all Korean children go to *private* preschool, particularly if their parents can afford it. Recently the government mandated a play-based curriculum for both types, but nearly all of them now have after-school "enrichment activities," such as mathematics, reading, writing, and English-language instruction. This seems more than a little bizarre, so I have to believe it's a political compromise of some sort. Even in preschool, some parents begin to hire home tutors for their children, or take them to *hagwons*, which are also known as cram schools. At these commercial tutoring centers, students receive reinforcement of their school subjects, and they typically remain in these classes until 10:00 p.m. A third type of preschool is not formally recognized by the government. It is commonly referred to as "English preschool," and most of the instruction is definitely *not* play-based. Here, children take advantage of early exposure to a second and very economically important language and drill on future school subjects. These English preschools can cost up to $2,500 per month, making them typically the domain of the very wealthy.[33]

South Korea's official implementation of a play-based early childhood curriculum seems to be part of an official recognition that parents are pushing their young children excessively hard toward academic success. In many cases, children as young as 3 and 4 are already feeling this pressure, and the government's attempts to stem this tide have not been terribly successful.[34] Much of a South Korean student's entire life can depend upon a few crucial standardized examinations, and parents are willing to do anything they can to maximize their children's scores on these tests. Nationally, society acknowledges no alternate pathway to success, so parents pour everything into their children's education from the very start.

When South Korean children leave preschool and begin formal schooling, the pressure only intensifies. Public school teachers have very high social and economic status and quite a lot of control. Parents often issue formal apologies and offer gifts whenever their children misbehave in class. The school day typically begins around 8:00 and ends at 5:00 p.m. After that, most children do not go home but go directly to private tutors, if their parents can afford them, or to *hagwons*. Until recently, many of the *hagwons* ran later into the night, but the government imposed a curfew, and any student caught studying in a *hagwon* after 10:00 p.m. is now subject to a penalty. Imagine that: a country where too much studying has of necessity become criminalized.

After leaving the *hagwon*, children do their homework. When they are done, they sleep for a few hours and repeat the routine. Because of their long hours of studying, many Korean students struggle to remain awake in class.[35] It's easy to see why they are now topping out the PISA test.

But, in South Korea, the most common cause of death under age 40 is suicide, and the rate of alcoholism is high. The culture determines social status less by family wealth and more by the children's educational achievements. For the student, everything depends upon school performance: social status, university acceptance, employability, and even marriage prospects. Many Korean families take on huge debts to pay for their children's education, and children are under a lot of pressure to help pay off this debt when they finish school. However, getting into a good university in Korea is very competitive. This explains why many South Korean students elect to study abroad, in spite of the cost.[36]

In Shanghai, China, the educational system resembles South Korea's. Officially, all preschools are play-based, and teachers are *forbidden* to teach writing or foreign languages. But parents who can afford it send their children to private preschools that place much more emphasis upon academic subjects, including English, from the very start. In public preschools, the government outlawed Korean-style enrichment classes, but interested parents find workarounds. Many young children from affluent families have private tutors and attend commercial learning centers similar to *hagwons*.[37] The most elite international preschools are conducted in English, utilizing native English speakers as instructors.

Like in South Korea, many Chinese parents make huge sacrifices for education. Some will sell their apartments and forego medical treatment in order to pay for their children's tutoring and other educational expenses. Some go deep into debt. As in Korea, the university system is very competitive, so many Chinese families save and borrow in order to send their children to foreign universities. Many students prepare for studying abroad by taking English classes and SAT-prep courses. Since the SAT is not offered throughout China, parents must pay for trips to Hong Kong so their children may take this test. Just like in South Korea, success in the Chinese educational system depends upon a student's scores on a few very crucial tests. Students spend years preparing for these grueling exams. Perhaps more so than in South Korea, extended families and relatives contribute what they can to a child's education.[38]

Though the American scores on the international PISA test are lackluster, when viewed separately, the scores of Asian American students have been found to be almost as high as those from Shanghai and even higher than those from South Korea. In the United States, about half of all Asian American children attend preschool. When compared with other immigrant groups, they tend to come from relatively wealthy and very well-educated families. Many of their parents arrived on special work and student visas, so they probably come from backgrounds favoring academic success. Asian American students tend to study about 6 hours more per week than their mainstream peers. Those who come from more impoverished, less well-educated backgrounds, namely, Southeast Asians, do not fare as well in the American school system.[39]

Of late, there has been some interest in the parenting practices of Asian and Asian American families. Recently, the phrase "tiger mom" has been introduced into our lexicon, and some speculate that typical American families do not push their children hard enough to succeed academically. Whether this is actually the key to Asian Americans' school success remains under speculation. Certainly, the fact that Asian American students spend more time studying than do their mainstream peers suggests this might be the case, but a recent study showed that children in Asian families who adopted harsh and very pressured parenting styles did *less* well in school than those with Asian American parents who were more supportive. Thus, the key component might be the value placed on education rather than the particular parenting style.[40]

That's my conclusion, at least. In Finland, where students are not exposed to high levels of stress, particularly in the preschool years, the standardized exam scores have been very impressive, even though they are no longer the best in the world. A completely opposite system in South Korea has led to somewhat better results, but at a cost. Either method seems to be effective. What seems crucial is the value placed on education and the investment made in it. That goes for parents as well as the society as a whole. In order to have a top-tier educational system, I believe a country needs to prize its education above all other worldly pursuits. If education is just a means to afford McMansions, fancy cars, and designer clothing, then we really don't value it all that much. As demonstrated by your willingness to read this book, I'd bet that you care more about it than that. Whether you favor Finnish or South Korean parenting styles, I hope your children do very well on the PISA test one day!

In the United States, preschool has not been shown without a doubt to provide permanent value, and it has not been proven necessary for later school success—though it may be beneficial. However, in countries where students go on to be the best students, or at least the best test takers, they do spend significant time in preschool. You'll have to make up your own mind, because now you know as much about this complicated and politically charged issue as I do.

If I had it all to do over, if my children were once again preschool age, I don't think I would feel an urgent need to send them to preschool before kindergarten. However, just to hedge my bets, maybe I'd enroll them in a good one for 6 to 12 months, for a few half-days a week, right before the start of kindergarten. I think that would not interfere too much with their multilingual development. One thing I might do differently would be to look harder for a truly bilingual preschool where they could interact with lots of native-speaking children. If I were an immigrant or an expat whose children's home language differed from the future school language, I think I would go heavy on the school language preschool before the age of 3, if possible. We'll talk more about this particular subject later.

When our children were younger, I'd have to say that Laura and I were what I might call "mediocre hyper-parents." Maybe we didn't pressure our children all that much, but we got them into *everything*: choir, piano, swimming, martial arts, preschool, and, of course, languages. Looking back on it, much of our efforts proved to be a waste of time. On most fronts, we started far too early. We needed to learn the hard way about fade-out.

We started our daughters on piano at about age 3, but most of their accomplishments have come since about age 7. My oldest daughter is now 10 years old, and I have to say she has friends who only started playing the piano a year or so ago who can already play much better than she can. We started martial arts at age 5, and some children in the class who have been practicing for less than a year have already surpassed my daughters. The same can be said of swimming. Both of my daughters attended preschool for 3 years, half-days, about 3 times per week. They're both in grade school now, and they're doing pretty well, but they both have classmates who attended no preschool at all who are doing much better in math and reading.

Both attend language immersion classes at the local public school, and here is where, as parents, we feel we were right to start early. As our daughters have been hearing and speaking multiple languages since birth, it's pretty clear that they have a *permanent* advantage over their friends. Some of their classmates are really bright and will probably go on to have spectacular educational careers, but because they started later, about age 7, they will never be as proficient in the immersion language as my daughters. That may be empty bragging, but it's also the very best advice I think I can offer you.

CHAPTER 4

School Immersion

● ● ●

I'll need to mention school immersion programs and bilingual preschools again before we're done, so we should talk about them in a little more detail. I wouldn't necessarily rate them as the most valuable tools that you as a trilingual parent will ever have, but they do have their place. As we saw on our world preschool tour, countries using very different approaches can all end up with well-educated young people. The same seems to be true of highly multilingual countries. In Scandinavia and Luxembourg, where just about everyone speaks two (or more) languages, preschool basically provides reinforcement in children's native tongue only. But in some Asian countries like Singapore, preschool is a major instrument for making sure that all children speak English at a high level. There, English is not really anyone's native tongue, but it is the one used by just about all the schools.

It's fair to say bilingual preschools are not all that common across the world. Why not? Let me boil it down for you: (1) multilingual societies don't really need them, (2) monolingual societies don't really value them, and (3) parents of ordinary means can't really afford them.

Let's say you were a child in Luxembourg. Most likely, your parents would know at least three languages: Luxembourgish, French, and German. Even if your parents spoke exclusively Luxembourgish to you in the home, you would hear French and German whenever you went out into your world. Most of the television and radio programming, including your favorite cartoons, would be in one of these major world languages. (Many

Europeans, by the way, swear that watching TV is actually very valuable to a child learning a new language.) When you entered preschool, if you even went, your teachers would speak to you in Luxembourgish most of the time, but you would probably hear and use two other languages from the very beginning of life. As you left preschool and entered grade school, you would be called upon to read and write in German and eventually in French. For most students, English would be thrown into the mix too.

On the other hand, if you happened to be born in China, the odds that your parents would be able to speak a foreign language to you would be considerably less. In the public places of your world, you would hear mostly the local Chinese language. When you entered a public preschool, your course of instruction would be entirely in this language. In fact, your teachers would be forbidden to teach you English or any other foreign language. However, if you were lucky enough to have wealthy parents, they could probably manage to place you in an international school, where you would begin to learn English. Hopefully, this preschool would have a reasonable number of native speakers in attendance—perhaps the children of foreign diplomats, visiting professors, or international business people. If your parents were wealthier still, they might be able to hire a private tutor or nanny from the English-speaking world.

In Singapore, where bilingual preschool actually works, most households claim some combination of Mandarin Chinese, Malay, Hindi, and Tamil as first languages. However, since English has been the school language for several decades now, a majority of the population speaks it fluently. Educational success depends on English proficiency, so most parents spend a lot of time speaking this language with their children. Naturally, the government encourages them to do this. When both parents work outside the home, as is very common in Singapore, they hire a foreign domestic servant who speaks English. Typically, these housekeepers come from the Philippines or Bangladesh, and the parents expect them to speak *English* to the children they babysit. Thus, by the time children enter preschool (as most of them do), 60% of them are already fluent in English. By the first day of 1st grade, thanks to the parents, housekeepers, preschools, and the 60% of preschool children who are already fluent in English, virtually 100% of the children can speak it well. After that, they hear English every day of their educational lives, mixed with a smaller amount of their mother tongue.

Conversely, in mainstream America, most parents have probably never seriously considered raising multilingual children, and their elected officials have no reason to give them something they don't ask for. Most likely, the preschool experience will be in English. Maybe the teacher will introduce a little Spanish in the form of songs or random vocabulary words, but not enough to allow the children to use the language independently. When these children enter 1st grade, they'll still be monolingual. They'll usually stay that way their entire lives. In fact, the school system will probably not even offer them a second language until they get to high school, where the success rate will be utterly abysmal.

In a typical American suburb, you might be able to find a small handful of private "bilingual" preschools. They'd probably be of varying quality and price. Many of them would offer only light exposure to the language you want your children to learn, and they might just be throwing the word *bilingual* around as a marketing technique instead of making an actual commitment. Maybe such a school would only have a teacher of the second language who comes around for a few hours every week, introducing a few random vocabulary words, some numbers, and a song or two. Some might not even have that. Pitted against 15 to 20 rowdy children who don't know anything about this new language, the teacher would have to find a way to hold their attention while attempting to speak to them in this strange and confusing way. Maybe the experience would not be a total waste of time, but it could be close. The odds that the children would emerge from this preschool experience actually speaking a new language would be slim.

On the other side of town, there would be bilingual preschools of another type. Most of these would be publicly funded, designed to help disadvantaged children from immigrant backgrounds prepare for school. They would endeavor to gradually introduce English, the future school language, to children who do not know it yet. They'd make sure to preserve the children's home language, which would most often be Spanish but might also be Mandarin Chinese, Korean, Vietnamese, or Arabic. All the children, of course, would prefer to speak their own language to one another, and their only meaningful English dialogue would be with their teacher. As we'll see, many such children will emerge from their bilingual preschool experience unprepared to function in the English-speaking classroom.

Some of these preschools and pre-K programs on the other side of town might actually be available to you—even if your children are not from a disadvantaged immigrant household—if you have the foresight to go there. The most recent American trend has been to place monolingual, English-speaking preschoolers into classrooms with disadvantaged immigrant kids who do not yet know English. The linguistic results, you might predict, have been favorable. In that setting, your children would learn not only from the bilingual teachers but also from the many immigrant children who are perfectly fluent in the language you want your children to learn. Your children would have an excellent chance of emerging from the experience actually speaking the language of interest.

If you venture more deeply into the local immigrant enclave served by this bilingual preschool, you might be able to tap into a network of immigrant women providing home-based childcare or maybe even running a small preschool on their own. Their purpose would probably be to provide childcare services to fellow immigrant women needing to work outside the home. In this setting, 100% of the teachers would be perfectly fluent in the language of interest to you, and 100% of the other children would be perfectly fluent as well. In fact, many of them might not even know English at all. If you somehow managed to place your children into an arrangement like this, they would really have no choice but to speak the new language. If given just a little time, you could bet your bottom dollar that they would emerge from the experience perfectly fluent themselves.

If your home happens to be in a major world city like New York or Geneva, you might be able to find an "international preschool" of the type popular among the same foreign diplomats, global businesspeople, and visiting university professors we just encountered in China. If you could afford the tuition, you could enroll your children there, where they would interact with expat children who speak their country's language extremely well. The teachers, of course, would be perfectly bilingual. Though you could be bankrupt by the time your children were ready for grade school, they would most likely be bilingual, if not trilingual.

So what's the difference between a preschool that actually teaches a child a new language and one that's probably a waste of time? Though there's not necessarily a solid line, and there's plenty to suggest that preschool is not the best place for children to begin learning a new language, I think the criteria are the same no matter where you are in the world.

Look for a preschool that meets the following criteria:

1. At least half the kids in the school already speak the language you want your kids to learn.
2. At least half the full-time teachers in the school are highly fluent speakers of this language.
3. When the children in the school play with each other, on their own, they speak the desired language at least half the time.
4. Most importantly, children who have been attending the school for 6 to 12 months can actually hold a conversation in this language. They do not just sing songs or identify objects on a flashcard—they can actually hold a little *conversation*.

If the preschool does not meet these criteria, please be careful about assuming that your children will come away fluent in the desired language. It could happen, of course, but you shouldn't take it for granted. So when you walk into a preschool that professes to be bilingual or to teach a child a new language, have this four-point checklist with you. A preschool might be able to conceal the facts on numbers 1 and 2, but your ears will tell you what you really need to know when you do your walk-through.

Notice one thing that highly multilingual countries have in common: By the time their students begin grade school, they *already* speak multiple languages. They are already prepared to begin reading and writing them. Take note of that. Still, it would be wise to begin looking for ways that your local school system might help you out as your kids become a little older. In the Unites States, this assistance is occasionally offered in the form of the school immersion program.

Though this terminology is seemingly American, immersion programs don't really differ from the way Singapore uses English in its grade schools or the way Luxembourg uses German. The immersion language is not a separate topic of study, but rather the means whereby children learn their traditional core subjects. In Singapore, for example, 1st-grade teachers assume that their pupils already know English, and the children do not just close all their other books when it's time to study this language. Instead, they use English to learn other subjects. Similarly, in an American school immersion program, the bilingual teacher will begin addressing the class in the immersion language from the very first day. Teachers will use it to teach math, reading, history, and everything else from the very first day. After a week or two of confusion, the formerly monolingual children will be able to follow along well enough to participate.

You might conceptualize the American school immersion programs as just a monolingual nation's attempt to imitate the school experience of a very multilingual nation like Singapore or Luxembourg. In the public arena, these programs are not highly standardized, but they tend to fall into a few categories:

1. **90:10 Immersion** (also called total immersion). This type of program starts monolingual American kindergarteners or 1st graders with classroom instruction that is 90% or more in the immersion language and the rest in English. The immersion language is usually Spanish, but programs occasionally use others. As these students progress through the grade-school years, their course work usually moves toward 50% immersion language and 50%

English. That way, as these students enter high school, they can take specialized courses such as chemistry and journalism with their monolingual peers. By about the 5th grade, these immersion students perform at least as well in English as their cohorts in the monolingual English classroom.

2. **50:50 Immersion.** Here, the curriculum begins with about 50% immersion-language instruction and 50% English for the monolingual students. Some classrooms alternate languages every day, and some do so every half-day. Sometimes, they teach half the subjects in the target language and the rest in English.

3. **Two-Way Immersion** (also called bilingual immersion or dual immersion). In the other types of immersion classes, the bilingual teacher is typically outnumbered by around 20 monolingual children who would be perfectly happy to just go on speaking English the way they always do at home. Rest assured that when the classroom doors burst open for recess, when the children enter the cafeteria for lunch, or when they invite each other to off-campus birthday parties, this is exactly what they do. Children in two-way immersion can't necessarily do that because half of their classmates do not even speak the same language as they do. While half the children in the classroom come from mainstream English-speaking households, the other half come from immigrant households, where they speak another language virtually all the time. Both sets of children have no choice but to learn the other's language just to function in the classroom, which typically has a 50:50 split. Even on the playground, they still must continue their language learning.

The published results from studies of American two-way immersion classrooms have been very impressive, claiming a 92% success rate. Children from mainstream English-speaking backgrounds learn the immersion language better than children in other immersion programs. Disadvantaged children who do not yet speak English well do far better in school than their cohorts placed in quarantined limited English proficiency classrooms in which none of the students are fluent in English. Mainstream children eventually do better in *English* than do children in monolingual classrooms, while children of immigrant households do not lose their heritage language. Even more amazing, the non-English-speaking immigrant children go on to develop better-than-average English skills when compared with *native* English speakers in the monolingual classroom! It appears that both groups of children learn from native-speaking playmates who have no advanced degrees in education. Imagine that!

However, two-way immersion programs have not always been popular with skeptical mainstream parents. Some of them who place a high value on school achievement worry that enrolling their children into a classroom in which half the students are immigrants might bring the overall academic standard down. While the data coming from these programs does not support this concern, the perception persists. Some immigrant parents have not been all that enthusiastic either. Many would rather see their children dive in and learn English as quickly as possible, despite the expert opinion advising against it.

Overcoming these reservations, American immersion programs have slowly gained popularity, and parental demand for them has grown faster than the public schools' response to that demand. Imagine that your school district discovered that it did not have enough math teachers to meet demand. As a means of being fair, the district decided that it would just hold a *lottery* for the available slots. If your grade schoolers win the lottery, they get to learn math. If not, well, maybe they will have other opportunities in high school…That's how a lot of these immersion programs operate. It seems like a cruel bureaucratic injustice to me, but that's the way it is. If you think you might be interested in enrolling your kids in an immersion program, start investigating your options well ahead of time, and have a backup plan if the cards are not kind to you. Maybe you could start making some noise at your local school board meetings too.

These public immersion programs do have a rough equivalent in the private school arena: the international school. Such an organization typically serves an expat community in a large world city with a sizable international presence. For example, there is a French international school in New York, a German school in Beijing, an American school in Madrid, and a Spanish school in London. Across the globe, these schools are not common, but they're not rare either.

Typically, the students are the children of well-heeled globetrotting expats, though local parents who can afford their high tuitions find them attractive as well. For the local parents, these schools provide a great way to make sure their children not only speak multiple languages but read and write them too. Some foreign governments support these international schools for the benefit of their expat taxpayers. Virtually all of them prepare expat children to return to home universities one day, but a fair number also offer a standardized curriculum that will allow students to attend university almost anywhere in the world. To a varying degree, international schools divide instructional time between the expat language and the local one. Most offer additional languages to older students.

To be sure, these international schools expect their students to speak the expat language very well at the start of 1st grade, but many do offer assistance in the form of preschool for 3- and 4-year-olds. To find these schools, you could make a trip to a few foreign embassies, befriend a few expats who speak the language you want your children to learn, or just go to your favorite Internet search engine. There, you might try searching "expat schools" plus the name of your global city, or maybe "expat forum" along with your city's name. In any locale where there are sufficient numbers of expats, they will be using an online forum to share information, and they will know about the schools.

If you want to just kick back and let the schools mold your little babies into trilingual adults, you might do OK as a citizen of Luxembourg or Singapore. If you're wealthy enough, you might even get by in an international megacity. But if you fall into the "none of the above" category, read on.

CHAPTER 5

The Best Age to Start

● ● ●

WHEN IT COMES TO FORMAL reading, writing, and math, learning them before the age of 6 is probably not critical—at least there's good information to suggest that. On the other hand, when it comes to spoken language, the first 6 years *are* critical. Let me see if I can convince you of this so you will decide to begin teaching your children multiple languages as early as possible.

When children do not learn to read or do math problems until age 7 or so, as we've seen, they often end up doing better than children who learned earlier.[41] The same is probably true of music. Many experts do not recommend introducing a musical instrument before about age 7, the same age when many European countries introduce reading and mathematics. Prior to that age, they say it's important for children to develop an ear for musical sound, an enjoyment of the art, and definitely a love of playful, kinetic singing games. But trying to make a younger child sit still and actually play a piano or violin is a lot like trying to make a 3-year-old do math. You run the risk of taking all the pleasure out of learning.

But what if children did not have the opportunity to speak or hear a language until age 7? Would they eventually catch up to the early learners? Of course not; totally different story. In history, there have been some examples of this tragedy: children who grew up without human contact or who were subjected to the horrible neglect of complete isolation for many years, or hearing children of deaf parents who were not exposed to any verbal language when they were young. When these children were eventually found, professional caregivers made urgent attempts to teach them to speak, but they weren't terribly successful. Depending on their ages, some children were able to learn a little basic speech, but many of the older children never learned meaningful speech at all.

So what's the difference? Why is it OK to delay the introduction of reading, math, and musical performance, but not speech? Why must some skills be learned in early childhood? Like walking or sight, speech is what many scientists call a biological skill, what most of us just call an instinct.[42] Long before civilization began, we needed this instinct for our survival, and we have been using it for as long as we have been humans. Like beavers that build dams, lions that stalk prey, sparrows that fly, or spiders that spin webs, humans who speak to one another have an incredible survival advantage that keeps us from becoming extinct. And nature has done everything possible to ensure that we retain this ability.

Viewed in purely physical terms, we humans are pretty defenseless creatures. We're not particularly fast, strong, or agile. We don't have thick shells, we can't fly, and we're not able to endure extreme temperatures. What we do have going for us, however, is our amazing ability to communicate, to share information and ideas, the skill that defines us as a species. It's so important to our survival that it has become embedded in our chromosomes, a part of every living cell in our bodies—as important as sight or walking.

With time, we developed this superpower to higher and higher levels, and we found it advantageous to add layers of complexity to our civilizations: agriculture, architecture, art, and eventually reading and writing. Then, a little over 500 years ago, came the printing press. Before that, very few people knew how to read or write. In fact, it's only been about 100 years or so that half the world's population at a given time has known how. Today, the worldwide literacy rate is climbing, but it's still only around 85%.

All of these things we've learned since the advent of civilization, including reading and writing, are what scientists term cultural skills. They are magnificent but less fundamental to our existence than our instincts. They must be learned through practice, through trial and error, and we can learn them at any age. Generally, only infants and very young children can develop the instincts, but an ordinary human of any age, with practice, can learn to farm, to write, to paint, and to build a dwelling from a teacher who already knows how to do it.

Like the ability to see, walk, or grasp objects with our hands, speech is encoded in our DNA. That is how we pass the primal instinct from one generation to the next, and no one has ever found even one tribe of isolated people who did not use language. It's hardwired, automatic, inevitable. It's too important to leave to tradition or custom.

Cultural skills, on the other hand, must be passed in a more cumbersome way: by oral tradition, by schools, by long apprenticeships, or by conscious practice. To a degree at least, cultural skills depend upon the perpetuation of a civilization. If a civilization is destroyed, and its people are scattered, their cultural skills, their art, their music, and their written language can be lost, but their ability to speak, see, or walk cannot.

So how does a parent teach children to speak? How does a lioness teach her cubs to hunt? How does a mama beaver teach her kits to build a dam? In all cases, the answer is…they really don't. Instincts don't require much teaching, if any. The parents only have to provide the opportunity to learn. The young ones just need to be in the presence of others in the community who are using the skill. In many ways, they already have the skill inside them. They only need a little opportunity to fine-tune what they were born knowing how to do.

Though scientists do not know for sure how children almost universally develop this instinct of language, there are some pretty clever metaphors. Dr. Chomsky, our friend from Chapter 1, described it as a language acquisition device.[43] Others have called it a language bio-program.[44] This portion of the brain, wherever it might be, exists only in infants and children. It's designed not for speech itself but for the *acquisition* of speech and learning to understand the spoken word. Indeed, we just saw that the infant brain has many more neurons and synapses than the brain of an older child. We lose these by about age 3. Though we don't fully understand their purpose and can't seem to rescue these doomed neurons with brain toys or Mozart recordings, it is tantalizing to suppose that this portion of the infant's brain is the mechanism whereby a baby learns to see, to walk, and, of course, to speak. After developing these basic skills, the child no longer needs this particular learning capacity. This bio-program then fades away, having left the rest of the brain with these necessary abilities.

Experts say that a human is born with the ability to speak every world language, to comprehend and reproduce every subtle sound of every language in the world. Perhaps this is one of the reasons that infants have so many more brain cells than the rest of us. Babies cannot know whether they will be born in China, Argentina, or Morocco. Thus, they need to be able to learn to participate in the verbal communication they hear in their environment. If the environment has more than one language being spoken on a regular basis, then infants will need to learn each of them in order to get around. Since the majority of children in the world speak more than one language, there is every reason to believe that this language acquisition device is not limited to one and only one variety of speech. Though there are no studies on trilingual children, bilingual children acquire two languages as naturally as one, and at the same rate—without confusion.[45] Homeless children who grow up on the streets of large international cities, who might never have the opportunity to see the inside of a classroom or even learn to write their own names, can speak and understand an amazing number of languages just by being in the presence of them.

This bio-program we have just described, you must understand, is designed to help children speak and hear a language. We call this fluency. It's a biological skill. Being able to read and write a language, called literacy, is a completely different, almost unrelated skill. While our DNA and the language acquisition device guarantee us fluency, they do not necessarily offer us literacy. Literacy is something that our schools give us. It's a *cultural* skill. While babies and toddlers have an advantage in achieving fluency, they do not have the same edge when it comes to literacy.

Since this is a book about teaching languages to children 6 and under, its main focus must be fluency, not literacy. For the most part, becoming "tri-literate," as opposed to becoming trilingual, is something that might be a better goal for a little later on, just like math or piano. Most of this "tri-literate" information I'm saving for a sequel—this book will already be long enough without it!

Though not without controversy, many experts agree on the importance of achieving fluency in the early years. Literacy is another matter; most feel that a person can become literate equally well at just about any age, so there's no real hurry. Furthermore, as I hope to show you, becoming trilingual can be a lot of fun for kids. You want it that way, because you need them to be enthusiastic partners in your project. Learning to read and write in all those languages will be more didactic and less fun, probably better suited to older children who have already begun to lose their sense of wonder and curiosity. Early on, you can let the language acquisition device do the work so they don't have to. There will be plenty of opportunity for boring drills and handwriting exercises down the road.

So what are the facts about this metaphorical language acquisition device, this bio-program? We don't have any. How do we know it even exists? We don't. We have theories, of course, but they border on philosophy, little more than intriguing science fiction. But they're the best we can do right now.

Let me see if I can offer you some evidence that infants and young children really do have a bio-program for languages and really can learn languages far better than adults:

1. In the relatively new field of functional neuroimaging, where the brain's electrical activity can be viewed with special scanners from moment to moment, scientists have found that when a child learns a second language before the age of 3, the brain processes it in the same way as the first language. If a child acquires a second language after the age of 3, however, the pattern of brain activity is more chaotic and decentralized.[46]

2. A recent research study on bilingual immigrant children and school performance showed that a child who starts learning a new

language at 4 or 5 will most likely be less successful than a child who begins well before age 3. Children who begin learning the new school language prior to age 3 do much better in the classroom than those who learn the new language later on. In fact, children not adequately proficient in the school language at the start of kindergarten often need 5–7 years to catch up, and many never catch up at all. While being able to speak a language is a high-level skill, the ability to function in a classroom learning environment in that language requires an even higher level. The early learners can function at this level, but the later learners cannot.[47]

3. Numerous studies of immigrant children have shown that they learn the language of the new country better and faster than their parents do. Their parents never catch up, no matter how long they work at it.[48]

4. Children who begin learning a new language in kindergarten by means of a good language immersion program do quite well, but they do not catch up to children who begin learning their new language in the home at birth.[49]

5. A Swedish study found that adults who learn a new language never achieve the proficiency of a native speaker. Older children learning a new language sometimes manage to reach native proficiency, but rarely. Very young children usually do achieve native proficiency.[50]

6. There is no age that has been shown to be equivalent to starting a new language at birth. Every month that passes is slightly less ideal than the previous one.[51]

7. Most experts think that the earlier a child begins learning a language, the better the ultimate proficiency in that language will be.[52]

8. According to Dr. Susan Curtiss, professor of linguistics at UCLA, "The power to learn language is so great in the young child that it doesn't seem to matter how many languages you seem to throw their way...They can learn as many spoken languages as you can allow them to hear systematically and regularly at the same time.

Children just have this capacity. Their brain is just ripe to do this…there doesn't seem to be any detriment to developing several languages at the same time."[53]

9. The ability to learn a new language progressively declines with advancing age.[54] The decline seems to start at birth, says the most recent evidence.[55] And adult learners achieve lower levels of proficiency.[56] Puberty seems in some ways to be the edge of a cliff, at which point abilities fall more rapidly.[57]

10. Experts generally agree that high school is probably not the optimal time to begin studying a new language.[58] If you happen to know any Americans, then you probably know some people who began studying a foreign language in college or high school. So how is that working out for them? How many of them can actually converse in that language today?

11. Adults who try to learn a new language have a success rate of only about 10%.[59] The only people still claiming that adulthood is a great time to start learning a new language are the people who sell language learning products.

12. After 5 years in a bilingual school immersion program that starts in kindergarten, the success rate is around 92%.[60] For infants, it's probably quite a bit higher than that.

In case you haven't already guessed, let me tell you exactly when I think you should begin teaching your children multiple languages. If your children have already been born, you should start today. If your children have not been born yet, it would probably be OK to wait until that day comes! If such an early start is not possible for you, I would make every effort to begin by age 3, or as soon thereafter as possible.

Just one caveat here. Children under the age of about 3 months are quite susceptible to infection and should probably have only limited contact with people other than their immediate family. So, if you are planning to use outside help to teach your children, you might want to delay bringing them into service until your children reach 3 months old.

CHAPTER 6

Quality Defined

● ● ●

LET'S REVIEW THE DIFFERENCE BETWEEN instincts and cultural skills. Deep inside the brain, instincts like sight and walking are very complex processes, but they are incredibly easy for humans to learn—so easy, in fact, that they really don't even need to be taught, if you start early. Cultural skills like music and art are not so simple to learn, but you can pick them up equally well at just about any stage of life. For our purposes as parents, spoken language is an instinct.

Traditional school subjects like math and reading are cultural skills. Nevertheless, we try to teach younger and younger children these subjects, while we delay the introduction of new languages until somewhere around adolescence or even adulthood. It doesn't make any sense, and it's just not working particularly well. It may well be something he wishes he'd never said, but Dr. Harry Chugani, world-renowned pediatric neuroscientist, put it this way: "Who is the idiot who decided that youngsters should learn foreign languages in high school?"[61] Maybe it's the same person who markets the aptitude test that determines which 2-year-olds get accepted into the elite preschool world.

Where the conventional wisdom on educating our children is concerned, maybe we've spotted a few cracks in the foundation. We shouldn't ignore those, and we might have to figure a few things out for ourselves. With respect to childhood language learning, experts talk all the time about "quality exposure," but finding a consistent definition of that term is impossible. There's no real standard yet, and many have their own opinions. Personally, I'm OK with that, because it allows me to dream up my own definitions. Once you've gained a little experience in raising trilingual children, you'll probably be glad to do your own dreaming, and your opinions on quality will probably be about as valid as anyone else's.

At this point I need to define a few terms for you:

£ **School language**—the language spoken in a child's classroom. Usually it's only one, but there are exceptions.

Home language—the language spoken in a child's home. Usually it's only one.

Community language—the main language spoken in a child's community. Usually one.

First language—the language spoken in a child's daydreams. Also called the primary language.

Heritage language—the language occasionally spoken at a child's family reunions!

𝒫 **Target language**—the language you want your child to learn.

Native language—You might also see this term. Basically, it's the language a child began acquiring at birth. Usually it's the same as the first language, but not always. Some immigrant children lose their native language as the community language becomes dominant.

And now you're as ready as you'll ever be for my personal top-ten list of factors that determine quality language exposure for kids:

1. A real live human
2. Words per week rather than hours per week
3. Age-appropriate technique
4. A native speaker
5. A teacher who does not speak your children's first language
6. Student-to-teacher ratio of 1:1
7. Frequent exposure

8. Parental monitoring
9. Sustained exposure
10. Stress reduction for the parent

A real live human. Here are two extremely important points that the commercial language learning industry will never bother to tell you: (a) the first 3 years are utterly crucial to language development, and (b) the only thing that works in those years is a real live human. Tattoo that onto your cortex before you read on. Before the age of about 3, children really can't learn language from anything other than another human who is physically present with them.[62] Recordings or videos just don't work. Small children appear to need direct social interaction to learn, and they learn best from a loving caretaker, one they know and trust. They need to have a "bond," and it's far, far better if their teachers have some emotional skin in the game.

After the child turns 3, other media—cartoons, movies, and TV shows in your target language, for example—are of some value. Like the Europeans, I really believe they have a place if your kids find them fun and interesting. However, they will never be as good as a real live human to whom your children feel emotionally connected. We'll make a very clear distinction between "human time" and "electronic time," and we'll need to assign very different quality values to them. Rest assured, human time will receive a higher value. However, electronic time is cheaper. In fact, it's free if you know where to find it, so you'll probably want both types of language exposure in your overall plan.

Words per week rather than hours per week. Now, that's how I'd like to pay the language babysitters in my house. I'd like to attach a voice recorder to their collars and pay them based on the number of words they speak to my children! I would even be willing to pay them double for every word that my children speak in return. Unfortunately, most language teachers like to get paid by the hour, even when they're not feeling all that talkative. You'll probably end up paying by the hour too, even though it's not really the duration that matters to you.

Suppose that when your children are in the company of a quiet book-worm, they hear only 10 words per hour. On the other hand, if a chatter-box is tutoring them, maybe they hear as many as 10,000 words per hour. Might we say, where a child is concerned, that 1 hour with a chatterbox is equivalent to 1,000 hours with a soft-spoken bookworm? It's probably not that much better, but being with a chatterbox as opposed to a more reserved person is many times better. Definitely keep this in mind as you begin to strategize your baby's trilingual future. You want to hire motor-mouths, not pantomimes!

Infants and very young children learn by hearing words, not by watching some teenybopper babysitter from next door flip through a fashion magazine or send text messages to the guy from art class she has a crush on. Your choice in babysitters has ramifications that reach further than just your child's multilingual future. Studies have shown that children who hear more words before the start of school are more intelligent and more likely to have successful academic careers. So, even if you don't want multilingual children, be selective about whom you hire to watch your kids.

About 20 years ago, Drs. Hart and Risley conducted an often-quoted study showing that children who heard more spoken language in the pre-school years tended to do better in school than those who heard less.[63] They usually had educated parents who spoke to them more frequently, with more sophisticated grammar. By the time they reached the age of 3, these fortunate children had heard about 30 million words, while children from disadvantaged backgrounds had heard only about 1/3 as many. In case you were wondering, 30 million words over 3 years comes to about 38 words per minute for 12 hours of every day. Normal adult conversation includes about 300 words per minute.

Children from very verbal families tend to start out their educational lives at a distinct advantage, and they probably never lose that advantage.[64] We also know that the number of words a child has heard by age 3 predicts the vocabulary size, and the vocabulary at age 3 predicts reading and spelling skills through at least the 3rd grade, and probably well beyond that.[65]

So, what do you think? If Drs. Hart and Risley were trying to find a language babysitter for their children, what sort of person would they choose? I say it would be a talkative one. A chatterbox might drive you crazy, but your young child would probably love the attention, and the interaction just might lead to greater school success.

(Maybe you noticed I threw a new term at you—the *language babysitter.* I hope you're curious about that one, but we'll just have to define it as we go. Most likely, your first language babysitter is not far from you.)

Age-appropriate technique. Experts say that the most important emotional need of an infant is a feeling of security—a warm embrace, a soothing lullaby, a dry diaper, a meal, a reassuring tone of voice to chase away a moment of fear or loneliness. Infants learn best when they are held and spoken to in a loving, comforting manner. Though it's best if the babysitter is actually talking to the baby, not just talking to someone else in the vicinity, infants learn a lot even when they overhear live speech not addressed to them specifically. During this linguistic stage, you'll probably want a language babysitter with prior experience caring for babies and little children, most commonly from raising children and grandchildren of her own.

Once they're old enough to crawl and walk, children acquire a need to explore their environment. At that point, they learn very well when they have a trusted adult to help them in this conquest, someone to follow along behind them as their interpreter, guide, and protector—speaking as many words as possible, of course.

Once children become verbal, the language babysitter should keep up the chatter, but she must take greater care to talk *with* them and not just *to* them. Back-and-forth dialogue teaches far more than commands. With increasing sophistication, children develop a knack—a sometimes very annoying knack—for abstract thought. And so begins the endless barrage of "why" questions. As they reflect on things they have seen and experienced, they become increasingly curious about almost everything. They need an adult with the time, patience, and energy to keep answering those endless questions. Some of them are easy to answer, but others are utterly impossible. Your babysitter, however, gets credit for any answer, so long as the question is asked and answered in the target language. If that is happening, you can be well assured that language learning is going on, even if the answers fall short.

You want a language babysitter who can actually engage a child in a two-way conversation—a teacher who can ask the child a question and elicit an answer, and who can answer a child's question in such a way that motivates the child to ask another one. A teacher who does not give the child opportunities to return speech, teaches much less than one who encourages a child to think, formulate thoughts, and put them into words. (When you see this start to happen in a second or third language, most likely sooner than you think, be prepared to wipe away a little tear of amazed joy and give the teacher a nice little tip!) Since the ability to narrate a story in his or her own words is a major gauge of a child's school readiness, the teacher who can have your child doing this before the age of 6 (in whatever language) is doing you a huge favor. When that happens in your target language, celebrate! Your efforts have been successful.

Children, even babies, are no different from all the rest of us: We really like it when people talk to us, but we also like to be heard, acknowledged, and appreciated. Look for babysitters who can do that at all stages of early life. It doesn't require a lot of education. In fact, it probably can't be taught. But it does require some chattiness, an attentive ear, and a big heart.

A native speaker. Some evidence indicates that children who learn a language from native speakers might learn it better.[66] You probably don't find that too hard to believe. If you can, choose language babysitters who are native speakers, but understand from the very beginning that you may not always have that choice. If you find yourself in a situation where only non-native speakers are available to you, use them without hesitation; a non-native speaker is infinitely better for your children than no speaker at all. At some point, you might have to decide how much extra you are willing to pay for a native speaker. As far as I'm concerned, I value native speakers, but I just don't think a native speaker is worth 2 to 3 times as much of my money as a non-native one, so I often give the nod to non-native speakers even when I do have a choice.

This seems like a good time to go all philosophical on you again. In some circumstances, you might find yourself needing to hire language babysitters who speak a heavy dialect or use some nonstandard form of the language. For example, you might not be able to afford a French-speaking governess from Paris, but you might find a babysitter from Haiti or Senegal who already lives nearby. Though some experts might discourage you from doing this, I don't see a problem with it. If your children grow up learning to speak a target language in a nonstandard dialect, I think they can make the transition to the standard form of the language later in life.

Outside the United States, you might find that your only source of teaching your children English is from a Nigerian babysitter, or perhaps one from the Philippines. If you are seeking Mandarin Chinese, your only local resource may be someone who speaks the Fujianese dialect. I think that's perfectly acceptable. Again, if you have a choice, you might choose someone who speaks a perfectly standard textbook form of the desired language, but you may not always have that luxury. If you seriously want your children to learn a language, take inventory of your human resources locally, and go with what you can find. I happen to be a lover of dialect. I think it adds an element of sincerity to spoken language. I think a child who first learns a dialect is more likely to be perceived as a native speaker, and that child can transition to the standard form later in life. I myself had to do that. I grew up speaking Southern Redneck and didn't have to learn Standard English until I was in school. I think I turned out OK, though I guess there might be some dissenting opinions out there.

A teacher who does not speak your children's first language. Maybe all children are Southern Redneck at heart, linguistically speaking. They can be relied upon to take the path of least resistance when it comes to their language. If they discover that their babysitter actually speaks their own first language, they will work incessantly to convert the baby-sitter over to what is easiest for them. Since children are such persistent and energetic little creatures, they can sometimes wear a babysitter down.

Eventually, some will just give up and speak the children's preferred language, or at least acknowledge what the children say in it. This, however, is a huge step-down in educational quality.

When you have a babysitter who does not even know your children's first language, you have a language tutor who cannot be worn down. The children understand this, give up, and speak to the babysitter in the target language, which is exactly what you want to happen. Of course, you might find it difficult to have an adult conversation with a babysitter who doesn't speak your home language, but I'll help you figure that one out. The inconvenience is a small price to pay and an investment well worth making.

Student-to-teacher ratio of 1:1. If you have two or more children, rest assured that they will virtually always speak their first language to one another. How to change that, I don't think anyone knows. If you leave a group of kids with a single language babysitter, be advised that they will try to ditch the babysitter and go play by themselves—in their preferred language. The pie-in-the-sky solution would be one babysitter per child, but that could get expensive. Instead, you might have to train your babysitter to keep your children focused on her and to keep them in the target language at all times. If it comes to it, splitting time might be the only solution, giving each child half the time he or she might otherwise have received. Half as much time in the target language exclusively is probably better than twice the time with a babysitter who can't keep the young pupils from ignoring her and conversing with each other in their own language.

Frequent exposure. If your children get their exposure to a language only once a week, it will be 7 days before they hear it again. That's probably a little too much time between sessions—enough time to forget much of what they learned. Thus, you should probably divide the learning time into at least two weekly sessions. Ideally, the very best way would provide at least some exposure to the target language every day, but I think you'll quickly find that's not always practical. However, divide it into multiple sessions whenever you can. And when that's not possible, just do whatever is practical. A single weekly dose of a language is far, far better than none at all.

Parental monitoring. Though I hope to make your supervisory role as easy as possible, you still have to understand something: no one will be as concerned about your children's multilingual future as you will. That goes for school teachers, public policy makers, and babysitters alike. You can't micromanage, but you have to make sure your language babysitters are talkative, and keep the conversation in the target language. Any babysitter who thinks she can just plug in a foreign-language video and text her boyfriend while your children watch should not expect you to pay her. As I'll show you, you can find your own language videos, for free. You're paying a teacher for conversation, so make sure you're getting the service you've bought.

Sustained exposure. Quality begins as early in life as possible and doesn't stop until adulthood at the earliest. If you provide good exposure for a while but then stop, your efforts will be wasted.

Stress reduction for the parent. If it's no fun for the kids, they'll rebel against learning new languages. If it's expensive and stressful for you, you'll procrastinate. Then, one day sooner than you think, you'll all wake up and it'll be too late. So the highest-quality language plan will be the one that everyone can stick to: one that reduces the parental workload, not increases it. When you get right down to it, we're only talking about a common resource here—babysitters. Most ordinary parents use them to give themselves a break and increase their productivity. There's absolutely no reason the agents of your language-learning program cannot afford you the same luxury. In a sense, the only thing separating you from parents raising monolingual children will be how you select your babysitters...

If you start this program as early as I think you should, you'll probably hope for someone with considerable experience with very young children. Everyday skills like knowing how to change a diaper or prepare a kid-friendly meal can go a long way toward enhancing the learning environment. Perhaps you've noticed that many ordinary parents hire babysitters who double as housekeepers. Maybe your language babysitters could also serve the same dual role. Just maybe—if you don't mind your kids helping out a little—your tutor could use the target language to teach your little ones how to mop a floor, load a dishwasher, or make a bed. I just want you to consider the possibility that a good language babysitter not only might enrich your children linguistically but could lighten your load as well.

If you happen to be a multilingual parent, that's great. Maybe you could raise multilingual children all by yourself. But should you? I believe the answer is no. I've seen highly intelligent, extremely committed multilingual parents fail at it. Though it's not anything magical, not exactly rocket science, it takes a lot of time, and that's just something we never have enough of in the modern world. There are only 24 hours in the average day, after all. I firmly believe that your life will be less stressful, and your children will learn more if you do not try to do everything on your own here.

Being a good trilingual parent is a lot like being a good CEO: you cannot and should not do all the work yourself. Though you must retain some oversight, you have to resist the urge to be a control freak. Your job is to grasp the big picture and to motivate the people working for you to make it happen. Once you've done that, you have to get used to traveling first class! So, while your team is hard at work chasing your vision, you need to go for a pedicure at the nail spa, pick up some exotic ingredients at the Asian market, or (my personal favorite) recline your seat back—all the way back—stow your worries in the overhead compartment, and do some strategic dreaming!

But when the little control freak inside your brain gets the better of you, stress not. If you want to maximize your personal contribution to your children's education, the best thing you can do is follow the guidelines set down by our good friends Dr. Hart and Dr. Risley. Speak to your kids frequently and elaborately, and read aloud to them every evening for at least 15 minutes. Be there at the dinner table, well rested from your nap, and engage your children in two-way dialogue—genuine back-and-forth conversation the way our great-grandparents did before television. Encourage them to ask thoughtful questions, and let them recount their activities to you in narrative form. Now we know that the ability to tell a detailed story and the presence of a large vocabulary are very good predictors of future school success. Water those seeds; nurture those skills.

Your children need to hear you speak in the most elaborate, fluent, and grammatically complex manner you can, because that will one day be their standard, their reference point. If you're like most people, you can only do that in one language: your strongest language. Use this language even if it will not be the school language of their future. Immigrant parents who try to speak the community language with their children, when they themselves are not totally fluent, often end up with disappointing results. Some of these children ultimately do worse in the community language than their peers who spoke their native language at home. To add insult to injury, many of them lose the family's native language as well because they stopped speaking it at home.[67] I could fairly describe that as a lose-lose situation.

So, if you as a parent speak Spanish at the level of a college professor but speak English at the level of a 5th grader, speak to your children in Spanish, even if they will be attending school in English. The prevailing theory holds that deep inside the brain, underneath all the spoken language, the language processor (or whatever it might be) needs exposure to a rich vocabulary and a complex grammatical structure in at least one language to develop thoroughly. If the young brain is deprived of this sophisticated exposure, that might spell trouble down the road. But once the processor has become proficient in at least one language, then—so the theory goes—it can adapt its advanced processing to different languages at some point in the future. So if you can immerse your child's language processor in a bath of sophisticated grammar and vocabulary in any language, you should do it.

Let it be your job to make sure your children have all the complex grammar and rich vocabulary they will need to succeed in school one day. Rely upon your babysitters to make them multilingual.

● ● ●

Notice that I made no mention of the language teacher's educational background on this list. Assuming that you, as the parent, take the responsibility of having grammatically sophisticated dialogue with your family, as Dr. Hart and Dr. Risley would recommend, it really doesn't matter all that much whether your children learn their additional languages from a rocket scientist or a peasant fishmonger. If you want your children to learn a language, and the only person you can find to speak it with them has only a 3rd-grade education, I say no problem. Go for it, absolutely, without hesitation. Feed the language acquisition device in that little brain as early as possible with anything resembling what you want that brain to have as an adult! Your children can learn the standard textbook form of the language later in life, and the less highly educated babysitter will do an excellent job of laying the foundation for you. However, if you wait for a credentialed school teacher, that foundation might be difficult or impossible to lay down later in life.

Where your little language geniuses are concerned, professional educators don't necessarily add quality, in my book. Little children don't learn by their techniques; they don't need an expert to "teach" them a language. When your children begin formal schooling one day, a well-trained teacher will be great, but in the earliest years, I'm not convinced that a highly trained professional can teach children a new language any better than a lovingly talkative adopted grandmother type.

When we were just beginning our own multilingual journey, we found a bilingual teacher who had a PhD in early childhood education. We thought we'd hit the jackpot, but we soon realized that we were wrong about that. At the time, our daughters were 2 and 4. This teacher came with lesson plans, workbooks, flash cards, vocabulary-building exercises, memorization drills, and even homework assignments that neither of us as parents had time to review. Our daughters hated the sessions, refused to cooperate, and dreaded the teacher's visits. When she moved to another city, we all breathed a private sigh of relief. We replaced her with a stay-at-home immigrant mom who did not yet know the local language. She brought her own daughter along and turned our living room into a noisy but phenomenally educational language lab.

So let me finish this portrait for you, my ideal of the highest quality language teacher for your little children. You want a real live human, a loving chatterbox who thoroughly enjoys spending time with kids and knows how to speak with them. She doesn't mind caring for the youngest of kids, well below the age of 3. She should be someone whom your children really enjoy and trust. Ideally, she does not even know your home language. She's fun but firm enough to keep the children from drifting out of the target language. She would be willing to come for a few hours several times a week rather than just once a week for a longer duration. She's prepared to be a part of your children's lives for many years. She's a babysitter who teaches language, simply by interacting in her native tongue.

You won't always be able to find this person. Maybe you never completely will, but she's the one you're always looking for.

CHAPTER 7

How Much Will They Need?

• • •

IF YOU BEGIN EXPOSING YOUR children to three languages somewhere around birth and continue until they reach adulthood, how many hours of exposure per week will they need in each language? Obviously, it's an incredibly important question for us, but, alas, science does not have a satisfactory answer. I hope you're getting used to that.

About 20 years ago, a published article claimed that children needed to spend approximately 20% of their awake time in a language in order to learn to speak it.[68] If you assume that children sleep about half the time and are awake the rest, then 20% is roughly 17 hours per week. Most linguistic scientists do not accept this research study as definitive, but many bloggers and publishers of parental advice columns *do*. You're likely to see it if you do any independent reading beyond this book.

The research study, upon which so many opinions have been based, had shortcomings. It examined only 25 children between the ages of 8 months and 2½ years—a very small number of very young children evaluated over a very short period of time. The investigators gave the parents a questionnaire, asking them how much time their child spent with the community language and how much in the heritage language. They found that if the parent did not report that the child spent at least 20% of the time with the heritage language, then the child did not seem to want to speak it. Estimates of exposure time in the heritage language were subjective, as were the determinations that a child did not want to use this language. Furthermore, most of the children did not stay in the study for its entire duration.

I think this number has become a myth without firm scientific backing that gets rewarmed and re-served on a regular basis. Despite its limitations, it lives on, mainly because nothing else out there gives us an answer to this all-important question. So, if not 17 hours a week, then how many? I have no proof, but I believe the number is lower. Here's part of the reason I feel that way:

1. My own children started a new language before 12 months of age and learned it with only 5 hours per week of exposure. I wouldn't claim that they can use it as well as a native speaker in the native country, but they can use it well enough to communicate. Perhaps they were not doing that early on, but they are now.

2. Hearing children of deaf parents have been observed to develop speech and language normally if their family life is otherwise normal, and they have as little as 5 to 10 hours per week of exposure to hearing speakers. It also seems to be important that these children hear normal speech from adults before age 3.[69]

   (Age 3 keeps coming up, doesn't it?)

3. American public school kids in Spanish foreign-language immersion programs progress very well in their native English if they have as little as 1 hour per day of English exposure. These children, by the time they reach grade 4 or 5, are performing in school subjects taught in English as well as children in monolingual classrooms. That's an apples-to-oranges comparison, I know, but worth considering.

Most scientists will tell you that the amount of language exposure necessary to establish childhood fluency is just not known yet. Probably, it depends a lot upon the quality of exposure (and, in our dreams at least, we're already experts on that subject!) Parental motivation seems to matter quite a bit too. If you actually want your children to speak multiple languages, your chances of success are considerably better. I'm half joking: The fact is, many immigrant parents are not all that interested in seeing their children continue to speak the heritage language, and these kids often lose it. In many countries (the United States included), being an immigrant is stigmatized, and speaking a language other than the community language can be an even bigger stigma.

So this is where the science stops. This is where a lot of books on raising multilingual children stop too. However, there's just one small problem: Where's the action plan? How much practice do children need in order to learn a language? What exactly are parents supposed to do, particularly if they are not multilingual themselves? Our scientists are silent on the matter. And yet, with no scientists to guide them, children all over the world continue to grow up perfectly multilingual. But if we wait for scientific clarification, our children will not. If we wait until high school, our children will almost certainly not. We have to do something before then.

Why don't we just do what experts do when they lack data? Let's take what we know and extrapolate. That is, let's just start dreaming stuff up! We will create these rules ourselves, so we have to follow them only if they seem to help us. If not, we can just ditch them. At least they get us started, the hardest part.

A fashionable new school of thought out there, popularized in Malcolm Gladwell's book *Outliers: The Story of Success*, claims that it takes about 10,000 hours of practice to become an expert in any given field, to thoroughly master it. That includes engineering, medicine, golf, Spanish—whatever.

Shall we assume for the moment that this 10,000-hour rule is correct? If you start at or near birth, and want to give your children 10,000 hours of study in a given language by the time they finish high school, then, if you do the math, the number of hours per week is somewhere between 10 and 11. Let's choose a nice round number and say 10 hours per week. If that's good enough for you, try to avoid getting bogged down in the math in the rest of this chapter, because the details could get more than a little tedious. In reality, these numbers will matter a lot less than the big-picture concepts anyway. But, if you're a total numbers geek, you might actually find the rest of this chapter entertaining.

Ten hours per week for your children to become experts in a language before they get their own apartment or move into a college dormitory somewhere. This seems like a lot of time, and it is. But keep in mind that it's not terribly stressful time. For the most part, it's just ordinary, everyday play and conversation—the same stuff they would have been doing anyway…only in a different language. Whether Malcolm Gladwell's theory is correct or not, I think it's a reasonable starting point. And based on what I have observed myself, I feel quite comfortable that 10 hours per week sustained over the course of an entire childhood, adolescence, and early adulthood would give your children something that you as a parent would be extremely proud of. Can I back that up with any science? Not a shred. Take it with a grain of salt if you like, but I think you'll find it a very useful model, even if it's only an educated guess.

Keep in mind that this 10,000-hour rule applies to run-of-the-mill adult learning of cultural skills. It does not factor in the boost to learning that your children receive from the language acquisition device which, as best we can tell, is most active before the age of 3. I'm going to estimate that the language exposure your children receive prior to age 3 is 2.5 times as valuable. Probably it's more than that, but we'll say that learning boosted by the language acquisition device should count 2.5 times. I'll also say that language exposure from age 3 to 6 counts 2X, twice as good. Children who learn within this slightly later but still very early time frame also have a higher long-term success rate than older children and adults.[70] If, however, you don't think that children are better language learners than adults, or if you don't believe in language acquisition devices or linguistic critical periods, no problem. You don't have to use these multipliers if you don't want to. Just go with 10 hours a week for 18 years, and leave it at that.

Let me do a calculation just so you understand better. Let's say you start at birth and give your daughter 10 hours per week in a target language until she starts 1st grade. Then you drop the exposure level down to 5 hours per week so she'll have more time for her schoolwork and extra-curricular activities.

For the first 3 years, you accumulate the following: 3 years × 52 weeks per year × 10 hours per week = 1,560 hours. But, we're multiplying the 1,560 hours before the 3rd birthday by 2.5, so we make it 3,900 hours.

From age 3 to 6, we also accumulate the same: 3 years × 52 weeks per year × 10 hours per week = 1,560 hours. Here we multiply by 2, which equals 3,120 hours.

From 6 to 18, we drop down to 5 hours per week: that's 12 years × 5 hours per week × 52 weeks per year, or 3,120 hours.

Add the hours up: 3,900 + 3,120 + 3,120 = 10,140 hours. A Gladwellian expert!

Despite the fact that we're assigning 2.5X value for any language exposure prior to the age of 3, please remember that, at this very young age, the only type of exposure that does any good at all is a real live human.[71] Not telephone, not Skype, not any kind of video-chatting. Not videos, cartoons, or other electronic time. Electronic time will be of value later on, but not really in the first 3 years. In fact, the American Academy of Pediatrics goes as far as to say that children under 2 years should not be exposed to these electronic media at all.[72] Once your children are older, you can begin to use these less expensive resources to make your life a little easier; but, for the first 3 years, be prepared to use human time exclusively. (If "Skype" is a new concept for you, feel free to have a preliminary look at Skype.com, and we'll discuss it again.)

Also keep in mind that once your children reach school age, time available for a second and third language will drop considerably. Though you might be able to expose them to two different languages for 10 or more hours per week each in the preschool years, that might be difficult to do during school sessions, when there will be homework, extracurricular activities and the like. When your kids are busy teenagers with new driver's licenses, lots of after-school activities, maybe boyfriends or girlfriends, and seriously rebellious attitudes, you might be lucky to get them to spend any time at all on a language. For this reason, as a matter of principle, I would definitely recommend what I call "front-loading."

It's a term I'm more or less borrowing from the mutual-fund world, and I think the investment metaphor is entirely appropriate. I really think it's best to make larger contributions to your family's linguistic fund of knowledge in the early years and allow them to compound over time. Front-loading will be up to you, but, if you possibly can, I'd suggest trying to accumulate the equivalent of 5,000 hours of language exposure (half the total) in each of your chosen languages before your children start 1st grade. That might not always be possible, particularly if you cannot start near birth, but it's something to aim for.

Let's do another one. Say your son is 3 years old and you want to start a language program. You choose your 2 languages and place him with fluent speakers for 20 hours per week, each. Once he reaches grade school, you drop the level down to 8 hours per week, each. When he enters high school, you drop down to 4 hours per week, each.

3–6 years: 3 years × 52 weeks per year × 20 hours
per week × 2 = 6,240 hours
6–14 years: 8 years × 52 weeks per year × 8 hours
per week = 3,328 hours
14–18 years: 4 years × 52 weeks per year × 4 hours
per week = 832 hours
Grand total = 10,400 hours

Mission accomplished.

Let's now consider that, beyond the age of about 3, children who are learning new languages begin to derive some benefit from electronic time: foreign-language cartoons, TV shows, kids' movies, Skype buddies, and music videos. The American Academy of Pediatrics reports that the average American kid spends around 7 hours per day on these electronic media![73] Let me suggest to you that there is absolutely no reason why the bulk of this otherwise wasted time could not be in a target language.

Can I offer you any research data to support my claim that foreign-language cartoons and TV shows are beneficial after age 3? Not really. While I feel strongly that they are helpful, my opinions are based on personal observation, though the Europeans seem to agree. Shortly, you'll see that it's very easy to find totally free, virtually inexhaustible resources for foreign-language videos, so you might want to experiment with them yourself and draw your own conclusions. I think you'll decide that they have a role. Personally, I've found that permitting my children to watch a fairly generous amount of foreign-language videos allows them to feel a little more mainstream. In most American settings—indeed, in most world settings now—your children's playmates are exposed to huge doses of pop culture from an early age. Most of their parents are just not that into childhood multilingualism, so the mainstream pop culture exposure in a language the children already speak is of highly questionable educational value, I think. Yet, if you forbid your children from partaking of it, they could begin to feel like outcasts, alienated from their little friends. I believe that taking some target-language exposure and disguising it as pop culture cartoons, kids' movies, and TV shows will allow your children to feel like they're getting to do the things that their friends are getting to do, without the time being otherwise so unproductively spent. Being able to discuss popular cartoon characters with their little friends means a lot to them. And their friends don't even need to know that your children are actually watching them in German, Spanish, French, or Korean.

In our house, we have a rule: Our children have relatively free rein to watch Internet cartoons, kids' movies, and TV shows, once the homework and chores are done, but these must be in one of the target languages. If we catch them watching a video in their first language (English), they lose all electronic time privileges for a week. No more *Dora the Explorer* in Spanish. No more Selena Gomez dubbed in German. No more zany Chinese variety shows.

I'll show you how to find these sources of electronic time (mostly on YouTube.com) in a later chapter, but for now, just be aware that the online world has an incredible abundance of resources for you as a trilingual parent. They're almost all free, and they do an excellent job of holding a child's attention. It's a little scary the way they'll keep a kid mesmerized for hours, but if language learning is going on, it's at least partly a good thing…isn't it?

While I think these electronic media have value for language learning, I believe we need to view them as supplements to human contact rather than replacements for it. For the purposes of calculating exposure times, let's say that electronic time is half as good as human time. That means when we add electronic-time hours to our totals, we will multiply them by 0.5. I'll also repeat that they begin to count only after the age of 3. And one more thing: Let's say they count only after a child has accumulated *at least 500 hours* of real live human time in a language.

Another calculation should clarify this. When your daughter is 18 months old, you place her with carefully selected language babysitters so she can become trilingual. Until she's 3, she spends 10 hours a week with language babysitters in each of her target languages. After she reaches 3, you can no longer afford this level of tutoring, so you must drop down to 5 hours per week. However, you supplement this with 2 hours per day of target-language electronic time in each language—mostly cartoons and kids' movies. When school starts, you must drop the teaching time down to 4 hours per week, but you continue to allow her 7 hours per week of cartoons and kids' movies in each target language. You continue this until high school graduation. How many hours does she accumulate in each language?

1.5–3 years: 1.5 years × 10 hours per week × 52 weeks
$$\text{per year} \times 2.5 = 1{,}950 \text{ hours}$$
3–6 years: 3 years × 5 hours per week × 52 weeks
$$\text{per year} \times 2 = 1{,}560 \text{ hours}$$
3 years × 14 electronic hours per week × 52 weeks
$$\text{per year} \times 0.5 \times 2 = 2{,}184 \text{ hours}$$
6–18 years: 12 years × 4 hours per week × 52 weeks
$$\text{per year} = 2{,}496 \text{ hours}$$
12 years × 7 electronic hours per week × 52 weeks
$$\text{per year} \times 0.5 = \underline{2{,}184 \text{ hours}}$$
Total
$$= \underline{10{,}374 \text{ hours}}$$

What if your language program gets interrupted? What if you encounter a bump in the road? Suppose your family has to move to a remote area with no foreign-language babysitters, or someone gets sick, or a parent loses a job? Let's say that a child can miss language exposure for up to 4 weeks in a given year without any subtractive effect, but after that, you have to begin subtracting hours. After 4 weeks in any calendar year with no language exposure, you must begin subtracting 20 hours per week for each additional week without language exposure. (It seems like a lot, but as we'll see, children are excellent forgetters, forgetting even more readily than they learn.) And, of course, if your children only get 48 weeks of language exposure in a given year, use 48 in your calculations, not 52.

Very importantly, let's also say that if a child below the age of 12 goes more than a year with no foreign-language exposure, then you need to reset the hours to *zero*. Why? It's a puberty thing, and I'll discuss it a little more thoroughly in a later chapter dealing with older children.

Shall we do another? (The correct answer is yes. Sorry.) A 6-year-old American girl is learning Arabic. She has accumulated 4,950 hours of Arabic when she goes to her grandma's for the summer. She spends 12 weeks there and hears only her first language, which is English. Grandma doesn't have a computer and has TV only in English. When the child returns home at the end of the summer, what will her total hours be?

12 weeks – 4 weeks = 8 weeks of loss
8 weeks × 20 hours per week = 160 hours of loss
4,950 – 160 = 4,790 hours total

Next, imagine the same 6-year-old girl goes to live with her grandma for 18 months while her parents are working overseas. When the child permanently reunites with her parents and resumes her language time, what will her adjusted total in Arabic be?

0 hours.

4,950 hours of accumulated language time down the drain! The true observation might not be quite that bad, but it's not worth the risk of losing everything you've gained if you can help it.

How could this unfortunate language loss have been prevented for this 6-year-old? The simplest answer, of course, is to avoid long interruptions in a trilingual program. However, that's easier said than done, particularly when life is throwing you curveballs. But wouldn't there be some "life support" level of language exposure for your children, at which they would not lose ground, providing maybe just enough to keep them from forgetting? This would come into play if you had to interrupt your trilingual program for a relatively long period of time. Perhaps at this level, your children would not gain anything, but at least they would not lose ground. No one knows for sure what this number would be, but let's say that it's 3 hours per week. I would not be surprised to learn that it's a bit more than 3 hours per week for very young children and a bit less for older children, but we'll just use 3 hours per week as our life-support level for everyone. If you drop below 3 hours per week, let's assume your children are probably losing ground, and you should subtract hours from the cumulative total.

For children less than 3 years old, these life-support hours must be time with a real live human, and there are no acceptable equivalents. For children between ages 3 and 6, let's say that at least 1 of the 3 life-support hours must be real live human time. The other 2 hours may be what we'll call "supervised video-chatting time."

I'll show you what I mean by that. This is electronic time that involves real-time interaction with a human using a phone or a computer. However, it's still electronic time, so the hour counts are halved. Examples of this would be telephone conversations (with accompanying video whenever possible), Skype, and other video-chat programs. Since the young child cannot be counted upon to pay attention to a video screen for a very long period of time without supervision, an adult will need to be with the child during the entire video-chat session or telephone call. These sessions must also be 1:1 (that is to say, one child interacting with one adult online). Most likely, each session will have to be kept short, depending upon the individual child's ability to sit still and pay attention.

Indeed, the reason for the supervision and 1:1 rules has to do with the relatively short attention span of children. If you want to just plop your kids in front of a computer screen and expect that they'll talk to a video image of an adult without losing interest, without wandering off, then I think you're being unrealistic. Even if you supervise two children interacting with one adult via computer, maintaining adequate attention on the part of the pair will be next to impossible. Thus, if you use video chatting, you need to be present at every moment.

A child beyond the age of 6 will need the same 3 hours for a life-support level of exposure, but no minimum amount of real live human time is necessary. All 3 hours could come from 6 hours of supervised video-chatting time if actual human time is impractical or unavailable. (Keep in mind that electronic time, even supervised video-chatting time, only counts <u>half</u>.) Also, don't forget that electronic time counts only if the child has already accumulated at least 500 hours of human time. I know this is a little confusing, but I'll try to clarify with some more examples in a moment.

But first, let me deepen the confusion just a bit. I'm going to say that, beyond the age of 9, video-chatting time no longer needs to be continuously supervised, and it counts as much as human time, as long as it's 1:1. In this unique situation, again assuming that the child already has at least 500 hours of human time, you do not need to multiply video-chatting time by 0.5, and you no longer need to supervise the sessions every single moment. For example, if a 10-year-old is Skyping 1:1 with a language instructor, and you feel reasonably comfortable that the quality of the interaction is adequate, then this is as good as human time and counts hour for hour as much as human time. Maybe it's not quite as good as human time, but I think it's close enough at that age. If, however, that same 10-year-old is sitting with her 11-year-old brother as the two Skype with an online language instructor, then the time only counts half and must still be multiplied by 0.5.

Let's also say that, even when a child's languages are not on life support, 3 hours of human time or an acceptable equivalent of video chatting are the minimum. That is to say, a child's entire language exposure cannot come from cartoons or kids' movies. That'd be pushing the electronic thing a bit too far. However, in a pinch, this life-support-level explanation means that a child beyond the age of 3 can get by with only 1 hour of real live human time per week. A child beyond the age of 6 can get by with none. There are some heavy qualifications, and you'd have to spend a lot of time supervising, but it could be done. Most likely, it wouldn't be as effective as a language babysitter in your living room, but I think it would get you by, at least for a while. No doubt, real live human time is the superior way to go, but if you're in a remote location, or your life is on hiatus, in a situation where you have no choice, I think heavily using video chat can keep your children's trilingual voyage from getting shipwrecked. However, whenever possible, go as rich on real live human time as you can.

Clear as mud, huh? Let's trudge through a few more examples and see if that helps.

You move to a new area with your 2-year-old son. He already has around 750 hours in his target language. Unfortunately, the new area is remote, and you do not have the same access to language babysitters as you did in the community you moved from. However, through a local college, you find a language professor who is willing to interact with your son for 3 hours per week. His fees are more than you can really afford, but you decide to employ him just so your child will not lose ground. While you employ this professor, you are actively seeking a cheaper alternative of some sort.

After a year, however, when your son is 3, you still have not been successful in finding that alternative teacher in your chosen language. At that point you continue to employ the professor, but you drop his weekly time down to 1 hour per week, and you find a language teacher on Skype who is willing to speak with your son if you are willing to continually sit with him. You use the Skype instructor for 4 hours a week, bringing your son's total hours to 3 (electronic time counts half). You also allow your son to watch 2 hours per day of foreign-language cartoons. This actually brings his weekly total to 12 hours.

Professor:			1 hour
Skype:	4 hours × 0.5 × 2	=	4 hours
Electronic time (cartoons):	14 hours × 0.5 × 2 =		7 hours
Total		=	12 hours per week

As it happens, you also have a 7-year-old son. He has already accumulated 6,000 hours of time in his target language. For him, you find a Skype language instructor for 6 hours per week, which you directly supervise. This counts as his life-support level, and you also allow him to watch a generous amount of target-language cartoons, movies, and other videos. So far you're holding things together, but boy, you're doing a lot of supervising!

Skype:	6 hours × 0.5 =	3 hours
Cartoons and kids' movies:	14 hours × 0.5 =	7 hours
Total	=	10 hours per week

Wouldn't you know it? You also have a daughter who is 12. In this remote location, you arrange to have her converse with Skype language buddies in the target language for the full number of hours per week you think she needs. Since she's older, continual supervision is unnecessary, but you still need to monitor enough to make sure she's learning. She's also older than 9, so this Skype time counts the same as human time, hour for hour. In the evenings, she watches an hour of foreign-language movies after she finishes her homework.

Skype:	6 hours × 1	= 6 hours
Movies:	7 hours × 0.5	= 3.5 hours
Total		= 9.5 hours per week

I hope this makes a little more sense to you now. If not, you can always just start with 10 hours per week per language and circle back to these calculations later on…if you feel the need.

In the event that you can get some exposure to a language for a child, but not enough to constitute the life-support level, maybe you do not need to subtract the full 20 hours per week for every week without adequate language exposure. Let's say, if you get 2–3 hours, you subtract only 5 hours for the week. If you get 1–2 hours, subtract 10. If you get 1 hour or less, subtract 15. If you are unable to get any hours, subtract the full 20 hours. If you have no alternative but to try to get by with an amount of language exposure below the life-support level for more than a year with a child less than 12, do you still need to reset the total hours to 0? To a degree, this might depend upon the age of the child: a younger child will be more vulnerable to permanent language loss. It might also depend upon the number of language hours already accumulated, but I think the best answer to the question is "probably." No one knows for sure, though. So, if I were you, I would try my very best to avoid that scenario. And I'll avoid boring you with another calculation. This is a minor point that will probably be of interest only to the truly obsessive.

Let's add just one more special form of language exposure to our expanding repertoire. Let's discuss a technique we'll call "holiday loading," which is similar to the technique of front-loading previously described. During holidays and summer vacations, particularly as children move into the grade-school years, these blocks of school-free time can allow for more intensive language exposure. This could, of course, involve traveling to another country or visiting a relative who is a fluent speaker of the target language, but it could also be just the intensive use of language babysitters, and maybe even more electronic time, within limits. This more intense exposure probably enhances the language quite a bit, but more importantly, it allows lower-level exposure and more time for homework—more time for concentration on school subjects—during the school year. For example, if you choose to give your children only 5 hours per week of exposure to a target language, you could supplement this during the summers by increasing the level to 40, 50, 60, or even 80 hours per week. You would have to evaluate the particular opportunity and make your best estimate of its numerical value. I'd also like to make the point that anything your children might do in the summer in their first language—camp, piano, tennis, math enrichment, and so on—can also be done in the target language. Just a few illustrations:

1. Since you want to give your son as much time as possible while school is in session, you arrange for him to have only 4 hours per week of language time in each of 2 languages. However, during the summer, he spends several months with one or both sets of grandparents, who reside in foreign countries and do not speak his first language. In this setting, he's completely immersed, receiving an estimated 80 hours per week in the target language for an entire 12-week summer. (In the local language, at least, that adds up to 1,120 hours for the year, though it might be necessary to do a little summer Skyping in the second target language.)

2. You only manage to get your daughter 3 hours of weekly exposure in the target languages, but every summer, you go with her on an overseas working vacation with an agency such as Workaway. There, you exchange work for free room and board while your daughter gets 80 hours per week in the target language.

3. You have a neighborhood friend whose parents live in China. The parents have agreed to let you stay in their home, so your son can attend preschool for a few months.

4. You really want your child to learn piano. In your community, you have found an instructor who speaks Russian, and she is willing to give your daughter daily piano lessons for the summer…in Russian.

5. You want your son to improve his soccer skills. In your town, there is a summer league with an all-Spanish-speaking team that practices daily.

I guess you understand now.

At this point, I think a caveat is necessary. As far as I'm concerned, the future school language should be allowed to predominate, at least a little. It might not be necessary in every case—all your children may be exceptionally bright students who can thrive in a classroom while simultaneously learning its language. But there's also a risk that they will fall behind the rest of the class as they struggle to understand the teacher. I don't think it's worth that risk, so I'd suggest letting the school language be at least 40% of a child's exposure, and let it be the child's strongest language if you can. This might not always be possible in the complicated, international world, but at least give this matter some thought. One exception to this caveat might be a child who will begin school in a language-immersion program. In that setting, all the children will typically start school at square one, with little or no knowledge of the new language, lessening the possibility of falling behind.

Now, to help you swallow them, I'll encapsulate all these "rules" into a single pill:

1. Plan for approximately 10,000 hours of practice in a target language before a child reaches adulthood (10 to 11 hours per week average over 18 years).
2. Try to front-load these hours, getting around 5,000 hours by the start of school at age 6.
3. Hours accumulated during the first 3 years of life count 2.5X. Hours accumulated between age 3 and 6 count 2X.
4. After the 3rd birthday, and after the child has accumulated 500 hours of human time, hours from electronic time sources such as foreign-language cartoons, Skype, and kids' movies count half, or 0.5X. (Just in case you're wondering, yes, I think it's probably OK to double everything between ages 3 and 6...including electronic time.)
5. If a child goes more than 4 weeks in a year without language exposure, then you must subtract 20 hours from the total for every additional week without exposure. If a child under 12

goes more than a year without language exposure, set the hours to zero.

6. The life-support level of language exposure is 3 hours per week of real live human time or equivalent. If the child is less than 3, only real live human interaction will serve. If the child is 3 to 6, one of these 3 hours must be real live human time, but the other 2 may also include supervised video-chatting time, although each video-chatting hour counts only half. If the child is over 6, any combination of human time or supervised video-chatting time will suffice to make at least 3 hours per week. Beyond the age of 9, video-chatting time no longer needs to be continually supervised, and it counts the same as human time, as long as it is 1:1 with the tutor.

7. If a child receives some language exposure, but less than the life-support level, subtract hours weekly according to this table:

2–3 hours	subtract 5
1–2 hours	subtract 10
0–1 hours	subtract 15
0 hours	subtract 20

8. By the start of the school years, try to be in the habit of holiday loading, in which your child gets a hefty dose of language when school is not in session.

9. Allow the future school language to be the dominant language whenever possible, attempting to keep it at 40% or more of the total exposure.

For extra credit, let's do a few more calculations. Like visits to the gym, these are painful but beneficial in the long run. (Or maybe I'm a little sadistic, just like your 10th grade English instructor was.)

1. You start your son's trilingual journey at 12 months of age. For 2 years, until the age of 3, you provide 20 hours per week of real live human

time in each language. Then, when he turns 3, you drop the exposure down to 10 hours per week of human time but add 1 hour per day of electronic time. At the age of 6, he goes 26 weeks (around 6 months) without any second-language exposure. Then you resume it at 4 hours per week human time and 7 hours per week electronic time. At the age of 10, you stop the real live human time and replace it with 2 hours per week of video-chatting time (a Skype tutor). You continue to allow 7 hours per week of regular, non-interactive electronic time in the form of cartoons, movies, and other target-language shows until high school graduation at age 18.5. What is his cumulative number of hours?

Answer = 12,768 hours

Age 1–3:	$2 \times 20 \times 52 \times 2.5$	=	5,200
Age 3–6, real live human time:	$3 \times 10 \times 52 \times 2$	=	3,120
Age 3–6, electronic time:	$3 \times 7 \times 52 \times 0.5 \times 2$	=	1,092
Age 6–6.5, no exposure:	$(26 - 4) \times 20$	=	-440
Age 6.5–10, real live human time:	$3.5 \times 4 \times 52$	=	728
Age 6.5–10, electronic time:	$3.5 \times 7 \times 52 \times 0.5$	=	637
Age 10–18.5, video chatting time:	$8.5 \times 2 \times 52$	=	884
Age 10–18.5, electronic time:	$8.5 \times 7 \times 52 \times 0.5$	=	1,547
Total:			12,768

2. When your daughter is 5 1/2, she spends a summer in Germany with her grandparents. When she returns home, you discover, to your amazement, that she can actually speak German. You decide to start a trilingual program. Recognizing that you're off to a bit of a late start, you're unclear on how to proceed, particularly given that she will be starting kindergarten this year.

Just shooting from the hip here, but I think I'd opt for one rather than two additional languages at home. If the kindergarten were half-day, you could probably manage 25 hours per week in German, maybe adding an hour every evening of a language movie or cartoon.

Summer in Germany:	$80 \times 12 \times 2$	=	1,920
Human time with babysitter			
during kindergarten year:	$25 \times 52 \times 2$	=	2,600
Electronic time during the			
kindergarten year:	$7 \times 52 \times 0.5$	=	182
Total at the start of 1st grade		=	4,702 hours

For adding a third language, you could wait until school begins and place her in a language-immersion program there. With a somewhat later start, the mastery of the immersion language might be compromised a little, but the result would most likely still be quite good.

As your trilingual program advances toward the school years, you might begin to assess how much the local schools will be able to help you out. It's a good way to save some money if you can make the system work for you. If cash becomes a problem, it might be altogether reasonable to develop just one additional language in the preschool years, and let the school develop the third one if your district has a good language-immersion program. Of course, your child's grasp of this third language might not be quite as good as the second one, because you're starting later, but it will still likely be quite good. Since many immersion programs have waiting lists, I'd suggest checking out what your local schools will have to offer at least a year or so before your children are slated to start.

A school immersion program will not only advance fluency in the target language but also help your child develop literacy in it. Again, this is an issue I'm mostly avoiding in this book, because it really only concerns children over the age of 6. I'm not suggesting much in the way of literacy introduction in your target languages before the age of 6, because I think that firmly establishing fluency is far more time critical, and there just doesn't seem to be all that much advantage to drilling preschoolers on cultural skills. Much of literacy depends upon fluency anyway, and actually being able to speak a language is an incredible advantage when it comes time to learn to read and write it. There is also quite a bit of what experts call *transfer*. That is, once a child can read and write in one language, that ability can greatly facilitate learning to read and write in another. But this depends a lot upon how similar the two languages are, whether they use the same alphabet or not, and whether they use characters instead of an alphabet.

In most cases, you'll probably want your children to end up both fluent and literate in three languages, so this matter will probably be of concern to you one day. But for now, suffice it to say that the best preparation for literacy in three languages is fluency in three languages. I mention the literacy issue now only because you probably need quite a bit of time to begin to plan for the next steps beyond the age of 6, and a good school immersion program could be an integral part of that. If there's not one in your school district, maybe you'll want to start weighing your other options. You also might want to choose your target languages based on how much help you think the schools can give you later on.

So, thank you for toughing it out through a heavily number-infested chapter! If you're anything like me, the whole experience probably gave you flashbacks to your least favorite high school math class. Though I'm not really much of a numbers guy, I try to be sensitive to the fact that many parents are very interested in tracking their children's progress and in having a formula to follow. If you're just not that type of parent, though, you can pinch yourself now. It was all just a dream—maybe a bad one—of our own invention. But dreams have meaning, and if you happened to grasp the concepts that the numbers illustrate, we'll call that good enough.

I think this particular formula is best viewed as a starting point, just a tool to help you plan 10 or more years into the future. Later, we'll talk about how to monitor your children's progress in a new language. Once you're comfortable with that, and once you have a little more experience at being a trilingual parent, you just might find that keeping track of cumulative hours and doing all these calculations demands more work than you really want to do. It's OK; I'll understand.

And, having said that, I have a confession to make: We really don't do any formal calculating of total hours in our home either. It's my fault, really. I'm just not enough of a control freak. From the comfort of my recliner, I tell myself that it's better to stay focused on the big picture and that a rough estimate is good enough. I imagine it probably is.

CHAPTER 8

Your Secret Weapon

● ● ●

ONCE, I BOUGHT AN OLD railroad-era mercantile building in a nearly deserted midwestern town. The city council thought it was an eyesore and wanted to tear it down. I got it for almost nothing, but I had to pay the back taxes and fix it up or pay building-code fines. My German-immigrant great-grandfather had built it with the help of his four sons almost a century before. One son, my grandpa, had used hand tools to carve the family name into a parapet stone above the customer entrance between the display windows. Apparently, German immigrants were not only farmers but also respectable stonemasons.

Not long after I became its new owner, I invited a buddy of mine on a little road trip to have a look at the thing. From the main street, he took one long look at it, and just shook his head. Clearly, he agreed with the city council. After I cleaned it up and made the necessary repairs, I rented the space to a couple from Ecuador who planned to start a Spanish-language church.

Somewhere in your cosmopolitan metropolis, your suburban labyrinth of cul-de-sacs, your rust-belt factory city, your sleepy college hamlet, or even your forgotten little railroad town, there are little havens of language-learning opportunity for your children. These enclaves generally stay out of plain view and maintain a low profile. Inside them, people speak the language of the mainstream majority infrequently, if at all. These groups are often struggling financially, just getting started in a new life, looking for additional sources of income to support themselves and their families. They are generally willing to work longer and harder than most of the rest of us. We call them recent immigrants when we want to be politically correct; we use other labels when we don't. They have braved all varieties of hardship, deprivation, and persecution to join us, to have just a little taste of our dream life. Sometimes we dislike the fact that they want our jobs and keep our own wages lower. Sometimes we resent them, and they are wary of us.

But these people are your secret weapon! I've named them "language babysitters," though the term seriously understates the phenomenal impact they can have on your children's lives.

To be sure, there are many exceptions, but recent immigrants are not always highly educated. In my mind, it is an almost tragic misconception that you need someone with a college degree in preschool education to teach your children languages. That belief seriously holds us back in our quest to move beyond our monolingual past. Maybe some recent immigrants are only marginally literate in their native language—maybe they can barely write their own names. Perhaps they do not even speak the community language of their new home; perhaps they never will. Their children will, one day, but that's best left for another chapter. Right now, I want to convince you that they are your best resource for raising trilingual children, not in spite of their educational limitations, but because of them.

Why are they your best resource? They are abundant, and they are everywhere. Their numbers are increasing, and they are eager to find work. Many of them don't speak the local community language, so your children will have no choice but to remain in the target language if they want their needs met, or they just want to be understood. Very likely, these immigrants have not studied the latest ivory-tower theories of early childhood education and will not bore your budding linguists with drills and exercises. Instead, with your occasional guidance, they will just *play* with your children, speak with them about everyday things, engage them in their own ordinary real-world activities, and thereby teach them a new culture in its purest form. Meanwhile, all you have to do is relax, maintain a comfortable distance, read the news, or visit the nail salon! You see how easy this is gonna be? If you don't already have one, you might want to buy a recliner for yourself. (I refer to my own recliner as my multilingual command and control center.)

But before you get all recumbent, you still have to do two things. First, you have to actually find some immigrant enclaves, which don't necessarily want to be found. Then, you have to convince some of their child-friendly inhabitants, who might already be a little wary of you, to come and teach your kids their language. On how to do this, I'll go into lots and lots (and lots) of detail.

A hundred years ago, many new immigrants to the United States tended to settle in large urban gateway cities like New York, Los Angeles, Chicago, or Boston. They took sweatshop jobs or scraped out equally squalid existences in the tenements and lofts of the old inner cities. A defense against culture shock, homesickness, and an established society that didn't necessarily welcome a new source of economic competition, neighborhoods readily clustered into ethnic groupings: Chinatowns, Little Italys, Little Warsaws, Little Tokyos, and others. A lonely, bewildered, and hungry newcomer could just step off the docks and walk a few blocks to a neighborhood that looked, sounded, and smelled a lot like home.

There the immigrant would likely make contact with an old friend or family member whose journey had preceded his or her own. Compatriots helped each other find temporary lodging and, more importantly, jobs. Entire economic sectors became divided along ethnic lines, and the ethnic groups that depended upon them defended these lines. This phenomenon of immigrant groups helping new arrivals from their homeland is something that sociologists call chain migration, and it exists all over the world to this day. It is how ethnic enclaves are born, and perpetuated.

But then, with a little help from Hollywood and Madison Avenue, these ethnic areas became romanticized, gentrified, overtaken by movie stars, artists, and wealthy businesspeople. New immigrants generally couldn't afford to live there anymore. Sweatshop industries were also leaving in search of still cheaper labor, modern spaces better able to accommodate their changing technologies and increasingly consolidated global markets. Many new immigrants therefore found themselves unable to eke out a living in these traditional ethnic strongholds, so they sought their fortunes elsewhere. Like before, they followed their fellow compatriots to the new jobs. Only, the new economic opportunities were less clustered, less centralized. This has made the latest generation of Chinatowns and Little Jaliscos more mundane, less exotic, but far more plentiful.

Though you wouldn't necessarily visit one of them as a tourist, these new ethnic enclaves are more numerous and far more accessible than they used to be, even if you don't happen to live in a large gateway city. For you as a prospective parent of multilingual children, that's the mundane beauty of it all. You won't need your camera, and you probably can't buy any postcards there, but if you know how to look, you can find a new Chinatown, for example, brimming with babysitters eagerly waiting to teach your children to speak perfect Mandarin—or at least, a perfectly acceptable dialect of it. The Chinatown I'm talking about may be no more than a mile or so from your house, and you may have already driven past it hundreds of times without really even noticing it.

So why is there a new ethnic enclave so close to you? Well, the world's gone worldwide now, you might say, and jobs aren't clustered in inner cities the way they used to be. It's more than a little controversial, but employers love these immigrants—so much, in fact, that if domestic authorities try to stop them from hiring immigrants, they just fold their tents and move their operations directly to the immigrants' native lands if they can.[74] It's a political hot potato, a delicate truce; nobody whose job depends on an election or a tax revenue source really wants to rock the boat right now— at least, not publicly.

Wealthy countries tend to have declining birth rates, which lead to aging populations, which can strain public retirement and healthcare systems. Their governments don't seem to mind the immigrants who pay their taxes and thereby fund these public entitlements. Virtually any day of the week, any month of the year, you can go to your favorite world news source and learn about some new violent conflict, economic collapse, or natural disaster. Events like these displace people. Those people seek better futures for themselves and their families, fleeing to more stable and prosperous countries with better job opportunities.

Globalization is upon us, and sometimes it's painful. We're dealing with it slowly, perhaps as best we can. For employers now operating in fiercely competitive worldwide markets, immigrants can make a very attractive labor pool. They take fewer sick days, show more tolerance for the unpredictable cycles of layoffs and rehires, and accept lower wages. Many of them will work on Christmas, and they don't ask off for Super Bowl weekend! A savvy employer can further cut costs by avoiding the use of a staffing agency and hiring based on word of mouth. If an immigrant employee who's earned a good reputation has a cousin, a sister, a village friend from back home, or maybe a former coworker who can't find a job in Los Angeles, the employer hires them when they arrive. The trusted employee's reputation would be tarnished if the people he recommended did not perform well, so he makes very sure they do. If the employer is kept happy, maybe the entire work crew is speaking a foreign language before long. That further increases efficiency and eliminates the need for the immigrants to partially acclimate before going to work. Everybody's on the same page, linguistically. Another example of chain migration and the birth of another ethnic enclave.

If things continue to go well on the job, perhaps an immigrant worker can send for a spouse or even aging parents. Though they might be too old for regular work, maybe Grandpa could pick up a few odd jobs, and maybe Grandma could care for the children during the day while everyone else is working. Maybe she would be willing to babysit your children a little too…

She would be my choice for the perfect language babysitter: mature, nurturing, and experienced with young children; highly fluent in your target language with little or no knowledge of your children's first language; family oriented, maybe with a grandchild or two in tow to play with your children and thereby enhance the exposure; and interested in earning a few extra dollars to help make ends meet, but not necessarily looking for a full-time job. That's my vision for you. Maybe you want to modify the image a little to fit your own unique situation, but I hope you get the basic idea. Hiring her would be far less expensive than the typical tutor and infinitely more valuable in the long run. No waiting lists, no application fees, and no toddler aptitude test required.

Should you want to hire her, throw in a few perks to sweeten the deal: Let her bring her family's laundry to your house if she wants, and let your little children "help" her do it—a valuable life skill that might make your own life a little easier. Definitely let her bring her own child or grandchild along if the child speaks your target language. Let her cook for you if she's interested, and you'll have a hot, ethnically intriguing meal on the table by the time you get home from the nail salon. Just make sure she and the children make enough for her to take some home for her own family! That should motivate her to keep coming to your house. If you as a parent gain enough trust, maybe you'll even feel comfortable letting your children spend a little time at her house one day. I would bet you a nickel that there are invaluable life lessons under that roof too.

If you find this person, adopt her immediately! If you can't find exactly her, come as close as you can. While you're at it, just go ahead and adopt her entire household, taking them under your wing a bit. If you've ever experienced life as an expat, then you know how intimidating life in a foreign land can be. How do you request utility service? How do you fill out a tax form? How do you find a good obstetrician if you become pregnant? What do you have to do before you buy a car, enroll your children in the local school, or apply for a driver's license? Be a liaison and a giver of good advice. As you build a sense of respect in this symbiotic relationship, maybe you should consider making these very important contributors to your increasingly unique and multicultural life a genuine part of your social group. Without even trying, they'll open your eyes to some amazing realities and teach your children more valuable lessons than whatever exclusive circle the status-seeking neighbors are joining ever could.

Speaking of the nail salon, let's talk more about chain migration. If you ever go for a manicure, you've probably noticed that most of the people who work there are not necessarily ethnically diverse…Many are

Vietnamese. How did this happen? Chain migration, word of mouth. Established immigrants helping newly arrived immigrants get situated. Just for fun sometime, see if you can find a Vietnamese grocery market near your house. There, you will likely find a public bulletin board with a number of handwritten ads, mostly in Vietnamese, offering manicurist jobs.

In my mind's eye, I imagine the 1970s. I envision an entrepreneurial young lady fleeing for her life, packed into a noisy military helicopter with dozens of other terrified refugees, clinging paralytically to the open door as the olive drab bird struggled to gain altitude above an embassy compound under siege. Maybe she was the daughter of a prominent local executive with American military contracts, or perhaps she herself had been an operative of some sort. In any case, the helicopter was the only thing standing between her and certain execution. She was witnessing the fall of Saigon firsthand, peace with honor.

Nearly starving in a jungle refugee camp somewhere, she finally made her way to a US government relocation center, where they handed her off to a church in Shanghai, West Virginia. She didn't stay long, though, taking a job in a local beauty parlor. When she'd saved enough money for bus fare, she moved to California, where she'd heard a group of fellow refugees was starting a little chain of nail salons. They'd learned the trade from the manicurist of a Hollywood movie star who did charity work with women displaced by war.[75] She spent about a year learning from this fledgling network before setting out for Houston, Texas, where some friends and surviving family members had settled.

She knew she could share an apartment with them, and she had been told that a great number of Vietnamese refugees were finding their way there. As they all gravitated to the same neighborhood, a family opened a little Vietnamese market, where one could purchase a few specialty items from home. The store served as a sort of meeting point, and had a large bulletin board for posting messages and job opportunities. It even offered a money-wiring service so she and other immigrants could send US dollars back home to surviving relatives, if they still had any. Communist officials tolerated this practice—even implicitly encouraged it—because the growing trickle of American currency helped their postwar economy remain afloat.

So this fictional entrepreneur eventually opened a small nail salon around the corner from her shared apartment. When she needed help, whom would she hire but local friends and relatives? As some of her employees learned the business, they opened shops of their own. With very limited English skills, Vietnamese immigrants didn't necessarily have anybody else lining up to hire them, so they were happy to find work in one of these, for low wages. The concept spread like wildfire, and a quiet, mostly word-of-mouth, national if not international network was born, all conducted in the Vietnamese language. Before long, one of the ladies she had met in California opened a college for manicurists. There, all instructors spoke Vietnamese, as did most of the students. Eventually this college would train many tens of thousands of Vietnamese refugees to work in an industry they would come to dominate.

The vast network of Vietnamese salons were mostly plain, obscure little shops in declining, high-vacancy strip malls, well off the radar of understaffed federal immigration offices, city ordinance departments, and local law enforcement. In Asian cultures, it's polite to be quiet, reserved, and obedient. Public service officials appreciate that, and they don't go stirring up trouble where none exists. The network was decentralized and low-key, but strong; not necessarily excluding non-Vietnamese workers, but maybe not really welcoming them either. Try to see it from the perspective of a nail salon owner: what would be the point of hiring someone who doesn't even speak Vietnamese, who can't even communicate with coworkers? Nobody else really wanted those jobs anyway—at least, not for that kind of money.

And nowadays, these little nail spas are quite literally everywhere. Maybe you or your spouse has visited one. They exist in giant megacities, suburbs, mill towns, farming communities with six-man high school football teams where the quarterback plays the trombone at halftime—everywhere. We love the service they provide, and we like the price. Probably, the local mayor, the sheriff's daughter, and the building inspector's wife feel the same way. And the school district doesn't mind the tax revenue either.

Any ideas yet on how to start raising trilingual children? Let me mention that there are well over a million Vietnamese immigrants residing in the United States alone, second only to the Chinese as far as Asian immigrants go, and chances are, they're not far from you. They've been around in sufficient numbers for a few decades now, so many of them are probably mature enough to be your perfect babysitter.

But before you drive off to the nearest nail salon to start asking around, let me please suggest that you remember to be polite and reserved, because they just might be a little wary of you, and your initial inquiries might be met rather coolly, particularly if you seem a little too pushy or ask too many of the type of questions that a public authority might ask. Try getting to know them a little bit first. Patronize their business, even if you prefer your toenails grody, thank you very much, and send them a referral or two. Maybe bring a pot of hot tea during a Wednesday-afternoon lull in customer traffic, and share it with them as they dazzle up your cuticles. Ask about their children and learn their fascinating personal stories. Don't be surprised if you meet people who, in a previous, faraway life, were engineers, doctors, bankers—professionals of every kind. Even if you only manage to identify yourself as a sincere and genuinely curious face in their often condescending, resentful, and xenophobic world, I'd say your chances of getting help are pretty good.

I hope I haven't left you with the stereotyped impression that all Vietnamese immigrants are working away in nail spas. You know that's just not the case. The true reality of immigration is far more complex than the oversimplified, highly stylized landscapes I'll be painting for you. My goal is just to maximize your chances of success on your quest for the perfect language-tutor-masquerading-as-babysitter. Please keep that in the back of your mind as you read on. We're baking bread here, and I'm still assuming that you just want to prepare a simple loaf, still assuming you don't care very much about the DNA structure of yeast or the physics of thermal conduction.

If you happen to live near a university, you could probably find a handful of Vietnamese professors or graduate students to help you out. Maybe they themselves would be too busy for a babysitting gig, but perhaps they know someone. Perhaps they have inroads to their own local ethnic community. It never hurts to ask, but, generally speaking, professionally employed, degreed people are not going to be terribly interested in the type of part-time work you are going to propose. There are exceptions to this rule of thumb, as there always are. We will explore these other realms of possibility later on.

If you're old enough to remember the Vietnamese boat people, then you're probably not the parent of preschool children anymore. I guess I'm pretty unique in that one respect. Once I was in a city park walking my daughter in her stroller, when I encountered an elderly guy who chuckled as he sized me up. "You realize," he said, "it won't be long before she's the one pushing *you* around!" A little stunned, I tried my best to laugh, found my receding hairline with my fingers, and kept walking.

My younger brother used to live in Corpus Christi, Texas. He's an older father too, only to a slightly lesser degree. My family paid a visit to his family a few years ago, and they treated us to a nice seafood restaurant on the bay docks. I couldn't help noticing that there were an inordinate number of Asians around. They wore work attire—jumpsuits and rubber boots—so I knew they couldn't be tourists, and they probably weren't restaurant workers or manicurists either. Maybe, I reasoned, Corpus Christi was a bigger port city than I realized, and these folks were in shipping, unloading their cargo before heading back to Asia.

As it happened, they were commercial fishers and shrimpers. Vietnamese immigrants have apparently found another niche in this industry. If you take a quick look at a map of Vietnam, you can probably figure out why they gravitated to the fishing boats. Funny that they came to the United States as boat people, and many still are! Maybe not funny; sorry. In any event, if you live in an area with commercial fishing or shrimping, chances are you can find a pocket of Vietnamese language for your children. Probably a modest neighborhood with an Asian market, some telltale ethnic restaurants, a check-cashing center for sending dollars back home, and maybe an immigration attorney with a Vietnamese surname too. In an area with a shrimping industry, if you were interested in seeing your toddler learn to speak Vietnamese, maybe you could just hit the docks.

But if you're highly allergic to salty air, I have an even better idea for you. Just go to your computer and open your favorite online search engine, like Google.com. From there, search for Vietnamese restaurants or Vietnamese markets in the area. In case you don't know, I'm giving you a first hint at how to find a modern "Little Saigon" ethnic enclave. In that interest, let's try a first exercise. I suggest that you try this on your own computer, because I strongly believe it's a skill a trilingual parent will simply need to master. Go to Google or your favorite search engine, and type in "Corpus Christi Texas Vietnamese market" (without the quotation marks). If you like, I'll help you get started with a tutorial video: *Searching for language tutors online*. You can find the video at www.trilingualbysix.com. It's also on my Trilingual by Six YouTube channel. Please have a look at it; I really think it'll open your eyes to a thing or two.

What did you find? As of September 2015, I'm finding some possibilities. There's an Asian market with some Google and Yelp.com ratings. There's also a place called Saigon Asian Market. Both sound promising.

Next, see if you can round up the street addresses of these places you've found. If you don't see anything directly on the search-engine results, follow the links to the various pages, and find the addresses there. From my surfing, I find that the Asian Market is located at 4101 South Padre Island Drive in Corpus Christi, and Saigon Asian Market is at 5625 Saratoga Boulevard. Now, see if you can find them on a searchable online map. Google Maps is my personal choice, but you get to pick. Paste the address of the more generic-sounding Asian Market in the mapping search box to see where it is. Then, zoom the map down to "Street View" and have a look around. With a little panning and traveling, you can see what the market actually looks like from the outside, the next best thing to actually going there.

Now see if you can get more information about the area. Use Street View to check out the rest of the neighborhood. If you continue with me here, you'll quickly learn that the modern version of a Little Saigon is a pretty unexciting place to the untrained eye: just a collection of incompletely leased, declining strip malls in an aging suburban neighborhood. But let me train that eye of yours a little more. Did you happen to notice that the Asian Market is flanked on either side by reasonably authentic-looking Mexican restaurants? What about the Chinese-food establishment and sushi bar in the same complex? How would you feel about your children learning Mandarin Chinese and Spanish in addition to Vietnamese? Nearby, you might've seen a pay-by-the-minute phone shop of the type popular among immigrants.

There are several check-cashing centers within walking distance of the market. For a reasonable fee, they'll cash your paycheck and arrange a remittance for you. That is, they'll send some of your hard-earned dollars to your family back home in Vietnam, Mexico, China, or wherever you wish. Check-cashing centers are popular in neighborhoods like this one; they're immigrant-friendly and personable, operating on a first-name basis with many of their customers. When was the last time you walked into a more conventional bank where the teller actually knew your name? Most importantly, if you're spending only what you need and remitting all the rest every time you get paid, check-cashing centers are often cheaper than traditional banks.

I'd guess that the used car dealerships you can see in the area are also immigrant-friendly. Financing is probably available on the spot—and when the shrimp aren't running or the fish aren't biting, the cash-loan offices and the pawn shops would find a way to help a person keep up with the payments.

So, now a quick "congratulations" is appropriate: You've just identified your first Little Saigon, maybe your first Little Mexico, and perhaps even your first modern-day Chinatown all in the same average-sized North American city. And what exactly does that mean? I believe I did mention that modern immigration patterns tend to be more decentralized.

Maybe, if we're lucky, it also means that immigration is less segregated along ethnic lines than it used to be. And if you happen to live in a place like Corpus Christi, Texas, you just might be able to find several different languages being spoken on a significant scale. So it should be really easy to find immigrant families to raise your young flock on a steady diet of Vietnamese language for 18 years until they leave your house, right?

Not so fast. Go back to Google, and search "Corpus Christi shrimping industry." Snoop around for a while. You'll probably conclude that commercial fishing and shrimping in the area have entered a phase of decline. The future of your first Little Saigon might be in jeopardy. Some of the immigrants you were thinking of relying upon will likely move away, if they haven't already. Some, at least, will remain, but without a continued demand for skilled shrimpers, the chain of new migration might rust away from its anchor, interrupting your supply of new immigrants. Those who remain will assimilate, learn English, and find better jobs, and they will no longer be interested in teaching your children their language. Their children will know a little Vietnamese but prefer to speak English most of the time. They'll get smartphones so they can text tiresome nothings to their mainstream friends, buy designer sandals, and follow Taylor Swift on Twitter. Meanwhile, the Asian markets we just found might go out of business.

Do you now think that committing to Vietnamese for your trilingual children in Corpus Christi would be a good idea? Tough to say. Maybe you could check out the local nail spas and see what's happening there. That industry is certainly growing faster than coastal shrimping. If you were a parent of young children in the area, now is when you might have to do some real detective work, exercise some diplomacy, get to know some people, ask some questions, and see what else you could learn online. Vietnamese still might be an excellent choice of a second or third childhood language in Corpus Christi, but you'd need some more information before you committed to that long term.

I actually did do the search I just suggested to you. As I was doing my snooping, I happened upon a page featuring a local Vietnamese Catholic priest. Before Vietnam was even Vietnam, it was French Indochina, a colony under European hegemony, and missionaries liked to go there. But when the North Vietnamese Army started marching into Saigon, if they had any sense at all, the missionaries ran like hell (pardon my French). My guess is a fellow like that priest has never taken his finger off the pulse of the local Vietnamese community. He would probably be an excellent source of information.

Just for grins and practice, let's see if we can find the beauty parlor where our fictional entrepreneur got her start back in Shanghai, West Virginia. Go to Google and type in "Shanghai West Virginia beauty." Hmm. No beauty shop there anymore. Not even a gas station, by the looks of the aerial map. Nowadays, you have to drive over the mountain into Martinsburg to get your hair done. And what if you want to get your nails done in Martinsburg too? On Google, type in "Martinsburg West Virginia nail salon." Quite a few of them. Some appear to be run by people with Vietnamese surnames…

Next, let's see if we can catch up with our entrepreneurial protagonist way down in Houston. On Google, search the term "Houston nail." Way too many hits; we'll need to narrow it down a bit. Next try "Houston nail salons." Still too much information. Now try "Houston Vietnamese nail salons." Not much at all. It seems that the Vietnamese nail salons are not necessarily interested in advertising themselves as such. Finally, try searching, "Houston Asian nail salons." That seems to return a more manageable body of information, but it's still difficult to tell which nail spas are staffed by Vietnamese and which aren't. Unless you're a better web searcher than I am, your next step might involve some networking.

Very possibly, during your Houston search for nail salons, you may have stumbled across an article or two about nail salons being used as fronts for money laundering—maybe prostitution. It's not necessarily a huge problem, but it exists, particularly in the larger cities, where there's more opportunity for anonymity. If you live in a large city, and this whole idea makes you uncomfortable, you're not out of luck. Metropolitan areas are absolutely teeming with alternative opportunities for preschool language learning, and I'm still a long way from showing you all of your options. Truth is, if you happen to live in a major urban center, you probably don't need anyone's help as much as you might imagine. In the smaller towns where everybody knows everybody else's business, there's unlikely to be any shops run by conspicuously foreign people that local law enforcement doesn't at least know about, so keep that in mind. If you happen to know a police officer or a sheriff in your town, you could just ask for an opinion. In any event, it's always a good idea to use your very best judgment.

If there's a problem, ideally you would want to figure that out by just driving by and peering in the window, but if you enter a place, and anything seems even faintly below-the-table, just get a quick trim, pay the person, and exit. In many cases, if you see the word "massage" on a sign out front, it might not be the ideal place to find a language babysitter. (Some massage businesses are totally legit, but I don't know which ones, and I don't care to research the matter for you!) In most places, you can tap into an online review source like Yelp or Google ratings to get an idea of an establishment's reputation.

OK, so it's time for a word about safety: These days, in order to enter a school and help your child's teacher by reading stories or even making photocopies, you often have to subject yourself to a rigorous screening process that might include references, interviews, and criminal background checks. Schools are careful, as they should be. You entrust to them your little reasons for living, and they don't want to let you down. Unfortunately, you might not always be able to go to these great lengths with your language babysitters. Actually, you could, but it would be very expensive. Employment agencies will find multilingual nannies for you, screen them, interview them, perform psychological testing on them, do background checks, evaluate legal work status, and follow up on references. Some also provide health and accident coverage, clothing allowances, and relocation services, passing all the costs and then some to you. If you could afford all that, you could just move to Luxembourg or Singapore, and your children would grow up trilingual as if by osmosis.

The vast majority of us, however, must make more pragmatic decisions. Actually, as a society, we've already made them. Since the dawn of recorded time, human migration has harbored an alluring, shadowy element. We love it when Hollywood sells us an exaggerated action movie, and we don't buy glossy magazines at the grocery checkout line just to read about how well immigrants are behaving in the pork processing plants of the Midwest. When we feel like being entertained, we don't necessarily want the whole truth, because most of it is just too dull.

For as long as the United States has existed as a nation, we have allowed our recent immigrants into our homes to clean our floors, fold our laundry, cook our dinners, and yes, even care for our children. Nowadays, they also give us rides to the airport, manicure our lawns, install our appliances, spiff up our nails, roll our sushi, and fashion our slaughter hogs into cute little breakfast sausagettes. There has always been a modicum of risk involved in letting a relative stranger into our homes, but it's a calculated one. A colleague of mine once made the sage observation, "If you tiptoe into your house, lower the shades, dead-bolt the door, and be very quiet, nothing bad will happen to you. But nothing good will happen to you either." Embrace it. As Americans, we have always taken our security with a little bit of risk, because we like it that way. We also like it when Hollywood and news anchors glamorize the risk angle, just a little.

Let me ask you some questions: How much do you know about the lady who cleans your neighbors' house? Better yet, how much do *they* know about her? How can they be sure their Saturday-night babysitter isn't selling their social security numbers to identity thieves or dealing drugs from their front porch? What's to keep the guy cutting the grass next door from slipping into your bedroom and helping himself to your jewelry while you're away on vacation? How can you know for sure that you really weren't abducted by extraterrestrial aliens last night? No need to answer those questions; just think about them (except for the last one, please).

Rivaling the word-of-mouth grapevine that immigrants use to keep food on the table and protect themselves from us, we have our own informal networks to improve our lives and keep us secure. If your next-door neighbor says the same guy has been cutting his grass for a decade without a single problem, then maybe you'll let him cut yours too. The same basic principle applies to the lady cleaning the house down the street. We also have online networks like Yelp and Angie's List to steer us in safe directions. If a nail salon has enough positive ratings on one of these review sites, you can probably feel reasonably comfortable in going there. But, having said all that, you still must remember that, as an employer of grassroots, native-speaking tutors, you're more than a bit of a pioneer. There might not be a perfect grapevine of quiet information for you to tap into. Be prepared to connect your own dots; be resourceful, even innovative.

Personally, I find that houses of worship (foreign-language ones, to be exact) give me an added sense of safety when I choose a language babysitter. I find a belief system reassuring. Whether the members observe them or not, ethical maxims are professed at least once a week. What's more, demographically speaking, most congregations tend to be overrepresented by my favored subpopulation—experienced, aging empty nesters who could still figure out how to change a diaper if the need ever arose (and if you start this trilingual journey as early as I think you should, the need *will* arise). Furthermore, socially isolated immigrants flock to them, and many congregations return the favor by filling a vacuum in social services and political advocacy. But stick to your own life philosophy, and decide for yourself whether seeking language babysitters at religious institutions is right for you and your children.

While we're on this little demographic tangent, I think I can tell you, without even doing any research, that most immigrant groups tend to be skewed in favor of sturdy men of prime working age. Often, they are away from home for the first time in their lives. The lucky ones are eventually able to build enough of a life in their adoptive hometowns to send for their wives and children, if they have them. But that usually takes time and hard work. A few of the unattached ones will marry local girls, but most won't. Sometimes when they feel homesick and lonely, it's not exactly spiritual comfort that is the object of their yearnings, if you get my drift. Some of the entrepreneurs at the local Asian massage parlor seem to understand this. This same general type of implicit understanding can also be found in other places, too, like the dean's office of your favorite university—or the Pentagon. I have to imagine that this all-too-human desire helps to partially explain why a small handful of seemingly innocuous immigrant-run businesses serve as quiet fronts for less socially acceptable enterprises.

I hope you feel a little emboldened now and can summon some courage, and I hope I haven't weakened your resolve by calling your attention to some reasons to be vigilant. In all fairness, though, you probably need to exercise the same care when you hire monolingual babysitters as you do when you hire multilingual ones. Nothing ventured, nothing gained, I believe. If you choose to raise your kids trilingually, you have to think independently. You have to take a few careful risks, because you will be ranging beyond the safety of the herd. Most likely, there will not be a culturally accepted pattern for you to follow. But forge ahead: Explore strange new worlds; seek out new life and new civilizations; boldly go where no man has gone before. Just keep a careful watch out for Klingons!

CHAPTER 9

My Friend

● ● ●

IF YOU WERE ABLE TO use an online search engine and interactive mapping program such as Google to locate an immigrant enclave in the last chapter, you are well on your way to becoming a trilingual parent. However, if you feel that the reward does not justify the risk, you can always just raise your preschoolers as monolinguals and leave the task of bringing up the next generation of international decision makers and innovators to braver, more visionary parents. You can join the herd and let those little language acquisition devices in those little brains melt away. While you put that in your pipe and smoke it, I'll tell you about someone I knew once.

I met a guy a few years ago while passing through Kansas with a buddy of mine. Frankie was working in a little Chinese buffet along a two-lane highway in the shadow of a huge grain elevator in a tiny town. If you ever travel the back roads, you've probably seen a place just like it.

Before the town's population dwindled, the buffet used to be a Dairy Queen, where the local farmers came to drink hot coffee and discuss the upcoming district championship basketball game or feeder steer market prices. Then, a Chinese family bought the aging property and all the kitchen equipment inside for cents on the dollar and opened shop. Since they paid their taxes and often gave free lunches to the local uniformed public servants, the town pretty much left them to themselves. Nobody really bothered to get to know them, and they didn't really bother to get to know anybody. With the help of an uncle and his wife, they ran the place. A teenage son, not much into basketball or 4-H, and hardly a social butterfly, helped out after school. Since his English was better than every-one else's in the family, he was nice to have around.

From time to time, though, the family needed a little extra help, and that's where Frankie came in. He was working long hours and sleeping in a tiny office in the back. If the local sheriff's deputies knew about that, they didn't say anything. It wasn't really even within their jurisdiction to ask questions about the citizenship status of their constituents anyway. Immigration was a federal matter, and no government agent had come to this town since the repeal of Prohibition in 1933, except for the guy who inspected the grain elevator once a year.

A rail line still runs through the town, and the freight train still stops at the elevator, sometimes. The old mercantile strip paralleling the tracks on Main Street has seen better days, but a bank out of Kansas City still has a branch there. A few antique malls, a pawn shop, and an insurance agency also remain. Since the town is too small to attract the attention of any regional chain, the old family grocery store is still open, but it's now owned by a Korean couple. Next to it, a nail salon. Then, a Mexican restaurant.

When I met him, Frankie had been working at the buffet for only about 3 months. Though he'd been in the United States for decades, he didn't drive and had never owned a car. He'd often thought of owning one and maybe even buying his own restaurant someday. His favorite news-paper down in Houston often listed Chinese restaurants for sale all over the country, but he found it hard to save for that sort of thing. His parents back in Fujian depended on him, and he'd been helping his daughter with college tuition whenever he could.

His English was pretty limited. Always working over 70 hours per week, he'd never really had time to learn, and he'd never actually needed to know more than a few words with customers who usually just helped themselves to the buffet. The extent of his higher education was a class in restaurant English back in Fujian. Over the years, all of his bosses had spo-ken his dialect, except one. When he was just getting started, he'd made the mistake of taking a position at a restaurant in Los Angeles owned by a

Hong Kong family who spoke Cantonese. It had been a total disaster. He couldn't understand his boss, and Frankie was pretty sure the place was keeping most of the tip money to itself. He also heard whispers that the boss had often been late with the paychecks. In those days, however, his green card was just a fake, and he didn't want to risk a disastrous deportation, particularly with his family smuggling debt still unpaid. He therefore decided to keep quiet about his concerns, leaving after only 3 days on the job, after a few free meals, without pay.

Frankie didn't really know how long he planned to work this time in the little Kansas town, but he was content to stay there for the time being. The money was better than average, as it usually was outside the big cities, and this particular employer happened to be from his hometown. He felt like he was being treated reasonably fairly. He was willing to work long and hard for minimum wage—or sometimes even a little less—but he disliked being flagrantly cheated. He had legal work status by then, if not English proficiency, so he could draw the line if he chose.

During his decades as a Chinese restaurant worker, Frankie had moved around a lot. From time to time, he would leave whatever job he happened to be working and catch a bus back to Chinatown in New York, Los Angeles, or Houston. New York was still his favorite, with entire neighborhoods speaking his particular dialect of Mandarin Chinese on the streets, but the city had grown increasingly expensive, and he wasn't picky, particularly when he wasn't with his wife. Chinatowns had always put him at ease; he liked the language, of course, but also the home-style food (unlike what the so-called Chinese buffets served up), the movies he could actually understand, income-tax assistance, newspapers—whatever he wanted or needed. He had always been able to rent a cot for a few bucks a night, get some badly needed rest, catch up with old acquaintances, and, of course, wire some money back to Fujian—and Minnesota.

Whenever he was ready to get back to work, he would go to a local Chinese employment agency that, for about US$35, could nearly always find an opening for him. He preferred to work in the more remote areas because the pay was better, and his expenses were lower. The employment agency would arrange a phone call to the prospective employer, and they would quickly negotiate the terms. Directed to a Chinese-owned bus service, he would make a long overnight journey to his next kitchen job. When Frankie awakened the next morning, his new boss would be waiting for him at a predetermined drop-off point.

His wife, Ivy, had worked the same way, for the most part, though at that moment she was back in China for a while, caring for a mother in failing health. Upon return to the United States, she was planning to spend some time in Minneapolis, so Frankie would likely be working solo for a bit. In their nomadic lives, childcare had always been an issue for the couple, and Frankie often wished he'd had more time for his kids when they had been younger, but long family separations and heavy sacrifice had always been a part of his seafaring culture.

Frankie had come to the United States as a much younger man, by himself, leaving Ivy and their infant son behind. Very difficult economic conditions in China had left him unable to support his family in farming or fishing. With a promise of financial assistance from his extended family, he'd been able to make travel arrangements with a local "snakehead," a human smuggler. Within a month, he'd left for America.

Several days before this voyage began, the snakehead had contacted Frankie and told him to go to a small tea house near the docks of Quanzhou. The port city was a several-hours' bus ride from his home in an agricultural region of Fujian, Southern China.

With just one small plastic bucket of belongings, Frankie had met up with several other passengers, and after a shared pot of tea, he was taken to a small fishing boat. When the port guard had been adequately bribed in American dollars, the captain of the small vessel pulled away from the dock and headed for open waters. The next morning, off the coast of Taiwan somewhere, Frankie was transferred to an Indonesian freighter, where he encountered other groups of wayfarers also on the first leg of their journey. The freighter then headed west until it reached a port in Vietnam, where local officials were again paid off. Then, the group disappeared into the adjacent city for a few days until a crew of local men ordered them into a small gravel truck that transported them into the nearby jungle. At that point, they began a long march along poorly marked trails, eventually reaching Laos, then Thailand. From this border, they were transported by train to another port city, and they again stowed away in the cargo hold of a freighter, sandwiched between containers of recycled plastic bottles. Next stop: Somalia, or so they were told, but the craft developed engine trouble and had to spend 10 days in Southern India first.

Apparently, the ship's entry documents contained some irregularities, and Somalian customs officials refused to allow the ship to unload its cargo. After several days in port, the still-loaded vessel headed back into open waters, where it anchored for several weeks as angry crew members yelled over the ship's radio. On one occasion, the boat was boarded by local pirates, who, after an exchange of currency and an inspection of all the cargo, left without further incident. Eventually, they returned to the Somali port, where, as the crew unloaded cargo, customs officials handcuffed the ragged stowaways and ushered them unceremoniously into police vans. Several days later, after a meal or two, from behind the rusted bars of their little cells, they saw their snakehead negotiating through an interpreter with a man who appeared to be the chief of the precinct.

Officers returned their meager belongings and escorted the stowaways back to the docks. They boarded an old boat manned by teenagers brandishing Kalashnikovs whose serial numbers had been ground away. Issued only a few bottles of water, they travelled in this manner to Kenya, where, after a week or so of further negotiations, they were placed on a connecting string of passenger buses and transported overland to Angola. At that point, they linked up with a hundred or so of their compatriots, mostly men, but a few women. All of them climbed aboard a small but reasonably seaworthy vessel flying a Romanian flag. The crew, as best they could tell, spoke Portuguese.

Shortly after this vessel crossed into international waters, Frankie and several other young Fujianese men were ordered onto scaffolds, where they covered the name of the boat with paint. Later, they stenciled on a new name: the *Modern Journey*. The recommissioned vessel then lowered its Romanian colors and raised a Nicaraguan flag as it churned its way farther west.

After a short refueling stop and change of crew in Cuba, the ship set sail for Guatemala. There, the refugees were divided randomly into parties of ten or so and delivered by vans to the outskirts of some unknown port city, where they began another treacherous journey by foot across another unfamiliar jungle. When they finally reached the Pacific Ocean, Frankie's party boarded a series of small boats that gradually ferried them up the coast of Mexico. Transfers from one boat to the next usually occurred at night, but not always. Eventually, they were handed over to a drug cartel that, at gunpoint, placed a few kilos of cocaine into each of their little containers of belongings and transported them into the hands of a "coyote" awaiting them at the northern border. A hundred miles or so west of Juarez, they were ordered to cross this border and instructed to walk toward a radio tower they could see on the night horizon. They were intercepted by yet another group of armed teenagers, who took their contraband and loaded them into the back of a tractor-trailer rig that eventually dropped them off at an isolated house, where they all fell asleep.

At dawn, they were placed into a motel courtesy van and delivered to a truck stop along the interstate, where they slipped quietly into a small, empty tour bus bound for Los Angeles. The decals below the rows of passenger windows read "Asia America Adventures." They were given assorted sun hats, khaki pants, polo shirts (all of which fit them reasonably well, more or less), cameras, and stolen Chinese passports. As the group approached the sprawling city, they were ordered to lie down on the floor, and the bus arrived at a dirty garage behind a tour agency. As they stepped down, the tourists dutifully returned the cameras and the passports, but kept their complimentary first set of gaudy American attire. Given scuffed-up suitcases filled with someone else's used blue jeans and T-shirts, also compliments of the house, they climbed into an airport courtesy van and took an excursion to a nondescript, single-family house in a graffiti-riddled part of the city, all the while followed by a newish Ford Escort.

A new group of multiply tattooed Asians with handguns chained them to beds in this house, and ordered the tourists to call their people back home for final payment of somewhere around US$37,000, a little more than the agreed-upon price because of the problems encountered in Somalia. Nowadays it costs a lot more than that, Frankie told me. Though the group offered the hostages an occasional cigarette and fed them regularly, they threatened Frankie and the others at gunpoint and slapped them around until the necessary deposit appeared in a bank account in Quanzhou or New York. Frankie was among the first in the group to be released. He was fortunate enough to come from a close-knit and reliable family that paid the smuggler's debt immediately. After his former guard motioned him off in the general direction of Chinatown, he vanished, rolling his complimentary American Tourister carry-on behind him.

When he'd first started working the restaurant circuit, Frankie didn't have legal work status, but after Tiananmen Square and an easing of immigration policy, he was able, with the help of a good immigration lawyer on the fringes of New York's Chinatown, to successfully apply for refugee citizenship status. He had some loose connections to the Fujianese Christian minority, and therefore his asylum petition received a favorable ruling from a sympathetic federal judge. His boss at the time, also Fujianese, of course added a supportive recommendation to his application. Such an application wasn't cheap, but it was not a terribly risky proposition; if he were to be turned down, he'd learned quite well how to silently vanish. Though an upgrade to US-citizen status didn't necessarily change his daily life all that much, he was proud of it, and he walked a little more confidently down streets where local people didn't necessarily appreciate his presence. Plus, he was then able, after he'd saved enough money, to bring his wife to the United States with him, even finding Ivy a more comfortable, direct route than he himself had taken. When she arrived, Ivy worked the restaurant circuit too. She could usually find work in the same buffet with him, but not always. Since this necessarily vagabond life didn't lend itself to having a child in tow, their son stayed behind in China with grandparents until he reached school age. No longer restricted by Chinese fertility laws, the couple had a second child, a daughter. As soon as the child was a few months old, the couple paid a woman they knew to take the child to China. There, the grandparents took her in and took proper care of her, with remitted American dollars. It was common practice for American-born children to return to China, and the local officials, themselves profiting from the infusion of greenbacks, didn't bat an eye.

Frankie knew a few people who came to the United States unmarried. When they obtained citizenship status, they were able to make extra money by agreeing to an arranged marriage. Most of these unions were not intended to last forever—just long enough to gain legal status for the "trailing spouse." There were agencies on both continents to set it all up, including doctored wedding pictures and certificates with official-looking stamps.

The province of Fujian is an area of Southern China about the size of Delaware, yet the majority of American immigrants from China over the past 30 years or so came from this little dot on the map. In terms of human chain migration, this compares in scale to that seen a century ago among the Italians, Germans, Irish, and Poles. The province supports this migration and depends on it for its livelihood: restaurant-English courses, lenders to help families pay the snakehead fees, a more or less underground trade in US dollars, currency exchanges for those who trust the Chinese banks, all kinds of contractors who don't mind being paid in dollars either...and a shipping industry. In this manner, the region has actually prospered.

For centuries now, the Fujianese people have fled to the sea during tough times—famines, wars, exploitative dynasties, and economic disasters. The result is a hardened, well-established chain of Fujianese ethnic enclaves in the port cities of Asia, Arabia, and Africa. And now, their network extends all the way to the New World. However, in the recent era, the migratory gene on their chromosomes has been so successful that Fujian has been largely depopulated of working-age men and women. It now relies on migrant workers from the rest of China to keep the economic wheels turning. Many of the older people are busy raising their grandchildren, nieces, and nephews.

But Frankie and Ivy were eager to bring their children to America. When their son was 8, and their daughter 3, they were finally able to work a deal with a great-uncle in Georgia, whose son, Frankie's second-cousin, had just bought a restaurant in a suburb of Atlanta. Frankie's great-aunt would take care of the children, see them off to school, and board them while the rest of the family operated the restaurant. Frankie and Ivy would stay in makeshift sleeping quarters in the business, at least until they could afford a place of their own.

The arrangement worked well enough until their son, Eric, started getting into trouble at school. He was a 2nd grader when he arrived, spoke very little English, and had trouble understanding the teacher. Finding himself an outsider and the target of bullies, he gradually fell in with a gang of local Asian toughs with loose connections to New York and Los Angeles. As his truant behavior intensified, his great-aunt kicked him out of her house. The couple had to find a nearby apartment and deal with his problems themselves. But since they both worked long hours, there wasn't a lot they could do.

When Eric was 15, he ran away to New York and joined a Fujianese street gang. For several years, he had no contact with his parents. His youthful rebellion had put a strain on his parents' extended-family arrangement back in Georgia, where profit margins were low, and the restaurant was struggling to stay open. Frankie's relatives couldn't always afford to tolerate the distractions in his life. As the relationship became unworkable, Frankie and Ivy decided to take their daughter and move to New York, hoping to find their son.

Eventually, Eric kicked his drug habit and joined the US Navy. (Something had always made him feel comfortable around ships.) He even managed to earn his GED, which got him the rank of petty officer and a new assignment down in Corpus Christi, Texas. He was unmarried, but since his next tour of duty (if he got promoted again) would likely be in Taiwan, his parents were hopeful he'd find a good Chinese wife.

In New York, Frankie and Ivy settled into a humble Brooklyn tenement, and their daughter, Iris, enrolled in a public school. Her English was very good, and she had been an excellent student from the very start. In no time, Frankie and Ivy found an employment agency in Chinatown and took local restaurant jobs. They learned, however, that kitchen wages were abysmally low in the city. So many Fujianese people resided there—many of them recent arrivals desperate for a first job—that restaurant owners could get away with paying their employees next to nothing. Struggling to make monthly rent and pay the light bill, Frankie decided that he would try to earn a little more money in more distant area codes. Ivy would stay behind to keep an occasional eye on Iris, while working for less money around the city.

Ivy managed to hook up with a small group of Fujianese women in the Brooklyn neighborhood. They encouraged her to join a little Fujianese Baptist Church, where some of the older women saw to the needs of neighborhood children while their mothers were out working the carry-outs. The church offered a few after-school activities, an unlicensed informal daycare network, and an occasional meal. The organization recognized that Sunday was typically a busy day for most restaurant workers, so it provided plenty of workarounds. Ivy joined the organization, and Iris was looked after while her mother worked 12-hour shifts 6 days a week.

But by age 11, Iris was already more than a little self-sufficient. Essentially raising herself, she was awarded a partial academic scholarship to a small Baptist college in the Midwest. With some help from her parents and her brother in the navy, she received a degree in chemistry. Throughout those years, she held down a part-time job bussing tables and restocking a salad bar…at a pizza franchise.

When Iris left for college, her mom gave up the little apartment, said goodbye to a few friends at the church, and joined Frankie on the national Chinese-restaurant circuit. The minister saw her off, urging her to phone in to his weekly tele-sermons when she was in the hinterlands. She politely nodded as she watched for her bus. The minister had himself worked the restaurant circuit in his earlier days, so he knew the system pretty well and did what he could to try to keep his transient, scattered flock together. He was old enough to remember the days back in China when Christian missionaries of all types established congregations throughout the land. He remembered nearly starving to death under the Japanese military occupation and, of course, the red tide that came shortly after its dissolution. His father had been a Baptist minister who fled to Taiwan from Fujian.

Separated from their parent organizations in the West, the Fujianese congregations on the mainland went underground. They were not terribly persecuted—not usually, that is. But they were generally prohibited from holding their meetings in public places. Most of them moved their activities into living rooms and kitchens. They honed their skills at compliance, maintained a low profile, and networked through unofficial channels. Their existence was officially prohibited, but local authorities usually dismissed them as irrelevant, a relatively small minority, not a threat. The little groups found creative ways to appear passive in the face of external pressures, and as the decades passed, they gradually lost most of the characteristics of the overseas institutions that had founded them back in the empire days. They developed their own flavor, their own customs, and sometimes even hybridized with Buddhism a little. They were stoically polite and superficially compliant, while remaining determined, tolerant of adversity, but always wary.

From the little midwestern Bible college, Iris was accepted into a PhD program at a state university in Minneapolis. To support herself, she'd most recently worked as a teaching assistant in an undergraduate chemistry lab. Maybe she even taught you or someone you know, or maybe it was just someone like her. Almost finished with her dissertation, Iris had already been offered several assistant professorships, but she was keeping her options open for the moment. She'd been seeing a young man from the local medical school, a senior internal medicine resident originally from a southern coastal city in Western India. As it happened, his great-grandfather on his mother's side had been from the Fujian Province. Small world.

His parents owned a roadside motel near Leesville, Louisiana. They weren't necessarily too thrilled at the prospect of their son getting romantically involved with a non-Indian woman, but he thought they'd probably warm up to the idea eventually, if anything came of it. From beneath the grain elevator, Frankie wasn't necessarily thrilled himself, but he managed to keep a healthy, long-term outlook. He was excited about the prospect of having a grandchild—maybe even two. He looked forward to a little redemption, hoping to have more time for his daughter's children than he'd ever had for his own.

As I left the little Kansas buffet, I urged Frankie to keep in touch. He nodded politely and glanced toward the salad bar as I handed him a business card. He didn't call, of course. Last summer as I was passing through Kansas again, I decided that a foray through the same little town wouldn't be too far out of the way. I pulled up to the joint, entered, and encountered a vaguely familiar face. The same family was still running the place. Of course, I immediately asked to see Frankie, but the woman curtly informed me that he no longer worked in the restaurant. I couldn't help but ask her if she knew where he'd ended up. She just frowned a little.

"Somewhere in Louisiana. Working in a motel."

CHAPTER 10

My Spanish

● ● ●

AT THIS POINT, WE'RE READY to talk more about who speaks your target languages. Try this: do a Google search of the term "English speaking countries" or "French speaking countries" or whatever you choose. Many languages from former colonial empires are now spoken in a surprising number of places. For example, many African and Caribbean countries use English or French as their official language. The same can be said for Portuguese and, of course, Spanish.

If you want your children to learn one of these languages, you most definitely should not limit your search to a language babysitter from the original country. For example, if it's French you want them to learn, you might be hard pressed to find a local immigrant from France. However, you very likely could find one from the Democratic Republic of the Congo, Algeria, Haiti, or maybe even Vietnam. If you want your children to learn English, and you don't know any people from England, see if you can find an immigrant population from the Philippines, India, Nigeria, or Jamaica. If you can't find such an immigrant population, see if you can identify a local college student needing extra money who has studied the language at a reasonably advanced level.

Similarly, if you are in an even more remote area with no colleges, immigrant enclaves, or other resources of any kind, you might consider paying a visit to your local high school. Talk to the foreign-language teachers, and see if maybe one of them has an exceptionally bright student with enough verbal fluency to help your children. In a pinch, a diligent teenage student might do well enough as your language babysitter. Though it might not be a perfect situation, it might occasionally be your only resource.

But whatever your resources happen to be, utilize them. Where childhood language acquisition is concerned, anything is better than nothing, and waiting for a more perfect situation to come along is always a mistake. Even if you could find one—even if you could *afford* one—the conventional definition of a qualified teacher probably doesn't apply to your little linguists in diapers anyway. You wouldn't hire an ophthalmologist to teach your children to see, you wouldn't need a kinesiologist to teach them to walk, and the person you need to teach them a new language just might not be the highly trained expert you imagine.

When I was 28, I started learning Spanish, which basically means I'm monolingual. I've tried to learn the language, but I'm pretty far beyond the critical period. I've done all the usual things—bought workbooks, listened to audiotapes, and taken community college courses in my spare time. I even married a native speaker, but my brain has apparently become Teflon coated. I've honestly tried hard, but I've never really gotten to the point of being able to participate in a spirited dinner-table discussion with a group of native speakers, like my in-laws. Usually, just about the time the conversation starts to get interesting, they get tired of slowing down for my benefit, the tempo quickens, the dialect thickens, and the metaphors get more esoteric. My daughters can follow along, but I often find myself reading a book in the back bedroom, washing the dishes, or feeding the dog. Sometimes, though, I linger out of politeness, or to see if I can get a little practice. I listen intently and smile a lot, but when they go into Spanish overdrive, I'm lucky if I catch every fourth word.

I'm not sure, but I think I've learned that my wife probably has almost as much family in the United States as she does in Mexico. Some of her family members, the ones who migrated in early childhood, are fluent in English. Others don't really speak the language at all. Most have settled in the American Southwest, so they can get by perfectly well on a day-to-day basis without speaking a single word of English, if they want. They have their own Spanish-speaking networks of friends, small businesses they patronize, churches they attend, strip malls they browse, banks they use, professionals they consult—all in their native tongue. In case you hadn't noticed, those networks are vast and ubiquitous.

The stories of how they all came to live in the United States are fascinating, I'm sure, but they always conduct those conversations in Spanish, so I'm a little foggy on the details. I believe some might've just walked across the desert back in the days before heightened border security. Others were sponsored by employers. Some married US nationals, and most of those relationships were actually permanent. By whatever means, they've all obtained citizenship now, as far as I know. They're all productive members of their adoptive society, and they work in just about every industry you can name. I'm grateful that they've been around to advance the Spanish skills of my children, but still I wish I'd been a better student for them myself.

If you hope for your children to learn Spanish, and marrying into a Mexican family is no longer an option for you, don't worry. A native-speaking network is probably not too far away. In the Western Hemisphere at least, Spanish speakers are expert networkers, and once you've encountered someone who is speaking Spanish at a local supermarket or restaurant, you've probably found the only contact you'll need to get you started. Be polite, be sincere, and inquire. Just don't wait until your child is 28! Expose them to Spanish overdrive as early as you possibly can.

Muncie, Indiana. Population: about 70,000. A place I chose randomly from a US map. Let's say you live there, and you want your children in diapers to learn Spanish. On Google, search "Muncie Indiana Mexican." Looks like there are at least a dozen Mexican restaurants. Some have favorable Yelp and Google reviews. Try to choose the ones that might be locally owned, not national franchises. You can do this from your laptop by going to Google Maps and going down to Street View. Pick out two or three, and plan to stop in. If you find one where at least some of the clientele are speaking Spanish, you've found what you want. Establish yourself as a customer, get to know a few people, and describe what you are look-ing for in understandable terms: a babysitter or maybe a housekeeper who preferably speaks only Spanish so your children can learn the language. Someone probably knows a nice grandmother who would be glad to help you. Leave your contact information, be gracious, and keep looking if you don't get any immediate takers. Most likely, the person you talked to will have to do a little asking around. Plan to go back in about a week.

If that doesn't pan out, well, it seems that Muncie is an agricultural community. Local farmers are probably hiring Spanish speakers when it comes time to harvest their crops or care for their livestock. If you don't know any farmers personally, try the local tractor dealerships, feed stores, or livestock sale barns. You might also try some of the local construction companies, lawn-maintenance firms, and remodeling companies. Maybe you can find some Spanish-language churches in the area. Use Google to search the term "Muncie Indiana *iglesia* [church]," and see if you find any-thing. If that doesn't work, just call a few local church offices, and ask the person who answers the phone if there are any churches in the area that have services in Spanish. Another possibility is the local check-cashing center. Drop by on a payday, look for dollars being sent to loved ones back home, and listen for Spanish. See if Muncie has any colleges or universi-ties with Spanish-language departments. If so, call or email some of the professors to see if they have any ideas. And, of course, if you're driving around and you see a business advertising in Spanish, drop in.

A very important resource I like to use is Craigslist.com. As with using Google Maps, a video is worth a thousand words, so please, *please* go to www.trilingualbysix.com and find a video called *Using Craigslist to find childhood language tutors*. It's also on YouTube. It'll show you how I use this online classified ad service. I'd strongly suggest you understand this tech-nique before you move ahead. Sometimes Craigslist can put you in direct contact with a language babysitter, but far more importantly, it can nearly always help you identify a Spanish-speaking community.

• • •

When you're a Craigslist expert, let's take a moment to see how well the technique might work in Muncie. First, try some broad searches and narrow them down if you find too many results. Start with the term "Spanish" under both the "Services" and "For Sale" tabs. Next, do the same for *"espanol"* and *"habla."* Most likely, you will find some car dealers or other merchants trying to attract the local Spanish-speaking population, maybe a Spanish tutor or two. If you call any one of them, they might be able to point you in a helpful direction.

We'll do more of these, to be sure.

CHAPTER 11

Very International Childcare

● ● ●

HUI ZHONG IS FROM BEIJING, China. She's lived there all her life, except for the time in her early teenage years when Chairman Mao sent her and her schoolmates to a farm in the North. She studied Russian in high school and kept working on it thereafter. But as the Sino-Soviet friendship cooled, she gave it up. By then, she had managed to get a job mopping floors at the US consulate in the city. She picked up some English and worked hard. Someone must've noticed, because she gradually moved up the employment ladder. Now, 30-odd years later, she's a coordinator in the embassy's Fulbright Scholarship Program, and she holds several university degrees, including one in English that she obtained by online correspondence. Because of her many years of reliable service, she's now eligible for US citizenship in a land she's visited only briefly, if she wants it.

She's not sure yet; she's waiting to see where her daughter sets down roots. Her husband, Xu Guan, is an accountant. He doesn't know English, but he does like kids. He's played crazy rhyming number games in Mandarin with mine—could be an accounting thing, for all I know. As I was unable to appreciate the finer points of the apparently hilarious exercise, I just nodded politely and stared at the passing bus outside the window of the couple's compact fifth-floor home.

Hui Zhong and Xu Guan received official permission to visit the United States one year, not coincidentally overlapping our local school's spring break. Hui Zhong was even allowed to bring her brother's wife along—and her niece, of course. Yaya, you can imagine, happens to be about the same age as my two daughters. You can be sure we invited them all to stay at our house.

Everyone really wanted to see the desert Southwest, you see. Hui Zhong and my wife Laura went online and booked a tour through an agency catering to foreign visitors. The trip would be air-conditioned and guided in Mandarin Chinese, which was perfect, since most of the people in our party were reasonably proficient in it, Laura being the only real exception. I can't seem to recall the name of the agency, but if you ever want your children to learn about the Grand Canyon in Mandarin, you can probably find it and many more by just searching online for "China tour agency Grand Canyon" or words to that effect. Naturally, pick one with favorable online reviews. Most of them are less expensive than the typical American bus tours that cover less ground. Some of them are downright cheap—*really* cheap—leaving one to wonder how they ever manage to turn a profit...

In one short week, our group took in not only the Grand Canyon but also Las Vegas, Los Angeles, the Hoover Dam, Yosemite Park, San Francisco Chinatown, and Stanford University (which I suppose must be an Asian parent's fantasyland). I was unable to go along, regrettably. I had to work my half of the holiday, but I'm pretty sure I got more sleep than everyone else that week. The tour was rigorous by mainstream American standards, and I can't imagine they had much more time at each destination than to snap a quick photo and climb back aboard. What else does one really need, after all? I prefer to do my sightseeing with Google Maps, as you already know, from the comfort of my reclining command and control center.

I was more than content just to hear about it all and see the pictures: random mismatches of khaki pants, polo shirts, sun hats, public fountains, sprawling landscapes, and newly formed playgroups of mostly Asian kids. Mandarin was the lingua franca among these national-monument-raiding intergalactic storm troopers, and I was glad of that. My wife told me that my youngest daughter got sick on the bus and threw up on Yaya's lap. After that, the two ordinarily close friends didn't speak to one another for a couple of days. My oldest daughter got in trouble three times for leaving her seat to walk up the aisle and trade candies with some Chinese kids. Recognizing that diligent little linguists will sometimes do that sort of thing, I interceded by cell phone to keep her from getting grounded.

Hui Zhong's daughter went along too, her spring break coinciding with that of my little flock. Following in her dad's footsteps, Cynthia was an accounting major at a university about 15 minutes from our home. One semester we rented her a room in our house at a competitive rate, and she was kind enough to share her language with our daughters. However, she had to take public transportation to school, and that burned up a lot of her study time. As her course load grew more rigorous, she moved out in favor of an apartment closer to campus. But first, she passed us on to Lin, a friend in her chemistry class. Lin's husband had been a doctor in China, and he was studying for his medical board exams here in the United States while holding down a research job on campus. Lin needed a little income stream, and that worked well, since she had a girl about our youngest daughter's age. Obviously, we encouraged her to bring little Hope along whenever she babysat. Another win-win. Lin also played the piano and gave lessons to our girls, in Mandarin Chinese, until she completed her nursing degree.

But Lin didn't leave us in the lurch either. Her husband was friends with a fellow who was a professor of mechanical engineering. One of his colleagues had a daughter who was in her junior year of high school, a recipient of University Interscholastic League math competition awards. So Melody began coming to our house every Saturday after her math-team practice sessions. My daughters bonded with her immediately, even though she spent a few minutes every week reviewing math homework with them (in Chinese). Since she knew about teen fashion, smartphone apps, and pop icons, Melody was of great value to our blossoming daughters.

Like Frankie, we were finding that the route to our destination was not exactly a straight line: it depended upon a network we knew very little about. It was as if we had placed ourselves into the hands of a linguistic snakehead operation, and each babysitter was assigned to transport us a little closer to our final destination. Many of the details were being worked out for us behind the scenes, Fujian style.

When we began our voyage to childhood fluency in Mandarin, we were totally clueless. My oldest daughter was almost 2 when I had to attend a meeting in Las Vegas. Since my aunt and cousin lived there, the family decided to go along. Over coffee one night, my aunt described her new job remodeling casinos. Apparently the carpet wears out fairly often in those places. Anyway, most of the remodeling materials were now coming from Chinese suppliers, who had recently awarded my aunt a free trip to Asia. She had lots of nice pictures to show me as I nodded approvingly and occasionally glanced at that big green glass pyramid I could see off in the distance out her window. She predicted that the Chinese suppliers would gain an increasing market share of the Las Vegas remodeling supply business, and I really couldn't disagree.

I got to thinking that maybe Chinese would be a good language for American children to learn. Without too much trouble, our daughter was already picking up a little German, my heritage language, but I didn't necessarily see any great future economic opportunity there. Most Germans I knew spoke English very well, and my ancestral homeland wasn't really hiring many Americans. It was cute that my little daughter could babble a few words to her great-grandmother and all, but maybe it was time to get more serious about my family's education. At that time, we were living in a small town in northern Texas, and I just didn't see any opportunity on this front. As far as I knew, people in China spoke a language called Chinese; I had no idea how to proceed. It didn't occur to me to scout the local colleges, and I never paid much attention to who was staffing the local Chinese buffet.

Then we moved to San Antonio, a larger town with a far greater predominance of Spanish, Laura's first language and my in-laws' *only* language. Since our children's births, Laura has always insisted on speaking Spanish with them, even in public, and she has always steadfastly refused to acknowledge any word they utter to her in English. Maybe you think that's a little militant, but rest assured that both my children can speak

Spanish very well. As a parent, if you or your spouse has a first language that differs from the dominant community language, and you're not addressing your own children in much the same way, I honestly believe you are missing a wonderful opportunity. But I digress again.

Settling into our new home city, I started a blind search for opportunities to learn the Chinese language. Still clueless, I didn't find much. Finally I decided to post an ad on Craigslist describing basically what I was hoping for—just a babysitter type, someone to communicate with my girls once or twice a week. After a week or so, a middle-aged couple responded to my ad. Laura and I met them at a local Dairy Queen. Though polite, the couple said that the type of work we were proposing was not of great interest to them, but they thought they knew someone who might be willing. It seemed that the couple was connected to a local Chinese Baptist Church that helped new immigrants transition to American life. Several days later, they introduced us to a woman by the name of Joy who had just moved into the area from Shanghai. Joy had a daughter about the same age as our eldest. She was looking for some additional income to support her husband, who had just been hired by a local software-development firm. She liked the idea of being able to bring her daughter along when she babysat our children. Eventually, we learned that she was a flutist. Later she would join the local Chinese orchestra, where she would meet Cynthia (Hui Zhong's daughter), who played the Chinese harp.

As we got to know Cynthia and Joy, Cynthia suggested that maybe we would like to spend a summer in Beijing. Cynthia felt that her mother could probably help us find a preschool for our daughters, where their Mandarin Chinese skills would surely receive a huge boost. Through her contacts with the embassy scholars program, Hui Zhong was also starting a business venture with an American man. The two were both helping exchange students in their respective countries find housing. Hui Zhong found rooms for rent for American students in Beijing, and her associate found rooms for rent for Chinese students in San Antonio.

When Hui Zhong and Xu Guan offered us their spare room, we accepted. Hui Zhong asked us to deposit money into Cynthia's US educational account as payment for the room and board as well as the preschool tuition for the summer. This saved Hui Zhong the expense of wiring money to her daughter and kept us from having to carry significant amounts of cash into China.

Needless to say, the summer was a magnificent milestone for our daughters' linguistic progress. By the time fall arrived, Hui Zhong trusted us enough to give us some cash to take back to Cynthia, to cover expenses for the upcoming semester.

So now let's see if you can find your own versions of Hui Zhong, Cynthia, Joy, and Lin. You might start by just asking around. I would suggest asking people who have a good working knowledge of the community you happen to live in: politicians, chamber of commerce representatives, law enforcement officers, Realtors, religious leaders, and teachers.

However, if simple networking proves fruitless, do not be deterred. This just means that you will have to do your own snooping around. But hey, maybe it's better that way. In the initial stages of your search, I think you have to remember that the first speaker you meet is probably not going to be the person you are actually looking for. Initially, you are really just seeking an inroad into an ethnic enclave—a way to find out where the native speakers of interest hang out, how you can make contact with them, and how you can gain their trust and acceptance. Let's bring what we know about the day-to-day needs of a new immigrant into sharper focus:

1. **Housing.** Not infrequently, when new immigrants arrive, they first find lodging with friends or family who play a crucial role in helping them to get oriented and perhaps also to get employed. As they begin to look for their own lodging, they will probably opt for something in the same general area as their first support group.

2. **Food.** Though it might be more convenient to adopt the local diet, one of the first things new immigrants miss about home is the food. Definitely, businesses spring up to meet this demand, with ethnic markets selling food specialties not necessarily available in mainstream stores.

3. **Language**. Where one does not speak the local language, just getting around can be a very daunting task. Ethnic enclaves reduce this shock, and, of course, support businesses spring up around them.

4. **Employment**. This can be a matter of pressing concern. When the need for income is strong, as it usually is, immigrants are usually not too picky about accepting a first job.

5. **Childhood education and daycare**. When parents bring preschool-age children to a new country, enclaves tend to have informal networks of childcare available. When possible, many immigrants will make arrangements to have an older relative come and join them so they can help out with this. They are, of course, required to enroll older children in school, where some developed countries have language-support services for them. Teachers and school administrators will nearly always be aware of these students, and therefore they will know something about local immigrant populations of interest to you.

6. **Banking**. It's not universally true, but many new immigrants do not start out with enough capital to make an account at a full-service bank cost effective. Furthermore, some new immigrants, lacking legal work status, are not necessarily interested in keeping their money in a form that might attract the attention of federal agents. But they still need to cash their paychecks and remit money back home to dependents. Many new immigrants find alternative institutions to fill these needs: check-cashing centers. Some check-cashing centers will also sell auto insurance, send electronic payments to utility companies, and make short-term loans. A traditional bank in your community that seems to be catering to non-English-speaking clientele is probably a telltale sign of a larger, better established (and more affluent) immigrant community.

7. **Legal aid**. Many new immigrants seek permanent citizenship. Those who can afford immigration attorneys find help in law

offices. Those who cannot will look to refugee-assistance organizations, religious institutions, and other charitable groups.

8. **Medical care.** Most new immigrants are young and healthy, but children still get sick or need immunizations, women sometimes need obstetrical care, and trailing parents can develop all the typical age-related conditions. Healthcare offices that cater to a specific immigrant group will usually advertise their ability to speak an additional language.

To be sure, there are others.

Let's have a closer look at where your future language babysitters might go to have these needs met.

1. **Places of employment.** While stereotypes are usually unfair generalizations, some immigrant groups really are disproportionately represented in certain industries. Some of these have been described as the Three *D*'s: dirty, dangerous, and difficult. That's one way of saying that immigrants often take the jobs that nobody else really wants.

    If you want your children to learn Vietnamese, visiting the local nail salons would not be a bad idea. If you seek Spanish, considering farms, ranches, construction sites, lawn-care companies, and housekeeping services might get you started. If it's Mandarin you seek, Chinese restaurants might actually be a helpful place to look. In fact, ethnic restaurants of just about any flavor are good places to begin your search. Many Asian grocery markets sell oriental food of all varieties and really are operated by Koreans. Motels are often owned by Indians, and a lot of convenience stores doubling as gas stations are Pakistani family businesses. Many French- and English-speaking Africans really do sell clothing accessories and trinkets in pedestrian zones.

    Immigrants who are still looking for permanent work might be functioning as day laborers. Typically they show up early in the morning at an established pick-up point and wait for someone to hire them for the day. A lot of construction and agricultural employers hire day laborers for short-term jobs, so you might ask a carpenter, builder, farmer, or other tradesperson in a labor-intensive field. Many of these networks are informal, word-of-mouth affairs, but some are organized into more structured businesses. If you can't find anything by asking around, try searching the term "day labor" in your town, and see if you find anything helpful.

2. **Ethnic food markets**. As far as I'm concerned, these stores are the surest sign of a nearby ethnic enclave. They are typically on the small side, though some of them can be huge, full-selection supermarkets if the local immigrant population they serve is large enough. Some function as anchors for other immigrant-oriented businesses: insurance, banking, apartment-finding, and employment agencies. If it's Chinese, Vietnamese, or Korean you seek, try a Google search using the term "Asian market" plus the name of your town. If that doesn't work, also try "Chinese market" or "oriental market." For Spanish, try "Hispanic market," "Latin market," "Mexican market," or "Mercado." For Arabic, try "Middle Eastern market" or simply "Arabic market." In some areas, other terms like "Turkish market," "German market," "French market," and "Indian market" might work. Very often, these stores will have bulletin boards for posting job offerings. The messages will usually have to be in the ethnic language, so unless you happen to be literate in it, you might have to get a translator to help you write yours. If you don't already know one, find a translator on Craigslist. If you can't find a local translator this way, Craigslist can probably find you one in New York, Los Angeles, or Houston.

Naturally, you could also just strike up a conversation with the cashier on a slow Wednesday afternoon.

Just for grins, let's find some ethnic markets. On Google, search the term "Middle Eastern market Memphis Tennessee." Now try "Indian market Lincoln Nebraska." If you still want more, search "Turkish market Cologne" or "Asian market Madrid."

3. **Ethnic restaurants**. Though most of these are indeed operated by fluent members of the ethnic group in question, some are not. Some Chinese restaurants are owned by Koreans or Vietnamese, some Mexican restaurants are operated by corporations, and many Italian restaurants are run by families that immigrated to the host country so long ago that they no longer know the heritage language.

4. **Refugee assistance organizations**. At the time of this writing, the United Nations is announcing that global refugees have climbed to levels not seen since World War II. Many of these are children who could play with your kids in whatever language you wish. Their parents would probably be happy to take work as language tutors for your family. Many refugees of all ages are looking for a place to live, even if only temporarily, as they adjust to their new lives. Perhaps you might consider boarding a refugee family who speaks your target language.

My children are a little older now, but if I had it to do over again, I would consider owning a duplex rather than a traditional single-family home. That way, I could always keep a target-language family close at hand. I'm no expert on income taxes, but it would not surprise me in the least if making half a duplex available to refugee families at a discounted rate would be considered a tax-deductible charitable donation of some sort. If you feel brave enough to consider such a prospect, ask the tax professionals in your life, and see what they have to say. Maybe the local refugee organizations would have some opinions. Most people, when they dream of home ownership, do not envision a duplex somewhere, but it could be a relatively temporary affair during the critical ages of language learning. When your children are older, you could sell the duplex at a modest profit and move into something more along the lines of the stock, mainstream, mass-produced dream home, if that's your desire. Just a thought. Maybe with a little brainstorming, you could come up with a variation of this idea that works better for you.

Of the many refugee agencies, the most well-known is probably the International Rescue Committee (IRC), which has branch offices all over the world. Others include Refugees International, United Nations High Commissioner for Refugees, and the Women's Refugee Commission. Many smaller nonprofit organizations operate at the local level. Religious groups are very active in this field too. Perhaps the most well-known of these is Catholic Charities. If you attend religious services, it's entirely possible that your congregation, whether you know it or not, is providing some form of refugee assistance. Ask around.

These organizations assist refugees with housing, legal aid, medical care, crisis intervention, resettlement, job training and placement, citizenship, and childcare. Intriguingly, the IRC has begun training refugee women to work as childcare providers, a prospect you might like to pursue if the IRC has a branch in your community. Where refugees are concerned, the need will probably always outstrip available resources. For this reason, if you are willing to help out in some way, you might find yourself with an abundant supply of language-learning resources. Probably all you have to do is contact some local refugee agencies and figure out a scenario that works. I would suggest just doing a simple Internet search using the term "refugee" with the name of your community. If that leaves you empty handed, make a round through the local churches.

5. **Check-cashing centers**. When looking for an immigrant community, perhaps you might like to swing by for a chat with the teller in one of these shops on a slow Wednesday. With some

respect and tact, you could learn a lot. Alternatively, you might just drive by after 5:00 p.m. on a payday to see who's cashing checks and remitting money back home.

These places have catchy but predictable names like Quick Cash or Payday Express or Easy Advance. Like Chinese restaurants and nail salons, they're just about everywhere. Some of the smallest of towns that don't have one will often have a convenience store providing a similar service. In these places, look for a Western Union or MoneyGram decal on the front door or a sign advertising international prepaid phone cards.

Generally, a check-cashing center's fee for wiring money overseas is less than a full-service bank would charge, particularly if the amount to be wired is just a few hundred dollars or less. These lower wire fees probably help explain their popularity. Lately, Walmart and other corporate grocers have begun to make a move in this market, with some offering money-wiring services in a partnership with MoneyGram. For that reason, you might consider doing some grocery shopping on a Friday or Saturday evening after paychecks are distributed and listening for the sound of foreign languages in the aisles. You just might bump into your next language tutor there.

6. **Houses of worship**. All spirituality aside, they offer camaraderie and familiar language. Many religions try to provide a culturally familiar environment, along with various forms of transition assistance like classes in the local language, childcare, community orientation, and even legal aid. Some immigrant groups have started their own organizations, while others have simply formed subcongregations within mainstream institutions. The best way I know to find these places is by word of mouth. The next best way is, as usual, an Internet search.

7. **Military installations**. Particularly since World War II, the US military has maintained a presence all over the world. Koreans we've already mentioned, but American soldiers have also been

marrying German, Italian, Taiwanese, Filipino, and Japanese civilians for decades now. As far as I know, the latest rounds of conflict in places like Afghanistan and Iraq have not yet resulted in the same degree of social intermingling, so this same phenomenon might not apply. If you're not American, sorry, I'm afraid I don't know a lot about your military system.

Let's find a pocket of another language around an American military installation. On Google, search "German Fayetteville North Carolina." Yes, there is a big army post there. Though the American military no longer has the same presence in Germany that it once had, there are still a good number of German expats in the vicinity of many installations.

It might be helpful to know that the American military offers citizenship to some immigrant students who have necessary language and technical abilities. After a defined period of active duty, these immigrants receive full citizenship for themselves, their spouses, their children, and maybe some extended family members. For this reason, the environs around many military installations may be even more multilingual than I've described.

8. **College campuses**. If you have a large university in your area, you can probably find student organizations for ethnic groups speaking many different languages. You can usually just do an Internet search with terms that include the name of the language as well as the name of the university. For example, you might search the term "Chinese student Ohio State University" or "Arabic student University of Oregon." For smaller colleges, you might need to do a search along the lines of "foreign student," "exchange student," or "international student" with the name of the college. This search might only lead you to an office coordinating international student affairs, where you would need to inquire with the administrator. Sometimes, professors and graduate students in the foreign-language department will know how to make contact

with local immigrant enclaves. Non-foreign upperclassmen or graduate-degree candidates studying a language would probably have sufficient proficiency to help you, even if they are not native speakers. I would not rule them out, particularly if they prove to be the only source of a desired language in your area.

An important point: many international students are not permitted to seek employment in their host country. Often, if they are caught in gainful employment outside of campus, the government can revoke their student visas. You might have to offer other forms of personal assistance or contribute to their education in ways other than employment. It might be legal to make utility payments on behalf of a student or help out with books and tuition costs, but I would definitely seek a professional opinion on this before proceeding. Some cash-strapped international students are probably willing to do a little work under the table, but you have to understand that this is not necessarily legal. Given that they are a well-spoken, highly literate, educated, and ubiquitous language resource, I count this as a great missed opportunity.

9. **Social and charitable organizations**. Many immigrant groups form clubs of various sorts, the majority of which emphasize some aspect of their native culture. These organizations perform many functions, including helping new arrivals get acquainted, effectively supporting chain migration. Typically, the founders have been in the country long enough to be fairly established socially and economically. In some major cities, ethnic chambers of commerce exist to promote business ties.

10. **Hospitals**. Immigrant healthcare professionals must at a minimum pass a tough licensing board exam in the official language, even if they were already licensed back home. This is not an easy thing to do if you're newly struggling with the language. For this reason, in hospitals, one often finds immigrant healthcare providers from countries with a common language, at least as a widely

used second language. In the United States, this helps explain why many hospital providers come from places like India, the Philippines, and Nigeria.

If you happen to know of another locale where you can find foreign-language-speaking immigrants, by all means go there. Additionally, as you go about your daily routine, just listen for the sound of interesting foreign languages.

CHAPTER 12

Monitoring Progress

● ● ●

IN THE MOST LINGUISTICALLY DIVERSE, most immigrant-rich nation the planet has ever known, Americans often blame their monolingualism on lack of opportunity. Many academic experts who don't travel the back roads join the lament. But I hope you no longer do—lament, that is.

And now our quest brings us dangerously close to another scientific black hole: We will need a navigation system, some way to know that we are on course to our destination, some assurance that we are making progress. How will we know that our children are becoming multilingual?

Early on, by 4 to 6 months of age, a child should make eye contact and "bond" with the language babysitter as she speaks. Speech should elicit a change in facial expression and maybe cooing, subtle telltale signs of phenomenal learning. By 12 months or so, depending on when you started, look for the ability to follow (or refuse to follow) simple commands and respond to the language babysitter's comments. Look for evidence that your little team is interacting and understanding one another, even when they don't see eye to eye.

When a child begins to speak, you'll have a better measure of quality, as well as a reason to celebrate. In fact, a child speaking in a second and third language is *the* measure! When should that happen? Tough to say, even if this journey starts at birth. Many prominent linguists claim that multilingual children who start at birth develop all their languages at the same rate and on the same time frame as monolinguals, but others say there's a bit of a delay (with "bit" remaining undefined—probably a matter of a few months at most). Nobody knows what happens to children who receive a lower level of exposure to a second or third language, say, 5 hours per week. My guess is they develop that language almost but not quite as fast as their first language, but I have no proof of that. If they start later than birth, it's even less clear; it might depend on how similar the secondary languages are to the first. As always, quality of exposure matters.

Let's say that a child who begins a multilingual journey prior to age 1 and who is getting reasonable-quality exposure should be speaking at least a few words in the target language by the 3rd birthday. Usually it will happen a lot sooner than that, but if you're at a relatively low number of hours per week, you might have to be a little patient. If you're impatient and can't wait that long, just increase the hours of exposure by about 50% every 4 months until you begin to hear speech. Here, your impatience might pay a nice dividend. Boosting exposure to the point that a child is actually using the language in an active way is probably a very good long-term investment. Once the child reaches that multilingual milestone, subsequent learning increases considerably. Speech from a trilingual child begets more speech. It's self-amplifying, a learning exercise all its own. Once that happens, you could drop back down again, but if the speech starts to taper off, go back up. Do the same if your children are not using the target language by age 3; increase the exposure every few months until you get the speech result you want.

It's caveat time again: if a child is not speaking at least a few words in the *first* language by age 3, this could indicate a true speech delay. We'll touch on this in a subsequent chapter, but if you suspect speech delay, consult your pediatrician. If the doctor recommends an evaluation by a speech pathologist, try to see one who specializes in multilingual children. This specialist will understand that being multilingual does not cause a pathological speech delay and will not try to convince you that stopping a second or third language will fix the issue. It won't.

If your children are older when you start the journey and already are chatting away in their first language, watch out for a "silent period" of up to 6 to 12 months. It doesn't usually happen, but it might. You can address it the same way: with patience or with increased exposure.

For children already speaking a target language, there are no rules on following progress. But that's OK—we play this trilingual parental game without expert supervision; we make our own rules, and we learn a lot! No wonder the play-based preschool educators operate this way.

And the great linguists too. One of the hallmarks of being a famous linguist is the ability to be taken seriously when you dream up a theory without actually proving it. I don't know if anyone will take us seriously, but at least we're thinking like great linguists now! Though your goals may be different, as a general rule of thumb, let's say that if your children reach the point of being able to maintain a two-way conversation with the language babysitter, you should just try to monitor the progress a little, making minor adjustments to the exposure level as you deem necessary. Let the course of many years of persistence and practice do its magic. If you and your babysitter agree that your children understand what is being said and are doing a reasonable job of holding up their end of the conversation, just let it ride.

However, if you need more structure than that, we could define a child's "end of the conversation" this way:

AGE	PERCENTAGE OF CONVERSATION SPOKEN BY CHILD
0–1	0+% (Not counting babbling)
1–2	1+%
2–3	2+%
3–4	5+%
4–5	10+%
5–6	10+%

That is, by age 4 or 5, you want a child to be able to do at least 10% of the talking in a two-way conversation with a fluent speaker. If a child is speaking more, say 25%, beautiful. This is probably an instance in which talkative kids have an advantage.

If you need your children to have an even higher level of proficiency, then they will probably need the ability to hold up an even greater percentage of a conversation. For example, if you think your daughter might one day attend 1st grade in another country, she will probably need to be able to tell a story or deliver a narrative in that language, with little or no input from the babysitter.

Let's say we want a babysitter who, by our estimate, averages at least 30 words per minute of speech, preferably more. And maybe you should give "extra credit" for words spoken by your children. If you sense the babysitter is habitually dropping below this level or excessively dominating the conversation, speak up. If that doesn't work, you might be ready for a change.

If you find yourself needing to increase your children's weekly exposure, it's probably better to do it with more human time if you can manage it. Most varieties of electronic time (the ones that are not interactive) will promote understanding of the language, but they ultimately do not require children to actually put their new skills to use. With excessive reliance on these, you run the risk of nurturing what many call a "passive multilingual," someone who understands several languages but cannot effectively speak all of them.

However, during some chapters in your life, you will probably have to fall back on electronic time. Judge its quality based on its ability to hold your children's attention. Usually, that's not much of a problem where cartoons and kids' movies are concerned—they can be downright addictive. Occasionally, make sure your children can tell you what the story line is or translate some of the comments for you. If they're laughing at the dialogue, that's an excellent sign.

So now, an ultrashort summary. In the earliest phases, evaluate for bonding and babysitter chattiness. Next, look for understanding. Then, expect speaking from the child followed by conversation. Finally, storytelling. Ultimately, more speaking from the child equals more learning.

Classroom teachers might not encourage children to talk more, but your language babysitters definitely should.

CHAPTER 13

Orienting Your Experts

• • •

By most accounts, the Asian country of Singapore is one of the most multilingual societies in the world. Nannies from places like the Philippines are very common there, and working parents insist that these domestic servants speak English with their children. By the time they begin preschool, over half the children are already fluent in English, and nearly all have learned it before entering grade school, where teachers require it from the very first day. Increasingly, students speak "Singlish" with each other, though their teachers probably don't allow this new language in the classroom. Not yet, at least.

On the other hand, the Japanese are generally regarded as more monolingual than other cultures in the region. They struggle with English in particular. Until recently, Japanese students began receiving exposure to English in junior high school. Since 2011, schools have been introducing English in the 5th grade, with so far unimpressive results. The current plan is to begin teaching English in the 3rd grade. Because of the strict immigration laws, foreign babysitters are uncommon in Japan.

Here in the United States, we really can't invoke that excuse. There is no reason we couldn't follow Singapore's lead and reinvent the whole babysitting thing. With just a little training, maybe your babysitters could have your children just as multilingual as a typical Singaporean kid. But maybe "training" is the wrong word. It's more of an orientation—a declaration of your priorities, your hopes, your goals, and your philosophy. In whatever way you can, you need to make sure that your babysitters see the big picture. You hope, of course, that your children will be trilingual by the age of six. You will be counting on these experts very heavily, and they will play a very important role in your family's life. They need to realize from the very beginning that they are more important than just domestic servants, more than mere employees. They are vital to your future plans. You would do well to remind them of this from time to time. They are more vital to your children's future than whatever elite social ladders you hope to climb, and maybe you would do well to remind yourself of that from time to time.

Once you've successfully instilled this sense of importance in your language babysitters, you may find they want to think and act like traditional classroom teachers. They may want to pull out workbooks and study guides and assign exercises, drills, and the like, in the interest of promoting your children's linguistic talents. If you're with me so far, you'll probably understand that you need to put a grateful but firm stop to that. Praise the effort, of course, but stop the "drill and kill." You want your language babysitters to understand that your preschoolers will learn best through play, social interaction, and participation in life's everyday activities. The children don't need to view this as work. It should be fun. Actually, it *must* be fun, if you want them to participate enthusiastically. Great if your babysitters take initiative and think of themselves as teachers, but you're after a very special, more spontaneous kind of teaching. Ultimately this type of teaching will be easier for the babysitter, more fun for the kids, and, in the long run, much more beneficial. Now that's a deal you don't get very often in life. Have fun, don't stress out, don't actually work at it, and you will be way ahead of the game. If only the rest of their education could be so easy.

Actually, it's easy, but it's not. While you don't want your babysitters to be academic drill sergeants, you do want them engaged 100% of the time. You want a running dialogue. Our rule of thumb, a minimum of 30 words per minute, is a good starting point, and you can spot-check this from time to time with a stopwatch or a mental count if you like. Remembering that normal adult conversation averages 300 words per minute, this is a comfortably low bar that should pose no problem for most language babysitters. If you want to raise the stakes a little, consider making your minimum standard 60 words per minute. If a stopwatch seems a little too compulsive for your style, fine. Just make sure you always hear words being spoken in the background. You really want to avoid the language babysitters who disengage and let you pay them to just sit and do their own thing—the dreaded texting teenagers. That's not language instruction; that's not acceptable, and those babysitters would probably be better suited to work in a kennel, though most kennels probably have higher linguistic standards than that.

So let me drive home these first few points before moving on. Your language babysitter needs to understand from the very start that you want talk, *lots* of talk, and you want back-and-forth dialogue. You don't want didactic, classroom-style instruction—just lots of conversation in the context of play and real-world activities that have meaning to your children. You want your language babysitter to understand her true importance in your children's lives, and you want your children to feel valued as little human beings. This may be enough to orient your babysitter, and in many instances, it will be all you can expect. That's certainly fine; a language babysitter who can carry on a conversation with your children and maintain a running dialogue will take you a long, long way toward your goals.

Beyond that, I think I run the risk of making this topic more complicated than it really needs to be, but you might try to encourage a few other things from your language babysitter. It's entirely possible that she might do a thing or two to maximize your children's future school success. The picture is a bit blurry here because most research studies on this topic have looked only at monolingual children. However, I think the information could be (and should be) extrapolated to the multilingual child. We've gone over the importance of reading to your children every evening and choosing storybooks that they genuinely enjoy. Reading aloud to them is perhaps the single best thing you can do to promote literacy later in life, and there is absolutely nothing to suggest that children should not be read storybooks in two, three, or even more languages. Perhaps if you were to provide your language babysitter with a small collection of storybooks, she could not only help your children learn additional languages but also promote their future literacy. It's a complicated, imperfectly understood phenomenon, but literacy in one language translates into literacy in other languages. So, for example, if your children who will be speaking English in school are being read storybooks in Spanish or French, you can reasonably expect that this activity will help them when it comes time to begin reading in English. Foreign-language storybooks are not that difficult to find in the modern era. Perhaps your language babysitter will even have a few lying around her house. If not, online booksellers such as Amazon.com tend to have sister sites in just about all the common languages, as we'll see.

We've already made abundant reference to the narrative concept. Studies have shown that a young child's ability to tell a story predicts 4th-, 7th-, and even 10th-grade reading comprehension.[76] Research also suggests that children use their most complex and sophisticated language ability when telling personal stories.[77] Make your babysitter aware of this. Properly set the stage, and you just might be amazed at how readily your child can tell your babysitter an elaborate story. If hearing your child do this in a second or third language would not make you proud, I honestly don't know what would.

To encourage your children to tell a story, simply ask a few open-ended questions. Then, just listen intently, letting them know that you are following along by providing little tidbits of feedback as the story unfolds. The stories can be basic, dinner-table accounts of how the child spent the day, or they can be elaborate, fantastic fairy tales of the child's own imagination. Either promotes literacy and improves language skills in whatever language the child uses to tell the story. Your babysitter might ask what happened at the park yesterday, for example, or maybe ask about some funny things that the family pet has done. Perhaps the child could tell some stories from the last trip to Grandma's house. Ordinary topics the child finds interesting will do. With more imaginative children, you might give a few opening lines to a fairy tale and then let them finish the story. For example, you could say, "Once upon a time there was a magic bird that lived in a castle in a dark forest," and then ask them to finish the story.

As the narrative develops, you or your babysitter can elicit further details: "Why did that happen?" or "Who else was at the playground?" or "How did the magic bird find the castle?" You get the basic idea. Another neat trick I've seen involves taking a storybook and, over the course of a week or so, reading it to the child several times. Then, you give the book to the child and say, "OK, you read it to me this time." If the book has enough pictures, the child will most likely be able to tell you the story, and you might be very entertained by the interpretations you hear!

While there is some indication that very young children will do quite a lot of language learning by just overhearing speech between adults, they learn better when the speech is directed at them personally. Actually, the amount of talk addressed to children predicts their rate of language development.[78] Starting from birth, you want your language babysitters to look your children in the eye and speak to them, even before they have the ability to give a verbal response. In some cultures, this is something of a foreign concept; not all parents across the world view their infants as conversation partners. In Western society we take this for granted. Parents carry on lengthy conversations with their preverbal infants. Babies respond by making eye contact, cooing, smiling, or perhaps frowning. Though it's not yet something you can hear or visibly measure, these very early conversations with infants are teaching them quite a lot about the language they will soon be speaking. Rest assured they are taking it in, processing the information, and learning from the experience.

It might be difficult if your language babysitter comes from a culture that does not generally accept the concept of an infant as a conversation partner. She may find the practice awkward and unnecessary, so you will want to find a way to emphasize its value of this to her. (Or him. Sorry. I've repeatedly made the assumption that most babysitters are women, but that might not be your experience.) Many cultures view talkativeness as impolite, as a sign of haughtiness or vanity. Being as gentle and diplomatic as you can, however, you need to help your babysitter move beyond this so that she will feel comfortable chatting away with your children. Unfortunately, if you find yourself with a reserved babysitter who will not be drawn out of her shell, you probably are not getting what you are paying for, and you might need to renew your search. I am sure that many quiet babysitters have big hearts and good intentions, but keep in mind that your children's future linguistic ability is at stake, and silence, however warm, is just not going to bring you closer to your goals.

Once again, if your language babysitter speaks your home language, you need to make very sure that she does not slip into this language at any point. As far as I'm concerned, the best way to handle this is to train her to simply say, "I don't understand," in the target language, and be persistent about this. If you can't do that, then you need to do what I like to do. Take the lazy way out and just hire babysitters who don't understand your home language! I have seen babysitters who speak the target language to their pupils 100% of the time but acknowledge everything the children say in their first language. The result is passive bilingualism, and that's just not the result you are after.

Having made a dogmatic, hard-line statement like that, I need to backpedal a little and explain that children learning a new language will sometimes substitute words in their first language when they don't know or cannot remember the word in the target language. That's called mixing or code switching, and it's not a problem as long as they are making a genuine attempt to speak in the target language. Your babysitter doesn't need to correct every mistake or be bullheaded about making sure your children speak the target language perfectly from the start. It's OK to allow some mixing. As your children gain proficiency in the new language, the mixing will gradually diminish. But children who attempt to speak to a language babysitter in their first language exclusively deserve to be thwarted—or at least "not understood." It might take a little time for your language babysitter to recognize the difference between mixing and rebellion, but she'll eventually figure it out. So will you.

Along the same lines, if your language babysitter has children near the same age as yours, this could be a real win-win. It could multiply the language exposure for your children and make working for you especially convenient for your babysitter. However (and this is a *huge* however), if the babysitter's children already speak your home language, it might not work out. For whatever reason, when children get together, they always seem to revert to the dominant community language. Your babysitter might try to steer the rowdy herd into the target language, but that could prove impossible. You could give it a try, but if it doesn't work out, you might just have to find another situation, or at least ask the babysitter to leave her kids at home.

By this time, it should probably come as no surprise that you might need a general rule against the use of electronics. If you permit your language babysitter to use her cell phone to make calls or send text messages, you need to keep this to an absolute minimum. I believe the same basic rule should apply to videos. With the best of intentions, many language babysitters will find cartoons in the target language for your children. While this promotes learning, it is substantially inferior to human interaction. Express gratitude to the babysitter but explain that the videos can be watched after she has left your house. If you find them appropriate, your children can watch them when the babysitter is off the clock. Stress to your babysitter that conversation is your priority. We've seen that older children do seem to learn a little from entertaining videos, but if you're paying for conversation, then that is what you should expect. Children can watch videos for free just about any time, but live conversation generally comes at a fair market price.

And finally, an observation from the real world. Most likely, you will never find a babysitter who meets all of these criteria and who can be oriented as completely as you would like. However, if you can find one who bonds well with your children and can conduct an ongoing dialogue in the target language, that's probably more than good enough. An imperfect language babysitter is far, far superior to no language babysitter at all. Just remember the sagacious words of the famous linguist Woody Allen: "Success is 90% just showing up." Merely taking the trouble to get a language babysitter is 9/10 of the battle.

CHAPTER 14

Choosing Wisely

● ● ●

REMEMBER THOSE TRIBAL VILLAGERS IN New Guinea I told you about? The ones who routinely speak five or more languages? Well, I'd like to tell you their secret, but I can't, because they can't remember how they did it. Apparently it was just something they picked up as very young children... sort of like walking. By the time they were old enough to form lasting memories, it had already happened.

For your own young children, there are at least three languages you'd like them to know: the home language, the dominant community language, and, of course, the future school language. However, for most of us in the United States, those three are all the same. Unless money is no object for you, the other languages you choose should really depend upon the human resources available to you locally. We now recognize that most children will need at least several language tutors before age 6. For this reason, a child's second and third languages will usually need to be ones with an ample, permanent supply of speakers in your home area.

So how do you make that determination? How do you know that your area contains a sufficiently large population of speakers? If you live in a large multicultural city like New York, Paris, or Hong Kong, you can choose just about any languages you wish. The rest of us, however, have to get to know our own neighborhoods a little better. The secret to long-term success lies not in finding one suitable language babysitter, but in finding a *community* of them. To illustrate, if you find a great person to babysit your children in Hungarian, you will have a devastatingly huge problem if that babysitter moves away, and there are no other Hungarian speakers in your town. You absolutely want to avoid that problem. You might find solutions, but they would not be cheap.

In the long run, I think you're better off choosing common languages that are spoken across broad geographical areas. Even if you live in a cosmopolitan metropolis with virtually unlimited linguistic variety, your life could change, and you could find yourself moving to an Ohio farm community or a paper-mill town in Louisiana. The last thing you want is to be forced to abandon your trilingual journey prematurely just because you can't find the resources you need. Modern life is unpredictable, so you want to choose languages that would probably be available no matter where you land.

Consider Italian, for example: a very beautiful language with many centuries of culture behind it. Unfortunately, there are not a lot of speakers living outside the country of Italy. A hundred years ago, there were lots, but these days not so much. If you lived in New York, you could probably still find an adequate number of speakers, but not in very many other places. On the other hand, a language such as French is spoken as a first or second language in many countries. A number of them regularly send immigrants all over the world. It might not exactly be the same dialect they speak in Paris, but it would be much easier to find a French-language babysitter than an Italian one. Similarly, maybe you have a special attraction to Finnish or Romanian, but your chances of finding enough speakers of these languages might be slim. However, if you can come up with a workable long-term plan for regularly exposing your children to one of these less common languages, by all means, go for it. Just be careful, and always maintain the long view. Usually you have to make rational choices rather than sentimental ones.

In the world right now, the most commonly spoken languages are Mandarin Chinese, Spanish, and English. There are approximately 7,000 other living languages, many of which do not even have a written form. A lot of them seem hopelessly destined for extinction as globalization advances. I have heard it said that a person who speaks the top three world languages can communicate with 75% of the people in the world, and it's certainly possible that these three will become even more prominent as less widely spoken languages fade into the history books. Also, these are spoken by a large number of immigrants settling all across the vast globe. Other languages with widespread availability include French, Russian, Korean, Portuguese, Arabic, and Hindi. Please understand that this is by no means an exhaustive list.

For some, widespread availability has a lot to do with world history of 200 years ago. During that time, many European powers were colonizing other parts of the world. Though the colonial era is basically over now, many of these powers left behind their languages in the lands they formerly occupied. The native languages of these colonies tended to be vast collections of tribal languages that were spoken only by a relatively small number of people. As the colonial powers retreated, the resulting independent countries often kept the language that had been forced upon them because it was the only one spoken broadly across the entire land. As an example of this phenomenon, the largest French-speaking country in the world right now is no longer France. It is the Democratic Republic of the Congo. Needless to say, England is no longer the largest English-speaking country in the world. That would be the United States, though many experts claim that India and China now have as many English speakers as the United States does. English is also the official language of Australia and many African, South American, and Caribbean countries. Additionally, it is the official *second* language of many more countries throughout the world. When a country is faced with having to conduct its official business in a single language, choosing one tribal language over another would only invite conflict, so many countries adopt a common world language as their official one.

At the moment, China is the largest immigrant-producing country in the history of the world, while the United States is the largest immigrant-accepting country ever. Outside of that context, it's helpful to know that, where there is ongoing conflict, economic collapse, or natural disaster, there are likely to be people who are migrating and resettling elsewhere.

Looking beyond the human misery caused by these disasters, I'd point out that the asylum seekers they generate could be a great opportunity for you. Many African refugees, for example, speak French, English, Arabic, or Portuguese. South American migrants usually speak Spanish or Portuguese. When they arrive in your neighborhood, they'll be looking for jobs…and you'll be looking for language tutors. Perhaps that is where you, as a trilingual parent, have a small role to play in world stability!

Quite a few refugees were highly educated professionals in their countries of origin, but they lack the necessary credentials to work in their chosen field in their new home. They might find a way to reenter their field of expertise one day, but that can take time, sometimes many years. In the meanwhile, they are prepared to take whatever work they can find as a bridge to a more stable life. As I perceive it, the way it often works is that a number of displaced refugees find their way into temporary internment camps, where they're relatively slowly "processed." Because accepting large numbers of refugees can be a tax-generating but politically unpopular move, many politicians decry the "invasion" and wait until whatever crisis that drove the refugees from their homeland fades from the headlines. Only then are they quietly accepted by their host countries. Other groups of refugees enter their host country illegally and maintain a low profile until such time as a turn of political sentiments eventually grants them some form of legal status.

In the so-called "graying" countries, those economically developed societies where the birth rate is low and the life expectancy is comparatively long, there is a growing need to recruit workers to fill skilled labor jobs that keep the economic wheels turning. Often these supposedly temporary laborers end up staying permanently. They help build the infrastructure that keeps the local economy prosperous, and they pay taxes that keep the healthcare and retirement plans solvent. Examples of this type of immigrant would include the Turks in Germany and, more recently, the Poles in Great Britain, as well as the Filipinos in Singapore and South Korea. Most Filipinos, I would quickly point out, have English-language skills. Saudi Arabia, as well as some other relatively wealthy Arab countries, contains large numbers of Indian immigrants. They are prized for their technical skills as well as their familiarity with English. If you are a parent in one of these countries and would like to see your children get a great head start on learning English, I hope you find this to be useful information.

And finally there is the phenomenon of brain drain. Economically prosperous countries are successful in attracting world scientists and professionals to their universities and highly technical industries. India is supposedly the world's largest supplier of these highly sought-after immigrants, but China probably also sends at least its share abroad. During a certain time in US history, which probably continues to this day, we had a shortage of medical doctors. Many physicians who trained in India or Pakistan were enticed in some fashion to practice here. Because of the colonial past, most of them already spoke English and found it easier to pass the requisite licensing exams. Engineers, computer programmers, and scientists from all over the world have also found they have an inside track to migrate to Western countries because of their highly developed and greatly needed skills. Many of them can be found not too far from universities, science-based corporations, hospitals, and other technical centers.

I know a little about universities because I was a college student once, but that turned out to be temporary. My physics professor was from India, same for computer science. Back in the days before Bill Gates was famous, we had to do our homework assignments at a computer lab, where we would enter our code onto punch cards before turning them in to an attendant who would feed the cards through a reader. Nightmare: a professor whose English I couldn't understand and a card reader that couldn't understand my commands. Nowadays I work in hospitals, so I'm still acquainted with a fair number of Indian immigrants—Pakistanis too. And, while I'm thinking of hospitals, did I tell you about Oma yet?

Didn't think so. I met her one evening when I was working a shift in the emergency room of our little town. Her husband, Bob, been diagnosed with cancer, and he was sick again. The couple had settled in the area after Bob retired from the military, in the days before the local air base closed. They'd met in Heidelberg, Germany, during one of Bob's overseas assignments. I'd been there, in Heidelberg, lots of times. It used to be a hub of American military activity back in the Cold War era. I'd even been engaged to a native German speaker once, but that also turned out to be temporary, just like some of the other very educational chapters in my life.

After Bob died, Oma agreed to babysit our first daughter, who was already 9 months old. As a result, the first word our daughter ever spoke was in German. I wish I could remember the word, but I can't. A few years later, our second daughter's first word would also be in German. Since my grandmother still spoke the language, and my other relatives were proud of their heritage, I got some family accolades for that during holidays and family reunions. Somewhere I think we have a video of two little girls conversing with their great-grandma in German.

When we moved away from that town, we actually tried to persuade Oma to come along with us, but she wouldn't. Eventually, though, she also moved away, to be closer to family. In real life, you see, she really was an *Oma*. Though we didn't realize it at the time, she'd been the first, totally unplanned leg of our linguistic journey, and she proved to be very difficult to replace. Germany just isn't sending abundant immigrants into the world these days. We had to search far and wide to find another German baby-sitter, eventually hiring a very reliable undergraduate at a local university to keep us from stalling. But, unfortunately, she didn't remain a college student forever either. We were frantically searching again. Resorting to Craigslist, we finally found a young man from Egypt who had spent a decade in Germany after his family, a religious minority, left home. It's actually going quite well, but eventually, he'll probably move on too.

If Laura and I could begin again, I doubt we would choose German. I'm proud that my children can speak my heritage language far better than I can, but continuing to find replacement babysitters will always be a problem for us. We've decided to grit our teeth and make the best of our early decision, hoping that, as our girls become a little older, they will gain the maturity to tap into the emerging world of online language pals.

We've already begun to use Skype for this. At some point it may be our only option.

An old friend from Germany now has two sons about the same age as our two daughters. She was able to pull some strings and get permission for our daughters to enroll in German public schools for the last 6 weeks of their school year, which runs through the middle of July. We have reason to believe that a donation we made to the school helped our cause! On the evening of their last school day in the United States, my daughters were with Mommy on a plane to Germany. Using VRBO.com, we'd reserved a small flat near my friend's house.

The progress our daughters made that summer was nothing short of amazing, but it was a huge investment, and Daddy was pretty lonely back home. Where German is concerned, we've so far been able to make the best of a hard situation—but I hope I can help you make wiser long-term choices.

CHAPTER 15

Wise Choices

● ● ●

UNDERSTANDING THE FULL EXTENT OF world immigration can be difficult. For one thing, many countries do not always keep accurate immigration statistics. For another, a sizable percentage of world migration is done illegally, and there's not a totally reliable way of gathering data. In your own neighborhood, there might not be any other way short of just getting out, doing your own detective work, seeing what sort of potential language babysitter groups you can find, and sizing them up to see if they'll meet your needs. I'd strongly recommend you do that, so you'll never run out of Omas.

Before you put on your detective hat, though, here's a little information you might find useful:

CHINESE

While Mandarin is not the only language spoken in China, it is the dominant one and the most common first language in the world by a very wide margin. Many Chinese who primarily speak another language or nonstandard dialect know standard Mandarin as well. Over the course of the last 60 years or so, China has conducted a very successful campaign to reduce illiteracy, and as a result, most of the population can read and speak Mandarin. Most think the country is the largest immigrant-sending land in the history of the world, and Chinese immigrants live just about everywhere. Though they work in many vocations, they are known in particular for their roles as scientists in the world's universities and high-tech industries—and for their utterly ubiquitous restaurants. In the United States, for example, Chinese restaurants, most of which are owned and operated by ethnic Chinese businesspeople, are reported to be more numerous than all the McDonald's, Wendy's, and Burger King restaurants combined. The largest Chinese enclave outside of Asia is supposedly in New York City.

Hindi/Urdu

Some say that the worldwide number of Indian and Pakistani immigrants exceeds the number of Chinese immigrants. Since India probably sends the greatest number of scientists and engineers to the world, you might find an Indian immigrant enclave not too far from your local college or other technological hub. Because of the past colonial connection to the United Kingdom, Indian and Pakistani immigrants are particularly numerous in English-speaking countries. However, their numbers are greatest in the Middle East, most notably Saudi Arabia, where their technical and English-language skills are valued. As with the Fujianese restaurant owners, the stereotype of Indians and Pakistanis owning convenience stores and motels in the United States contains a definite element of truth, however oversimplified. A huge percentage of all the motels in the United States are owned by immigrants from a single region in Northern India.

Spanish

In the Western Hemisphere, Spanish is everywhere. Waves of Central and South Americans have migrated north, where they are so numerous that it is difficult to generalize their settling patterns. However, many recent immigrants work in agriculture, construction, and various hospitality trades. In the Eastern Hemisphere, Spaniards are moving relatively freely across the European Union countries.

ENGLISH

Though some say French is the most common second language in the world, most people say that English holds this distinction. A surprising number of countries use it as an official first or second language. It is an official language in India and Pakistan, as well as in many African countries, such as Nigeria and Kenya. In the Philippines, a country that sends a striking number of immigrants to the rest of the world, 60% of all people speak English. In just about any country, if you want your children to have an English-speaking babysitter, you can probably find an immigrant or student group to help you out, even though they might not speak a standard dialect. You could count on your children to be able to transition to a standard dialect later on.

ARABIC

Arabic has close to 300 million native speakers worldwide.[79] Sadly, much of the Arabic-speaking world is fraught with chaotic violence and political instability, and it is generating more than its share of refugees. Many are finding their way to Western Europe, but they are seeking asylum virtually everywhere. Most tend to resettle in urban areas, but this might not always be the case.

In the predominantly Christian world, the prospect of fundamentalist Islam and religious conflict can cast a dark shadow over relations between the two rather different approaches to life. I think, however, it's important to make a distinction between the Arabic language and religious politics, because the Arab world is more culturally diverse than most of us in the West realize. If you seriously want your children to learn to speak Arabic, I don't think you should be deterred by what you see on the nightly news. In the United States, for example, well over 60% of all Arabs residing in the country are Christian.[80] Depending on where you live, it can be easier to find Christian Arabs than Muslim ones. The Arabic-speaking world just might be a far calmer place by the time your children are adults, and they just might feel very fortunate to be able to speak the language as they begin their own careers. Knowing what I know now, if I could go back in time 5 to 10 years, I would probably choose Arabic for my own children. Sometimes, the greatest opportunities of the future are connected to the worst difficulties of the present.

FRENCH

Regardless of whether or not French is actually the most common second language in the world, it is very widely spoken, with almost 50 countries across the globe claiming it as an official language. If the continent of Africa ever develops a more unified political system, French could very easily emerge as a far more important world language. As it now stands, many French-speaking countries in Africa and even Southeast Asia are generating quite a few refugees. Miami, with a large Caribbean immigrant population, has a number of French heritage language schools for children.

KOREAN

Over 60 years after an armistice, the United States continues to maintain a large military presence in South Korea, and a fair number of service people choose to marry Korean nationals. You can often find a cluster or two of shops advertising themselves in Korean script around domestic military bases. Additional streams of immigration have augmented these Korean enclaves in modern times. Many Korean immigrants work as shopkeepers (particularly grocers), and Asian markets are often owned by Koreans. Like their Chinese neighbors, the Koreans have traditionally been a migrating culture, and they have a sizable expat presence throughout the world. For more information, just use Google to search the term "Korean diaspora." In the United States, Korean parents often send their children to weekend schools, many of which are affiliated with Korean churches.

VIETNAMESE

In the wake of the Vietnam War, refugees flocked to the United States, gradually coalescing into large enclaves in Houston and Southern

California. Since those postwar days, however, Vietnamese people have continued to migrate. While they reside in greatest numbers in the United States and Canada, you can find them almost everywhere else.

PORTUGUESE

In addition to Portugal and Brazil, several African and Asian countries have populations that predominantly speak this language. Though Brazilians have not migrated as extensively as some other South American groups, you can often find them in major Latin American hubs like New York, Los Angeles, and Miami.

RUSSIAN

When the Soviet Union began to fragment, many ethnic Russians remained in the former member states, but others left for Western Europe, the United States, Canada, Brazil, and Venezuela. For whatever reason, a number of them opened Russian-style preschools. If you live in a large city, you might be able to find one of these.

POLISH

As members of the European Union, the Poles have found work in Western European countries, most notably in the United Kingdom. Poland retained its traditional apprentice system for skilled labor and artisanship at a time when many European countries were abandoning theirs. As a result, Polish artisans and skilled workers are finding their carefully cultivated trade skills in great demand.

BENGALI

Among the world's most commonly spoken languages, Bengali ranks very high. People speak it natively in Bangladesh and parts of Northeast India. While there are quite a few Bengali-speaking immigrants in the world, their numbers are smaller than those of many other groups. Bangladeshis, like their Indian neighbors, have recently been highly recruited because of their English-speaking abilities.

• • •

If you remain committed to teaching your children a language not mentioned in this chapter, that's great. Just satisfy yourself that you'll always be able to find an ample supply of speakers. From where I sit, within the borders of the largest immigrant-accepting nation in the world, finding language babysitters seems like a relatively easy task. But in countries where immigration is less common, that job is a little more difficult, although not impossible. Humans are migrating like never before, and you can find substantial numbers of immigrants all around the globe. I'll be so bold as to say that few places still exist where you could not find at least three languages being spoken widely and regularly enough for your purposes.

In the next chapter, we'll practice finding the resources you need, even in less-than-ideal environments.

CHAPTER 16

Searching, from the Recliner

● ● ●

I HAVE GOOD NEWS AND bad news: You'll be able to complete this chapter in the semi-recumbent position, but you'll need your computer on your lap. Now we'll apply all that we've learned, so if you can stay alert through this one, you'll be just about ready to go.

● ● ●

Let's suppose you live in Phoenix, Arizona, where your home language happens to be English. You'd like for your children to learn Spanish and Mandarin Chinese. If they can master these three languages, you reason, they'll be able to communicate with 75% of the planet.

First, let's see if we can find some local Spanish speakers. Since Phoenix is very close to the border with Mexico, the largest Spanish-speaking population in the world, this shouldn't be difficult. Go to Craigslist, and find your way to the Phoenix ads. If you get lost at any point, just review the video, *Using Craigslist to find childhood language tutors* on my website at www.trilingualbysix.com or on YouTube. Choose "Services" and make sure to search the entire text of the ads, not just the titles. Search the term "Spanish babysitter" or "babysit Spanish." When you've finished looking around here, try "child care Spanish" or "day care Spanish." With these searches, I found some ads written in Spanish, an excellent sign. Notice that some in-home daycare providers are willing to speak Spanish to your child for just a few dollars per hour. Remember that you can also use

Craigslist to find a translator if you need one. You could also try Google Translate.

I also picked up a couple of new vocabulary phrases: *Ninera* = babysitter or nanny and *Se cuidan ninos* = childcare. (If you happen to be a Spanish speaker, I apologize for not using tildes, but Craigslist doesn't use them either.) Searching these new terms, I found some more possibilities, including some offers for cooking and cleaning in addition to babysitting. When you're ready, search "housekeeping Spanish," "house cleaning Spanish," *"limpieza,"* or *"limpiar casa."* In a place like Phoenix, if you had trouble finding what you were looking for with these searches, you could probably just walk outside, knock on your neighbor's front door, and ask for some suggestions. Hiring Spanish-speaking domestic servants is a common practice in the southwestern United States.

If you answer one of these ads, and the prospective babysitter or housekeeper doesn't have the availability that you need, I would suggest that you ask if the creator of the ad knows anyone else who might help you. Chances are good they would. You have to respect those informal networks.

With all the political and economic unrest in Central America, it's a reasonable supposition that a lot of Spanish-speaking refugees are flowing into places like Phoenix. Do a quick Google search of the term "refugee Phoenix Arizona." A lot of information turns up: everything from government organizations to religious and secular volunteer groups to interesting news articles. If you were having trouble finding Spanish speakers in Phoenix (which seems unlikely), maybe you could contact a few refugee assistance organizations. There are probably also some refugees from the Arabic world, Asia, and sub-Saharan Africa, where people commonly speak French and Portuguese. Feel free to spend some time playing around with this. You'll probably find possibilities for many different languages.

Next, let's see if we can find some Mandarin Chinese resources. From Craigslist, search the term "Chinese babysitter," "Chinese nanny," or "Chinese day care." You might find something, but I didn't. Try searching broader terms, such as "Chinese" and "Mandarin." I find some ads for landscapers wanting to trim Chinese palm trees and a catering company that wants to serve egg rolls at your next party, but I also see a significant number of Chinese tutors. They seem a little on the pricey side. They'd probably prefer to work with adults, and they might be overqualified for your needs, but you might be able to negotiate a package deal in a pinch. You might also ask some of them if they know anyone willing to do some babysitting.

Before we move on, I'd like to show you one more important technique for finding language babysitters on Craigslist. Though it's not free anymore, you can post your own job offerings on the site. It's not expensive or difficult, but there's a trick or two you might like to know. Before you start, you have to open a Craigslist account. There's not a specific category for babysitting or domestic help, so most people who post ads of this basic type place them in the "education/teaching" or the "general labor" category. For us, "education/teaching" has worked well. Typically, our ad will read something like this:

Hello. We have children ages 7 and 9 who already speak Mandarin as a second language. We are looking for someone to spend about 5 to 10 hours per week with them, speaking exclusively in Mandarin. Just conversation and play—no lesson plans. No formal teaching experience is necessary. If you have children who speak Mandarin well, just bring them along!

Let's keep looking. Go to Google and see if you can learn anything about the local Chinese community. This time, let's start with a broad search and gradually narrow it down as much as we can. First, search "Chinese Phoenix Arizona." Not surprisingly, this returns a vast number of local Chinese restaurants. If you can't find anything else, you could always fall back on these, stop by a few of them to introduce yourself, and see if anyone knows someone who might do some babysitting.

When I do this search, I also find a Chinese cultural organization that hosts several festivals throughout the year. On their website, they give contact information. On this contact page, they've posted a number of links to other Chinese organizations in the area. One links to the local chapter of the Confucius Institute, which is partially funded by the Chinese government. In conjunction with Arizona State University, this institute supports a K–12 Mandarin Chinese immersion curriculum in several of the local public schools. You might want to very seriously investigate that sometime. If your children were to enroll in some sort of Chinese school immersion program starting in kindergarten and continuing through high school graduation, I think you could be fairly certain that they would become fluent and literate in Mandarin.

Among the web page's interesting links, I also find a couple of Chinese weekend schools. One of these, Hope Chinese School, has courses beginning at the pre-K level and extending all the way through advanced Mandarin, SAT-prep, and AP calculus.

I'm starting to wish my children were growing up in Phoenix! The school also offers music lessons, dance, art, and other cultural courses. If I were parenting there, I would have my children waiting at the front door of that school the moment they met the minimum age requirement! Much of the school's website is written in Chinese characters, so unless you know the language, it might be time for you to start making some immigrant friends locally. It wouldn't hurt to call to see if anyone at the school knew someone who might like to babysit for you every now and then.

Clearly, Phoenix has a sizable Chinese population, and it seems very committed to the education of its youth. Assuming you want your children to make good grades in school, maybe you could hitch a little ride on these coattails. Now, search the term "Chinese preschool Phoenix Arizona." There appear to be several, some of which advertise in Chinese characters. Using the criteria we've already detailed, you could visit a few and see how much Mandarin dialogue you actually heard.

Next, search the term "Chinese church Phoenix Arizona." You'll see quite a lot of results. If your spiritual convictions permit it, you might find that some of these churches offer children Sunday schools in Mandarin Chinese, or maybe weekend schools. If nothing else, this would be a free source of weekly language exposure. Since mature grandmother types who love children are usually overrepresented in churches, you might be able to find an excellent babysitter by paying a visit to a few of them.

Let's see if Phoenix has a Chinatown district. You probably guessed it: just search "Chinatown Phoenix Arizona." It appears that Phoenix once had a Chinatown neighborhood, but in modern times, it is nothing more than a historical relic. However, it's extremely likely that a city as large as Phoenix will have a more modern version. Perhaps we can find it by the technique we discussed earlier. Do a quick search of "Asian market Phoenix Arizona," as you recall that an ethnic food market is the surest sign of a nearby enclave.

Bingo. Phoenix has a Super L Ranch Market and a Lee Lee International Supermarket, both of which are large Asian grocery chains. There are also many smaller markets. Switching over to Google Maps, I see that both stores are anchoring a number of other Chinese businesses. The Super L is closer to the center of the city, and the Lee Lee is in the suburbs. I think it's fair to say that Phoenix has at least two modern-day Chinatowns.

Do you remember how to zoom down to Street View in Google Maps? From the Asian market search you just completed, click on one of the links advertising the Super L Ranch Market, and find the address of this place. I'm finding that it is 668 N 44th Street. Now go back to the main Google start page and enter this address. As soon as you've completed that, click on "Maps." If you zoom in just a little bit, you can see that this grocery store is located in a complex called the Cofco Chinese Culture Center. Now, drag the little yellow man in the lower right corner of your screen, and drop him on the street directly in front of the Super L Ranch Market. At this point you can maneuver yourself around the streets surrounding this grocery store. You probably get the idea that this is a thematically Asian shopping center. Maybe if you took your children for a walk there, you would meet a babysitter or two. Maybe the Super L Market has a bulletin board for posting job openings. If you were nice, maybe the clerk would help you write your ad, and you wouldn't even need a Craigslist translator.

If you feel left behind on this one, just review the video, *Searching for language tutors online*, posted on www.trilingualbysix.com and on YouTube.

● ● ●

So now, let's take this to the next level of difficulty. Let's say you live in a smaller town in the midwestern United States. How about Wausau, Wisconsin? This time, you've decided you want your children to learn to speak Arabic and Hindi, but you're willing to change your mind if you can't find any speakers.

Let's start with Hindi. On Google, search "Indian Wausau Wisconsin" and "Hindi Wausau Wisconsin." I don't know about you, but I didn't find much. Even the nearest Indian restaurant is more than an hour's drive away in Madison. Maybe Hindi is not a good choice in Wausau. But before we give up, let's do a little more detective work. Search "University Wausau Wisconsin." From what I can see, there are some smaller colleges and universities in the area. I went to the faculty/staff roster pages and scrolled through all the names, but I didn't find any that seemed to be from India. I did, however, find one or two that seemed to possibly be Arabic.

Next, search "hospital Wausau Wisconsin." From the directory of physicians at an institution called Aspirus, I was able to find a handful of ethnic Indian doctors. At least some of them attended medical school in India. At this point, not having found any other options, we might try contacting some of these Indian doctors to see if they know anything about a local ethnic enclave. We might come up empty handed, but who knows? We might also try stopping by some local convenience stores and motels. If we could find any Asian markets locally, we might also inquire there—some will stock Indian foods if there is a local demand. I also took the liberty of searching the term "Hindu temple Wausau Wisconsin" for you, but I didn't find anything.

So what about Arabic in Wausau? From the college faculty directories, we might see if we could make contact with the few possibly Arabic professors we found there. On Google, try the term "mosque Wausau Wisconsin." It doesn't look like Wausau has one, but from a page called "Islamic Finder," I was able to determine that Northeast Technical College has a prayer room for Muslim students. I also found the email address of the faculty director of the prayer room. Maybe it would be worth contacting this individual to see if there is a local Arabic-speaking community of any size. Why don't we go to the Northeast Technical College website and see if we can find more information about international students on this campus? Do you think you can find it? It looks like the correct name of the institution is Northeast Wisconsin Technical College. The website has quite a bit of information for international students, but I cannot tell how many of them might speak Arabic. It looks moderately promising, but we would probably need to pay a visit to the campus to get additional information. And we would definitely want more information about the size of the permanent Arabic-speaking community in Wausau before we committed our children to this language here.

Let's also search the term "Orthodox church Wausau Wisconsin." Here I found a few, but the closest one was a little over an hour away. Next, try "halal Wausau Wisconsin." Halal is a special Muslim way of preparing meat. There is a Greek restaurant in Wausau that prepares halal foods. Perhaps someone in this establishment would know something about a local Arabic-speaking population. I searched "Mediterranean market Wausau Wisconsin" but didn't find anything.

I would say that the prospects of finding an ample supply of Hindi-language babysitters might not be all that great. For Arabic, our chances might be a little better, but we'd need more information than we can get from our computer.

Maybe in Wausau, we should consider other languages. Search the term "immigrant groups Wausau Wisconsin" and see what you find. Then try "Mexican Wausau Wisconsin." You'll probably find a relatively large number of Mexican restaurants. At least a few of them will be staffed by fluent Spanish speakers. Interestingly, there are also several Mexican grocery stores in the area. With confidence, we can say that Wausau has an enclave somewhere. Maybe one of these markets has a bulletin board or a chatty clerk.

Let's return to Craigslist and get a little creative. Go there now and find the Wausau, Wisconsin, section. Choose "Services" and enter the search term "Spanish." I found a Spanish-language tutor or two, but not much else. Next, choose the "For Sale" option, and search *espanol.* Here I found a number of used-car ads in which the dealer was clearly targeting a Spanish-speaking market. By determining the addresses of these dealers, I could probably get a clue about the enclave's general location. If you need a little guidance, review the video, *Using Craigslist to find childhood language tutors.* Again, it can be found at www.trilingualbysix.com and on YouTube.

Using Google, try *"iglesia* Wausau Wisconsin," remembering that *iglesia* is the Spanish word for "church." Maybe you were more fortunate, but I did not find anything suggesting the presence of a Spanish-speaking church in the area. Next, try "Catholic Spanish Wausau Wisconsin." Aha—it looks like the St. Matthew Catholic Church has a weekly service in Spanish. This might be a very good place to find a Spanish-language babysitter. If you decide to show up one Sunday, you might also ask the priest if he knows anything about local refugee organizations. Now let's try "check cashing Wausau Wisconsin." If you locate these places on Google Maps and go down to street level, you can see that some of these businesses are located relatively close to modest apartment complexes of the type that recent immigrants might inhabit. If you were in Wausau, you could pay a visit to some of these businesses to see if they were advertising to Spanish speakers. You might also ask some of the tellers if they had any clients looking for some part-time babysitting work. Based on this investigation, it looks like Spanish would be a good language choice in Wausau.

Might there be other possibilities? Chinese, perhaps? Let's try "Chinese Wausau Wisconsin." There are lots of Chinese restaurants, not unpredictably. If I couldn't find anything else, I could always start exploring these. Try "Asian market Wausau Wisconsin." There are several. Why does a small city like Wausau have so many Asian markets? Some of them have names that sound Southeast Asian. If that doesn't tickle your curiosity a little, it probably should. It looks like the town probably has a permanent Asian population of some sort, and it's possible that some of them speak Mandarin Chinese. Should we try "Chinese church Wausau Wisconsin?" Though I don't find any, I do note that the local Hmong population has at least one congregation. What's up with that?

What about Vietnamese? Search "Vietnamese Wausau Wisconsin." Rather surprisingly, there seem to be a number of Vietnamese restaurants in the area. Isn't that interesting? Moving on to pages 2 and 3 of the Google search results, I find an interesting video called "Wausau - Hmong Journey." If you have 10 minutes to spare, I would recommend watching it. From this video, I learned that the Hmong comprise approximately 12% of the Wausau population, a striking number for a small city. It seems that the Hmong fought alongside the Americans against the North Vietnamese in the 1960s, which would mean that they had to flee for their lives during the Communist takeover.

I'm wondering if any of the older Hmong there might speak Vietnamese. The Hmong language might be an option too, if you were very sure that you would not be moving away from Wausau in the future. In any event, this would be a very significant immigrant population. Let's have a look at "nail salon Wausau Wisconsin." I'm thinking that the possibility of finding some Vietnamese speakers in one or two of these businesses would be better than good. Though you might want to be efficient and read some reviews before you go, you would need to drop into some of them and introduce yourself.

Any other possibilities in Wausau? Next, let's try "refugee Wausau Wisconsin." I don't find all that much, but there do seem to be a few additional interesting articles about the local Hmong population. On one result, however, I do find a reference to an organization called the Wausau Area Refugee Network. When I follow this link, I find the name of the person who heads the organization. He notes that there are a number of refugees from Somalia in the state, and he gives his contact information at the end of the little article. Maybe we could call him. Now let's see if we can find out just a little more about these Somalian refugees. Search

"Somalia official language." One of them just happens to be Arabic. We could also place some calls to the local churches to see if we can find any other refugee assistance activity in the area. We already found at least one Catholic church, and there are probably others, but let's search "Catholic diocese Wausau Wisconsin" to see if we can find some sort of central organizational office. I don't immediately find such an office, but I do find a link to the local Catholic Charities organization. When I go to this website, I find that this group is indeed active in immigration services. They provide a phone number, an address, and an email contact. It's a safe bet that if there are refugees in the Wausau area, this organization is participating in their resettlement. In the United States, there is another easy way of finding information about refugee organizations on a web page called "New Americans Campaign," located at http:// newamericanscampaign.org/resources/help . From there you can enter the zip code of the area of interest and find a listing of all the available refugee assistance organizations nearby. Go there and enter the zip code for Wausau. It's 54401.

I can think of another possibility: if there is an American military base near Wausau, there might be a source of Spanish, Korean, and maybe a small chance of some German or Japanese. When I search "military bases Wisconsin," however, I find that the nearest one is at least an hour's drive away. Not much help in this case. When you have an American military base in your area, you can usually just drive the streets around it and find evidence of other languages. You could also try a few creative Google search terms.

Last but definitely not least, let's check out the local public school system to see what we can learn. Use Google to search the term "Wausau Wisconsin school district." On the school district's home page, you'll find several interesting possibilities. Explore as many of these as you like, but we want to find some sort of course catalog detailing what languages each school teaches. For me, this proved a little difficult, so I'll save you the time and lead you directly to it. From the "Schools and Facilities" menu at the top of the page, choose "High Schools." Here, I chose "Wausau East

High." There you will find a menu button called "School Information." If you move your mouse over this button, you will see a drop-down menu that includes "Course Description Book." Choose this item, and you will be taken to the school's course catalog. It's a long document, but if you scan it a little, you'll find that the high school offers 4 years of Spanish, French, and German. If you found it necessary, you could probably contact several of the language teachers and find a responsible, advanced student in one of these languages to babysit for you. As you'll soon see, however, you would probably not need to go this route.

Now, return to the school system's home page by clicking on the "WSD Home" tab. Click on the menu tab called "Parents." There, choose "Student Demographic Report," which will direct you to another lengthy document. Scroll down until you find a very basic table of contents, and notice that Section III gives information about ethnic enrollments and Limited English Proficient (LEP) students. Continue scrolling down until you find this section. Sifting through the many graphs and tables, you will learn that well over 20% of children in grades K–5 are Limited English Proficient. Also notice that, out of 8,000 to 9,000 total students, almost 1,100 are Limited English Proficient. At least one out of eight students speaks a language other than English in the home!

With so many children who do not speak English well, if at all, it's a safe bet that there are some family members out there who would be ideal candidates to babysit your children, if only you could find them. One of the graphs in this section demonstrates that 6% of these children are Hispanic and 20% are Asian, probably Hmong, maybe others. We might have to place some telephone calls or even do some ground-level detective work, but I think we could find some native speakers of another language if we really wanted to. In fact, we could probably find thousands of them, even in a place like Wausau.

Finally, return to the system's home page and, once again, select the "Parents" menu. This time, choose the "Parent/Student Handbook" item. Notice that this document is published in English, Spanish, and Hmong. Try repeating this school-system exercise in your own hometown sometime. If you can't find anything helpful, just call your school district, and ask a few questions. If you don't get any information this way, put your detective cap back on, and go to the school system's main administrative office. You might be hard pressed to find an American school that does *not* have a Limited English Proficient student section.

• • •

Let's raise the bar another notch. The most remote town in the United States is a place called Barrow, Alaska, population 4,200. It's so far north that it's not connected to the rest of the world by roads, and it has to rely on air transport to bring in supplies and visitors, weather permitting, of course. Craigslist does not have a section devoted to the area. I'll go out on a limb just a little and predict that there are no Chinese weekend schools either.

But let me show you another little trick I think you'll find useful. Go to http://www.mla.org/map_data. The Modern Language Association (MLA) maintains this search engine, which relies on US Census data to determine what languages people are speaking in a given area. For our purposes, the data is a little old, drawing from the 2000 census, and it only reports legal residents, but we can still learn something here. In the lower left corner of the screen, you'll find a box to enter a city name. There, type "Barrow" and enter the information. You'll learn that roughly half of the population speaks English. The rest speak Inupiat and a variety of other indigenous languages, as well as Tagalog, Korean, and even Spanish. Next, near the top of this page, you'll find a link called "Show ability to speak English (all languages)." Click on it now. After you've taken a moment to digest this information, use this site to learn more about your own home area. Just keep in mind that the data is over a decade old, and the site reports only what the Census Bureau knows. If you want me to walk you through this, I touch on it in my video, *Searching for language tutors online.* Find it on my website (trilingualbysix.com) and YouTube.

Despite its remoteness, Barrow would hold possibilities for a prospective multilingual family. Certainly, Inupiat would be available, but so would Korean and Tagalog—maybe Spanish too. On Google, try searching "Asian restaurant Barrow Alaska" and "Inupiat Barrow Alaska." It seems that Barrow has at least three Asian restaurants you could visit, and a strong Inupiat presence. Next, try "Mexican Barrow Alaska." It seems there was a restaurant called Pepe's until recently, but it burned down. Maybe it will have reopened by the time you get around to reading this chapter. If you're so inclined, you might try searching for churches in an ethnic language. In just one minute, I was able to learn that the Inupiat have several and the Koreans have at least one. There might be others. Finally, in a remote settlement of just 4,200 people, you could always just ask around. Most likely the community survives on social cohesion.

● ● ●

Ready to level up? Imagine that you live in a typical city in South Korea. Arbitrarily, let's say it's Gimhae. If you would like, you could do a search of the city and find out more information about it. As a parent, you are interested in giving your children a head start on learning English, since the local public schools don't start formal instruction in it until the 3rd grade. First, see if Craigslist has anything going in Korea. They do, but only in the capital city of Seoul. Go there and surf around a little, just to see what you can learn. Don't forget to select the "Services" tab from the drop-down menu, and be sure to search the entire text of ads, not just the titles. Try the terms "babysitter," "nanny," and "housekeeper." Maybe "housemaid" would be better. Browse through these various ads, all of which are in English. You'll probably get the idea that a number of women from the Philippines are advertising these services. This would seem to suggest that there are quite a few Filipino immigrants in South Korea. Now, go back to Google and type "Philippines official language." One of them is English, but you already knew that, right?

Since Craigslist only operates in Seoul, we must look elsewhere to find information about Gimhae. Let's take what we just learned and see if we can find some English-speaking Filipinos there. On Google, enter the phrase "Gimhae Filipino" or "Gimhae Philippines." I'm finding an organization called Filipino Association in Gimhae, Korea. They have a Facebook page, where I see some pictures of Filipinos in a church and some references to prayer requests. Let's go that direction now by searching the term "Filipino church Gimhae." I found a little information on "Imho Catholic Church Gimhae." Though I can find an address for the institution, much of the remaining information is in Korean characters, which I don't know how to read. The next step might be to place a few calls or pay a few visits. I do find, though, that the church is associated with an organization calling itself "Gimhae Migrants Support Center." Search that term now. The results here seem to suggest a number of possibilities. I'm thinking we could manage to interact with the population of immigrants from the Philippines. If not, we might try some similar searches in nearby Busan, a much larger city not too far away.

Since Craigslist is not yet widely available in South Korea, let's see if we can find some similar classified ad pages online. On Google, search "Craigslist similar pages South Korea" or something like that. When I do this, I find a site called Naver, which can be found at http://cafe.naver.com/joonggonara. Unfortunately for me, it's all in Korean characters, so I can't use it. If you're from South Korea, you can probably do a better job of finding a site like this yourself. I would imagine that this particular page does have some listings for babysitters, English tutors, housekeepers, and so on. Also, do a search of "classified ads South Korea." This time I found some possibilities. With a little trial and error, I think I've decided that the best one would probably be Koreabridge. It looks to be a message board used primarily by expats. I chose the "Jobs Wanted" section, and I found some English speakers looking for part-time work of just about any kind. Some of the ads were posted by Filipinos, not unexpectedly.

Another option would be to search for Western Union or MoneyGram offices. We could do this in at least two different ways, either by doing a Google search or by simply going to the company website. We'll do one of each. First, in Google, search the term "Western Union Gimhae." It looks like Western Union has a substantial presence there. We could get the addresses of some of these, go by, and see what we might learn about international populations of migrant workers remitting money to their families back home. Probably, there are some Filipinos, Pakistanis, Bangladeshis, or other English-speaking immigrants doing exactly this. Most likely, they're also cashing their paychecks somewhere—perhaps at the same place. With a better understanding of the Korean language, we could probably learn a lot more. Next, simply use Google to search the term "MoneyGram." This should enable you to find a central website for the company. On this site, you can choose your country and city of choice. Once you do that, you can see that MoneyGram also has a significant presence in Gimhae. In South Korea, there might be other international companies offering a money-wiring service, but I don't know about them.

At this point I offer a little reminder that, once you find one or two immigrants from a given country, you can use a respectful and persistent approach to find out more about their local expat community. Now, let's see if Gimhae has any universities. Indeed it does, as we can see by simply searching "Gimhae university Korea" or entering a similar search parameter. If only we knew Korean, we could probably find out more about international students and professors from English-speaking countries. If you are proficient in Korean, go ahead and give it a try. Very interestingly, I happen to note that a university in Central Oklahoma has an exchange program with Inje University. That would mean that there are a lot of English speakers on that campus, and maybe one or two of them would be interested in spending some time with your children. If not, perhaps they could give you some more information about English-speaking resources in Gimhae.

Knowing that the United States still has some military bases in South Korea, we could search "United States military in South Korea" and find their locations. Doing that, I see that there is one in Chinhae, or Jinhae. Though it might be a bit far from Gimhae, we could still go there and investigate, looking for evidence of businesses serving a local English-speaking population. Maybe we would find something.

Since most South Koreans learn English in the public schools, and many attend university in the English-speaking world, you might be able to find a local person willing to do a little work for you. Maybe this would not be quite as good as finding a native English speaker, but it would be adequate, I strongly believe. With only this level of exposure to English, children would still be far ahead of their peers with no English skills before the time when the local grade schools begin teaching it. I would predict this might very well be a permanent advantage in a highly competitive educational system like South Korea's. As we've seen, there are English preschools in South Korea if you can afford them. If you want, search the term "English preschool Gimhae." I found a few in nearby Busan.

For a person who actually lives in South Korea and knows the area and the local language, this would probably have been a much more fruitful exercise. There are probably many more sites advertising babysitters and housekeepers as well as other resources of interest to Anglophiles. Feel free to branch out on your own again if you know Korean.

What about other ethnic groups in Gimhae? Let's try searching "immigration to South Korea statistics." I find myself connected to a helpful *Wikipedia* article, oddly enough entitled "Immigration to South Korea." It seems that the largest migrant worker group in South Korea is the Chinese. See what else you can learn.

• • •

Let's take an imaginary trip to Santiago, Chile, where you are the parent of a 2-year-old. You'd be thrilled if she could learn English before starting school, and maybe one more language beyond the community language of Spanish. Please stay with me just a little longer and search the term "immigration to Chile." For me, *Wikipedia* comes through again with an article by that exact name.

The long publication suggests an extensive history of immigration to Chile, so we should have a choice or two here. Since you're eager for your children to learn English, it's a little discouraging to read that much of the migration from North America has been from individuals who are economically well situated. That is, they might not be terribly motivated to work for you at babysitter wages, but we'll see what we can do. I thought it was interesting to see that Chile has a very large Arab population, including the largest Palestinian population in the world outside of Palestine. However, it seems that the Muslim population is small and that the majority of Arabs in Chile are either Christian or lacking religious affiliation. A substantial number of these Palestinians come from families that have been living in Chile for many generations. But quite a few came to the country shortly after World War II, and even more have come in recent times. Since somewhere in the vicinity of 4% of the Chilean population is of Middle Eastern descent, we can assume that there will be at least some chain migration continuing into the present day. Apparently, modern migration from sub-Saharan Africa is limited, but there appears to be a growing population of Chinese and Japanese immigrants. It also looks like Chile is home to a respectable number of Koreans.

Choosing Santiago, we've made it relatively easy on ourselves. Most likely, a significant number of immigrant groups have chosen to settle in this large international city, but still we're looking for a source of English for our little 2-year-old. Before continuing our string of Google searches, let's see if we can find anything on Craigslist. Once you arrive there, you'll see that the site defaults to Spanish. It's not yet broken down by city, but since we have chosen a major metropolitan area this time, we can expect to find quite a bit in Santiago. From the drop-down menu below the search box, choose *"Servicios."* Then type "English" into the search box. I happened to find one American student hoping to trade English lessons for Spanish conversational experience. This student planned to enroll at the University of Chile and hoped to improve her Spanish before beginning. Now that could be a good situation, and free is certainly an attractive price. I also see a few English teachers in Santiago trying to earn extra income, but their going rate seems to be somewhere around US$25 per hour. That could get expensive. I also see some ads from English teachers wanting to teach via Skype for significantly less than US$8 per hour. That would be great if your daughter were a little older, but it won't work at 2.

Next, let's search "*Ingles*," the Spanish word for "English." Here, I found a few additional ads in Spanish for English tutors, but I also saw a student from the United States who wanted to trade room and board for tutoring children. That might work. If you can't read Spanish, you could always use Craigslist to find a translator, if necessary. I also took the liberty of searching the term "tutor," but I only found a woman wanting to teach English via Skype. Maybe later.

With this encouraging data from Craigslist, let's go to Google. Start with "English Santiago." I've discovered that the University of Chile has an English version of its website, and I found an online English newspaper called the *Santiago Times*, the existence of which suggests a large English-speaking population. The site has a classified ad page with a section for language classes. Here I find a few individuals who are willing to teach children. Their services are probably at least as expensive as what we found on Craigslist, though.

I don't know about you, but I'm eager to explore the University of Chile's English website. The mere existence of this site strongly suggests that there are a large number of English speakers strolling around campus. Please find the site and snoop around. When you're done, search "Santiago universities" or "Santiago colleges" and see what else you might learn.

Maybe we could find another international student highly proficient in English to spend some time with your little daughter. I cannot claim to know whether foreigners with student visas are permitted to work in Chile or not. If you lived in Chile, you would have to check this out for yourself and make responsible judgments. If it's not exactly legal for international students to seek gainful employment in the country, maybe you could find some other way to support their education. Maybe you could find some native-born students majoring in English to help you. Each situation would be a little different.

Now try "English preschool Santiago." I found a few and visited the websites. None of them listed any pricing information, so I have to conclude they're expensive. Also, search the term "expat Santiago schools" and surf around until you find a discussion forum or two.

Finally, see if you can find some other English-speaking immigrant groups in Santiago. For background information if you need it, search "English speaking countries." There is a *Wikipedia* article that lists all of these, and it's a relatively long one. Pick a few that seem promising and formulate some search terms of your own. Maybe "Nigeria expat Chile," "Filipinos Santiago Chile," or "Indian restaurant Santiago."

Once again we could locate some Western Union and MoneyGram offices in Santiago. Most likely we would find a few migrants remitting funds back home.

We still need to find a third language for your little 2-year-old in Santiago. As we learned, Chile is home to an unusually large group of Palestinians, so why don't we just choose Arabic? Search "Palestinians Santiago," and you will find a list of articles that might net some promising leads. Since we learned that the majority of Palestinians in Chile are Christian, try "Orthodox Church Santiago." Indeed, there are a lot of them, as well as an archdiocese. When searching "Coptic church Santiago" and "Maronite church Santiago," a few more institutions turn up. My guess is you could probably find at least a few Arabic speakers at any of these. One of them might be perfectly happy to spend some time with your little toddler. Using the terms "mosque Santiago" and "halal Santiago," a few more possibilities turn up.

Maybe there are some refugee organizations in Chile. Search "refugee Chile" and "refugee Santiago." With a few clicks, I find that the United Nations High Commission on Refugees (UNHCR) has a branch office in Argentina, but it's probably too far away for our purposes. Maybe we could call the office to see if they have any presence in Santiago. Digging a little deeper, I see that some religious organizations are providing refugee support in the area. You could explore any of these if you were so inclined.

• • •

For whatever reason, a substantial number of immigrants seem to gather around religious institutions. I've heard it said that the act of immigrating can lead to a sort of spiritual awareness in a person. Possibly, becoming an outsider in a faraway land makes a person want to seek out something familiar, or maybe it's just that religious institutions are happy to take in the socially isolated. Certainly, a lot of mainstream religious organizations have outreach programs for new groups arriving in their areas. It's probably also true that many immigrants leave their homeland so that they can exercise their faith more safely. In any event, houses of worship are good places to go looking for prospective foreign-language babysitters.

When looking for speakers of Arabic in a place like Santiago, Chile, searching a term like "orthodox" usually uncovers something. As I understand it, most of the Christian churches from the Arabic-speaking world are branches of the Orthodox Church. I can't profess to understand the relationship that all these terms have to one another, but other words you might see (or even try searching) include *Melkite, Coptic, Syriac, Maronite,* and *Antiochian,* just to name a few. Christians are a minority in every Arab country, and when a region destabilizes politically, these Christians have tended to become refugees. When you think about the history of the modern and ancient world, this is not a new or isolated phenomenon.

You probably also get the idea that a lot of this information is country specific. The way to find a foreign-language-speaking immigrant population in one country might not be the same in another. If you happen to be raising children in a country not mentioned in this chapter, I hope you can use the skills you've learned to find the expat community that has the particular language talent you desire. Once you have found that community, interact with it.

Since our search has taken us in a lot of different directions, I want to boil things down for you. Look for your language babysitter in these places:

1. Internet search engines
2. Internet classified ad pages such as Craigslist

3. Ethnic grocery markets
4. Ethnic restaurants
5. Houses of worship
6. Local colleges and universities
7. Immigrant social and business organizations
8. Money-wiring and check-cashing centers
9. Refugee relief organizations
10. Typical ethnic businesses, such as nail salons and motels
11. Area high school foreign-language classes
12. Military installations

Your neighborhood might offer other possibilities. And no matter where you go, keep your ears tuned! You can find them if you try.

CHAPTER 17

More Resources

● ● ●

IF YOU DON'T LIKE THE idea of hiring immigrants as language babysitters, I understand. Personally, I think they're the best resource on the planet for teaching children multiple languages, but there are some valid reasons not to go that route. Please let me remind you that, until they reach a certain age, very young children really can't learn additional languages from any source other than a real live human in their immediate presence. And by the time they reach that certain age, their language acquisition devices are already beginning to lose their powers.

I'll offer you some alternatives that will probably be just as effective, though they are usually more expensive.

Private language tutors. We've already seen how much tutors cost in Santiago, Chile. In other countries they can cost a lot more than US$25 per hour. In a sense, they are overqualified and tend to be very educated. As a result, they want to use a lesson plan or a highly structured technique of the type that a preschooler would not take sitting down. With a little coaxing, though, perhaps you could persuade a tutor to just play with your children and have ordinary conversations. You can easily find a nice supply of language tutors in any classified ad publication or telephone directory.

Commercial language schools. Perhaps the best-known of these is Berlitz, but there are definitely many others. Some of them will accept students as young as 2 years, but I doubt any would be willing to teach a preverbal infant. Usually, commercial language schools teach in a relatively didactic style at a going rate of somewhere around US$40 per hour.

Bilingual daycare centers and preschools. Some of these are really valuable, and some are not. Listen for running dialogues between fluent teachers and fluent pupils. It's almost a necessity that a significant percentage of the other children in the school speak your target language at home, as their first language. It's even better for you if these children don't yet know your children's first language. That's just not a situation you're likely to find in an affluent American suburb, so be prepared to expand your search. In fact, if you find a bilingual preschool in an affluent suburb, evaluate it with a skeptical eye. The places you are looking for will normally be designed to serve the needs of immigrant children, not to help mainstream children whose ambitious parents want them to be multilingual. What marketing they do, if any, will not be directed at you, and you might have to locate them on your own, maybe by networking with some immigrant parents. The places on your radar will likely fall into one of several broad categories. First, the government-supported pre-K programs designed to help disadvantaged children who do not yet speak the community language well enough to function in a classroom setting. Second, those that are owned and operated by immigrants, with their own children in mind. Often, they strive toward future school readiness with a very heavy emphasis on preservation of the family culture and heritage language. Third, the more informal, home-based daycares staffed by immigrant women. Some of these function like co-ops—neighborhood immigrant women helping other neighborhood immigrant women trying to make ends meet. Fourth, the exclusive international preschools serving the needs of well-to-do expats in large, globally oriented cities.

Foreign nannies. There are full-service agencies that will find you a highly qualified, well-trained, very multilingual nanny from just about any country in the world you desire. Many of them hold university-level teaching certifications and have made a permanent career of doing this work. Some of them are so good that they can totally lift the burden of raising your children from your shoulders, including homeschooling, if you want. The agencies will do background checks, perform psychological screening, take care of visa applications, provide health and dental plans, arrange for international travel, offer clothing allowances—everything. In some countries, these elite babysitters are called governesses, and they can be expensive. You could probably expect a total annual cost of US$70,000 or more. All you have to do is make the call and write the checks. Other placement organizations can help you if your budget is smaller, but their candidates might have less impressive resumes, and their screening processes might be less rigorous. Many would still be very multilingual, however, even if they used a nonstandard dialect. If you're interested, start with a Google search of the term "international nanny" and branch out from there.

Au pairs. They're usually younger than nannies, with less experience, and they aren't necessarily making a career of caring for children. In many cases, they view their work as a chance to travel or maybe even immigrate to a new country. They come from all over the world and speak just about any language you could imagine. They provide limited services—usually just childcare. Most of them are not interested in staying in their position for more than a year or so, but there are, of course, exceptions. Most of them want to have a reasonably active social life beyond just playing with your children. Anecdotally, I have heard stories of good ones and bad ones. Some of them, I'm told, can be the equivalent of having an extra child in the house.

Travel. Perhaps the best way to avoid foreigners in your trilingual program is to become one yourself! If your life permits it, you might develop a habit of making frequent, perhaps even extended journeys to countries where your target languages are spoken. No doubt, that could be very expensive, but there are some neat tricks to doing it more affordably, with more interaction with locals for your language learners.

1. Work/lodging barter. Several organizations exist to connect budget travelers with home owners wanting to exchange free lodging for relatively light work. Many opportunities are child friendly. Some are available in amazingly exotic locations, so if you like the idea of an unconventional vacation, this concept is worth checking

out, even if you have no interest at all in raising multilingual children. I have found a website called Workaway.info that offers this service, but there are many others. Of course, if you have a spare room, you might consider using one of these sites to offer it to a summer traveler...in exchange for some free language babysitting.

2. Vacation rentals and house sitting. Lately a proliferation of websites has been advertising apartment rentals all over the world. If people have an extra room in their home or plan to be gone from their apartment for a while, they will just post an ad and rent their space out for a very reasonable rate. My favorite site is VRBO.com. Some homeowners who need to be away for extended periods are even looking for a house sitter: someone to keep an eye on things and maybe mow the lawn or feed a pet. Search "house sitting international" or a similar phrase.

3. Volunteerism. An incredible number of secular and religious groups recruit help. Try "volunteer international" or maybe "missionary international" and branch out from there. If you are looking for a region where people speak a particular language, you could try "volunteer French," for example, with which you would probably find some opportunities in Africa or the Caribbean. You might even find an opening or two in France.

4. Roadschooling. Some homeschooling families take things to the next level and hit the road. Some, you might imagine, do it internationally. Sounds like an exotically adventuresome way to grow up, doesn't it? Roadschoolers are a well-organized, very supportive online community. Simply searching "roadschooling" online will probably connect you to them.

5. Family and friends. If you are lucky enough to have foreign-language-speaking relatives, be nice to them, and maybe they'll invite you over. If not, see if you might cultivate some friendships on a Skype language exchange.

CHAPTER 18

Beyond the Living Room Floor

● ● ●

BEFORE YOUR CHILDREN REACH THE age of about 3 years, your only effective resource is a real live human. Once your children are older, you have a lot more possibilities, though human interaction will probably remain the most valuable one. When your children are 6 or so, the school system might help you out if you play your cards right. Long before you reach that milestone, I'd suggest you learn about any local school-based language-immersion programs. Though they might be free, some of the best things in life have waiting lists...

Let's discover the other possibilities.

VIDEOS/CARTOONS

When our children started showing an interest in watching normal cartoons, Laura and I found that they were perfectly happy to watch them in any language, even when they didn't understand a single word. The hypnotic and calming effect that animation has on children is almost frightening, but it's a phenomenon that we as parents have used to our advantage for a long time, whether we admit it or not! There's absolutely no reason not to extend this advantage to the language-learning realm.

Our first foray into the animated video world involved a series of language DVDs we bought online. They were marketed as "educational" videos, designed to teach young children rudimentary language skills. Many of them showed young children how to count to 10 in a desired language or maybe how to say a few random vocabulary words. Our children found them moderately entertaining, but as their overall language skills progressed, we found that these DVDs were far too basic. Furthermore, they were on the expensive side. We didn't really mind the investment, but after a while, our children just weren't learning anything from them. At that point, we branched out and began looking for children's videos from other countries. We learned that online retailers like Amazon.com have sister sites in many countries, but we soon discovered that many DVDs from other parts of the world would not play on our DVD player. DVDs are region specific, you see, and you have to have the right device specifications to play them. Back on Amazon.com, we were able to buy a multi-region DVD player that wasn't terribly expensive, but the viewing screen was a little small. Our children had no problem with this, though. They would sit in front of the little box for hours at a time and watch their favorite characters in their little Technicolor fantasy worlds. They actually picked up a respectable amount of language that way.

We had chosen Mandarin Chinese for our children, and neither one of us spoke a word of it. Since the retail sites weren't in English, we had to get a little help from our Chinese friends. In case you think you might like to introduce some foreign-language DVDs into your children's repertoire, please do yourself a favor and learn from our mistakes. Skip the educational ones and go straight to the cartoon characters who maintain a running dialogue. Once you're up to speed with this, I think you'll find a lot of familiar characters. Animated celebrities are strikingly multilingual in the DVD world! If you're feeling a bit more adventurous, buy some DVDs featuring local characters who are not famous in your own country. Pleasant Goat and Big Wolf, for example, are superstars in China.

To find Amazon.com sister sites all over the world, simply go to Google and search a phrase such as "Amazon France" or "Amazon Mexico." You will find something like Amazon.fr or Amazon.es. In Germany, it's Amazon.de. In China, it's now Amazon.cn. When ordering from this last site, do your best to order DVDs in Mandarin, unless you want your children to hear Cantonese. If you're not sure how to make that distinction, just ask a new friend. As an interesting aside, since 1957, mainland China has used the simplified Chinese character format, while Taiwan still uses traditional characters. Supposedly, this is very gradually changing in Taiwan, but it's a politically sensitive matter, given that Taiwan and China don't always see eye to eye on everything. In Hong Kong, people use both traditional and simplified characters, and most speak Cantonese. When your children become old enough to learn to write in Chinese, these two character types might be an issue, but I'm told that if you know one type, you can learn the other without too much trouble. As the name suggests, the simplified version might be an easier place to start. Most computer keyboards can be set to enter either simplified or traditional using the same keystroke.

Many online retailers, including Amazon (and now Netflix), are moving away from the DVD format in favor of streaming versions. This is mostly a good thing, because DVDs have a bad habit of getting destroyed when placed in the hands of careless children. The bad news is there are access barriers: these sites have regional blocks, meaning that you cannot watch them from a server outside the particular country. Currently, an Amazon subsidiary will let you rent a movie only if you use a credit card issued by a domestic bank, and Netflix will block you from viewing a French program if you try to access it from a server outside of France. There are ways around that, but Amazon and Netflix would prefer that you not know about them. If you insist on learning how to use these services as language-learning resources for your children, you might need to consult your friendly neighborhood techno-geek, or perhaps you could use a Google search phrase like "how to access French Netflix from the United States" or "how to rent German movies from Amazon." At present, the American versions of Amazon and Netflix do have a small but growing foreign-language offering for interested parents. In Netflix, for example, try looking for a "subtitles and captions" menu selection where you can choose a language and learn what's available.

If that seems like too much trouble, however, just go for the free stuff. There's enough of it out there to keep your kids entertained in just about any language you can think of for the next 1,000 years. My favorite place to get free language videos is YouTube.com. If you'll go there with me now, I'll show you how to save a pile of money.

Let's assume you want your children to spend some time watching videos in Russian. On YouTube, just type in the search term "Russian cartoons." If you're lazy and smart, you'll choose the ones that are at least 30 minutes long. You'll also discover cartoon "playlists" that go on for many, many hours. Just to reinforce this concept, search YouTube using the term "Arabic cartoons." I'll give you some *great* tips on this indispensable resource if you'll please just take the time to have a look at one more video: *How to find free language videos your children will enjoy* (available on my website, www.trilingualbysix.com and YouTube).

Next, let's become more sophisticated and find some French cartoons. Find a web page called "Google Translate." From here, enter the word "cartoon" and translate it into French. You'll quickly discover that the term you are seeking is *dessin animé*. Then, search the phrase "full movie" (*film complet*). Now, on YouTube, just enter the search term "*dessin anime film complet*." Adding the second qualifier to your search has the effect of eliminating a lot of the shorter clips. Your children might enjoy viewing a long collection of 3-minute videos, but you would probably be happier taking a longer break than that. When you feel comfortable with the skill, try doing the same thing on your own, in Spanish. When you're really feeling confident, see if you can find some Korean cartoons with the same technique (Hint: unless you have a Korean keyboard, you'll have to cut and paste). As before, it's easier if you see this done once, so do us both a big favor and review the video, *How to find free language videos your children will enjoy*. Exclusively (as far as I know) at www.trilingualbysix.com and on YouTube.

Once your children are just a little older, they might begin to outgrow cartoons and become more interested in kids' movies. At this point, your search parameters need to change a little. On YouTube, try something like "Russian movies for children." If you can't find any children's movies, select an adult one, and begin sifting through the additional recommended titles until you find something more age appropriate. If this doesn't work for you, just get a little help from a parent who speaks your desired language. They probably even know some video sites other than YouTube.

At their present stage of development, our children are big fans of "China's Got Talent." Search for that on YouTube. Next, let's try another language. I tried "Latin America's Got Talent," but I couldn't find very much. So I went to Google and searched "kids' talent show Spanish television." There I found a *Wikipedia* article that informed me that I was really looking for "LaVoz Kids." Search that on YouTube now. Perhaps you found something to your liking, but I could only find some shorter clips of less than 15 minutes. To get around this problem, try searching "LaVoz Kids playlist." That returned me something that would mesmerize my child for hours and allow me to have my own time.

For the next step, we'll assume that you want your children to learn Korean. Go back to Google and search the term "Korean television programs." See if you can find something that might appeal to your family. When you've done that, find the Korean name of the program you've identified and use those Korean characters to search for episodes of the program on YouTube. If you've watched my video, you should understand exactly what I'm talking about. If not, you can watch it now! (*How to find free language videos your children will enjoy.* At www.trilingualbysix.com and on YouTube.)

In our family, we've been so successful with this resource that we adopted the rule I told you about earlier. We allow our children to watch cartoons and videos whenever appropriate as much as they want, but it has to be in the target language. If we catch them watching videos in the home language, we take away the video privilege for a while. It seems to be a compromise that everyone can live with.

A lot of cable and satellite television providers will happily sell you programming in various languages. It can be a little expensive, but might be worth your while, depending on how old your children are. But an even better idea might be to try out some of this programming for free. Many television stations from across the world are now available online, and a simple search will get you started. Often, there are some tricks to getting connected, so don't be shy about asking your immigrant friends how to do it.

DAYCARE AND PRESCHOOLS

If you live in an area that has a foreign-language preschool, it could be a fantastic way to give your children another skill. If you find a good one, you might not need to do anything else. Unfortunately, most of the international preschools are expensive. Now that you know how to find and network with immigrant enclaves, you can learn more about all the others.

HERITAGE LANGUAGE SCHOOLS

When our children reached the age of 3 and were fairly reliably toilet trained, we began enrolling them in weekend Chinese-language schools. We've been very satisfied with the results, and the tuition has always been incredibly affordable. As it happened, a Taiwanese group ran the one closest to our home. It had programs for children through age 18, and some of the course offerings were college preparatory in nature, not unlike the ones we found in Phoenix, Arizona. However, most of our babysitters were from mainland China, and they convinced us that our children would be better in a program that taught the simplified Chinese characters. Now knowing what I have since learned, I don't know whether this was a wise move or not. Our current heritage language school takes place inside a local Chinese Baptist Church. It is of very good quality, but it doesn't have many students who are older than 12. There is another weekend Chinese-language school at a local university, but it's a long drive. This one is supported by the Confucius Institute, an organization run by the Chinese government.

In our current weekend school, our children are just about the only non-Asians in attendance, and they're probably the only ones whose parents are not fluent in Mandarin. The parental instructions and application forms are in Chinese, not English. It is definitely designed to serve the needs of children who speak Mandarin in the home, which is why we chose the school in the first place. We had to beg a little and use some polite persistence in order to convince the principal to allow us to participate. We had to get help from one of our babysitters with the weekly homework assignments that began somewhere around age 4. The class utilized workbooks and chalkboard exercises, but we decided that this level of didactics was not necessarily inappropriate, given the complexity of the Chinese character system. It was only a few hours every week, so it was not particularly burdensome for our children. When we move beyond the age of 12 in our family, I suppose we'll have a difficult choice to make. Do we drive the extra distance to the university-based school, or do we struggle to convert to the traditional characters of the one closer to our home? Some inexpensive SAT-prep and some help with calculus homework (in Mandarin, no less) might be nice later on.

For a while, our children also attended a German weekend school that was sponsored by a not-for-profit corporation. After a short while, we decided to give it up. Since most of the ethnic Germans in our community have been around for many generations, very few of them still speak the language at home. The school offered a very basic level of instruction, consisting mostly of songs, numbers, and a few rudimentary vocabulary words. The instructors spoke German with the children—some of the time. Most of the children were under the age of 10, and a lot of parents seemed to be using the school as an opportunity to run a few errands on Saturday morning. The recent German immigrants we knew were not interested in taking their children there. I didn't get the feeling that any of the graduates from this program would achieve fluency.

As you see, heritage language schools come in all shapes, sizes, and levels of difficulty. The best ones are sometimes the most challenging to find because they are not intended for the mainstream public. However, these are the ones that you probably want. Unless you happen to share the ethnic background of the school's membership, be prepared to make some sacrifices and enlist some outside support. If you're properly tapping into the appropriate immigrant community, as I think you should be, I predict you will find that support.

Weekend schools are a great resource, and in some cases you may want to choose languages for your children based on their availability in your community. If you want to find them, you might start at your Google search page. Use terms like "English school Madrid," "weekend school San Diego," "heritage language school Pittsburgh," or some appropriate combination. If you fail to find anything, absolutely do *not* give up. More often than not, you will have to rely upon your contacts in the local immigrant enclave to find them. Many of these are not designed to be community outreach projects, and you are not necessarily supposed to discover them.

Some of the larger weekend schools have two tiers: one for children who speak the language at home and another somewhat quarantined section for kids from mainstream households. Not infrequently, the latter tier is attended by adoptees who have already lost their native language. Unless you have no choice, choose the former, even if it involves a little extra pain and sacrifice. Honestly, the best way for you to gain access to a class with kids who speak the target language in the home is to make sure your children already know how to speak the language fairly well *before* you show up at the school. So, if at all possible, plan ahead, and find a language babysitter or two at least a year before you plan to fill out a weekend school application. Never lose sight of the fact that your inability to use the school's language with your children at home is *not* the school's problem.

Video Chatting

We've already seen that a number of more traditional tutors offer their services more affordably via Skype. If you happen to live in an area where the cost of living is very high, you can save a lot of money if you find a tutor in a less expensive area. Simply go to Skype.com and download the necessary software to use this online telephone and video-conferencing service. If you decide to find a Skype tutor, I would recommend looking for one who lives in a country where people speak the desired language natively. For example, if you live in Peoria, Illinois, and you want your children to learn Russian, don't go looking for a Skype tutor in Peoria—find one in Moscow. You might try something along the lines of "Skype Russian tutor Moscow" from your Google search engine. You might also like to know that our friend Craigslist has a section in Moscow. The worldwide network of Skype tutors has figured this out, and Craigslist ads for various forms of language instruction by Skype are commonplace. You would have to figure out how to go about paying a tutor who happens to live 5,000 miles away from you. Maybe PayPal or Western Union could be of assistance.

A lot of Internet websites will help language learners get connected. Many are willing to work for free, trading lesson for lesson. Someone in Venezuela might be willing to converse in Spanish with your children in London, if you would be willing to converse with him in English in return. Finding these websites is not too difficult. Use Google to search "Skype language buddies," "Skype language pals," or "Skype language exchange." A more recent trend, language students have begun video chatting with elderly people in foreign retirement centers. I am aware of some students of English in Brazil who have found retirement home residents in Chicago for conversation partners.[81] Both parties benefit. The students get language practice, and the elderly people with lots of free time get someone to talk to.

The biggest problem with video chatting is that younger children find it incredibly boring. If you happen upon a really entertaining Skype pal, maybe your children would participate without supervision, but I wouldn't bet on it. Usually, if you don't sit and supervise, children will use video-chatting time as an opportunity to play with their dolls, pick their noses, or run off to the kitchen for a snack. As a child matures, however, Skype becomes an increasingly valuable resource.

Music Lessons

While many highly respected experts in the field of musical education do not recommend formal instruction before the age of 6 or so, you might feel differently as a parent. Some immigrant groups seem to prefer music performance lessons for their children beginning somewhere around age 3. If you happen to associate yourself with an immigrant group that is musically inclined, you might be able to accomplish two goals at once. If you found a Japanese piano teacher, you might persuade her to give music lessons in Japanese. Some immigrant groups are fond of playing instruments not commonly used in their adoptive country. Northern Mexicans seem to have a special affinity for the accordion, and some Asians and Africans like to play instruments that I cannot even pronounce. It could be fun, and it could help you stay connected to the immigrant group.

Many ethnic groups, even those that have been overseas for many generations, like to maintain children's choirs or dance groups. This might be a good choice for younger children, since singing and moving to the rhythm are more natural than sitting perfectly still on a piano bench for hours at a time.

Sports Teams

Some immigrants like to assemble into sports teams so they can use their own language together and perhaps participate in a sport that's not so popular among the locals. A number of Chinese community centers have avid table tennis players, and English expats seem to enjoy getting together for rugby matches. In the United States, where soccer does not enjoy the same dominance that it does in the rest of the world, it is possible to find teams speaking languages other than English on the field. Some sports enthusiasts have gone as far as to create teams for their children. Perhaps your children could participate in one of these.

PLAYGROUPS

Across the world, expat moms like to get together while their children play. In the United States, we tried a few of these with our German and Mexican friends, but we found that young children very quickly develop a preference for the community language when they're in mixed company. Keeping English out of an American playgroup is like keeping weeds out of a garden. It's a never-ending battle, and most parents would rather use playgroup time as an opportunity to relax and chat while their children burn off some excess energy on a playground somewhere. No one is really interested in chasing after the group and hovering like a helicopter to make sure that everyone stays in the target language. On the other hand, if you yourself are an expat mom and can find some other parents with children who don't even know your children's home language, it could be a beneficial exercise. When you find that situation, however, usually you don't understand the language being spoken by the other parents, and you might find yourself marginalized. For exercise, outdoor time, and socialization, playgroups are fantastic, but beyond that I think they have their limitations.

SUMMER LANGUAGE CAMPS

Like everything else, these vary in quality and price. Typically their level of instruction seems pretty basic. Dollar for dollar, I would not rate them that high on the value scale, but I'm sure there are exceptions. If you find a good one and have a sense that your children will come home from the experience actually speaking the language better, go for it.

ETHNIC CULTURAL ASSOCIATIONS

Not too long after our children were able to walk without falling down every five steps, we found a Chinese cultural association that had a children's dance group. Actually, it was a girls' dance group because there weren't any boys willing to participate. The association held a few annual festivals in which the girls performed a little routine or two. It was fun to watch, but there wasn't a lot of language learning going on, since most of the other little girls spoke English perfectly well. The instructor was a skilled English speaker too. Participating in this dance group and attending all the festivals allowed us to make some friends within the local Chinese community and, of course, find some babysitters.

More often than not, immigrant groups will have been around awhile and established themselves before they organize cultural associations. Typically, the cultural association's mission is to preserve culture and heritage awareness, though they also often help new immigrants from their home country get established and acquainted. Your experience might well prove to be different, but in my eyes, these organizations are better opportunities for networking than language learning.

Houses of Worship

Regardless of one's spiritual orientation, houses of worship are a great linguistic resource. In a sense, you might think of immigrant spiritual centers as a subset of ethnic cultural associations. Before an immigrant group has the infrastructure and local sophistication to form its own cultural organization, it can always attach itself to a preexisting house of worship and use it as a type of community center. As you've already seen, these can be really excellent places to find tutors for your children, and many of them host weekend language schools.

CHAPTER 19

Bumps in the Road

● ● ●

ONE'S LIFE SHOULD BE *ABOUT* something. Something substantial—more than just making ends meet, more than achieving a higher standard of living, more than obtaining nicer clothes or fancier cars. There should be some greater goal, some purposeful endeavor that takes a lifetime to achieve. If we have children, maybe that goal should include them, leaving them with some tools to achieve the same sense of purpose beyond the ability to make good grades or land a higher-paying job one day.

The languages we choose to give our children can be a part of that journey. Choose thoughtfully, and be prepared for the fact that it's not always going to go perfectly well. There might be months when you feel that your children are making no progress, possibly even periods of lost ground in between advances. Remain focused on the horizon, not on the mud between your toes. Though they will not always thank you at the time, I can't imagine that your children will ever regret the fact that you sent them off into the world able to communicate with a substantially greater percentage of humanity.

No doubt, globalization will continue, and if you think about the way the world looked 100 years ago, 50 years ago, or even 10 years ago, it's perfectly clear that things are changing rapidly. There are lands of prosperity as well as abject poverty, fairness as well as horrific injustice, stability as well as unimaginably dangerous chaos. As we try, somehow, to grow together, we find that differences of opinion, competing interests, and varying beliefs can result in great tragedy and violence.

Through raising trilingual children, as well as through the preparation of this manuscript, I have found that I know a little bit more about the world than I did before I started. If you choose the same path, I think you will have the same awakening. Very importantly, I have developed a deeper understanding of the fact that many people in the world do not make the same assumptions about the meaning of life that I do. Being a Westerner, I have always imagined that comfort, prosperity, peace, and safety are just universal aspirations, but maybe they aren't. Maybe there's something deep inside each of us that yearns for hardship, suffering, and danger.

Just down the street from me lives a Palestinian couple who has lived in country for a long time, as far as I know. I don't really know their background or their attitudes about Western life, but I'm curious. I don't really have the courage to visit their homeland and learn firsthand about the culture, so maybe getting to know them a little better would be a safe alternative for me. Indeed, the Middle East seems to be very familiar with all forms of hardship. It's been that way for a long time, and some years it seems that it's never going to change. Many great writers have seriously pondered this matter and have arrived at a variety of conclusions. In some ways, what is happening there is beyond the comprehension of most of us in the West.

I think there's far more to it than religion and, sometimes, a fearful resistance to change. I think there are also some very firmly held beliefs about what constitutes a purposeful life and what does not, which roads lead to happiness and which do not. There are probably very different views on the ability of technology and modern conveniences to advance that purpose. I'm no political scholar, but I would like to know more. And that is one of the reasons I now wish that I had chosen Arabic for my children. More generally, I've decided that just about all new immigrants are better at recognizing the excesses of Western civilization than the rest of us are. And that's one of the reasons I'm so glad I came to raise my children multilingually.

I've seen research articles suggesting that immigrant families successfully pass their heritage language to their children somewhere around 70% of the time. That's a relatively low number, but I think I know the reason behind it. Many immigrant families aren't really trying. They're more interested in assimilating, fitting in. Host countries are not always terribly tolerant when they hear a person speaking a language they do not understand. Many immigrant families arrive at their destination with very little money in their pockets and have to work very hard to make ends meet, so they don't necessarily have a lot of time to sit around and teach an "unnecessary" language to their children. They're far more committed to helping their children learn the local language. If your family is already multilingual, then you might have the same problem. Probably you're already busy, and maybe you don't always have the extra time or energy to speak with your children in more than one language. This is one of the reasons I think you should recruit help.

As you embark on this trilingual journey, I think you have to plan for the possibility that the life you have when you begin will not necessarily be the life you will have when you arrive. You could experience job disruptions, moves, illnesses, divorces, and unforeseen changes of just about every kind. Try your best to develop contingency plans and build systems that will not be affected by any major life change. That might not be totally possible, but you should still give it some thought. If you have a spouse, then you should do your best to make sure that he or she is committed to your plan as well. If not, it could be a major source of conflict and frustration. You will need to function as a team, just as you will in every other aspect of your children's lives.

Being trilingual can also change a family's social-networking patterns. The parents at country clubs, golf tournaments, and elite charity foundations will probably have their children participating in activities that are very different from your children's. At some point, you just might find yourself a little on the fringes of your usual network. To achieve your own goals, you might find yourself needing to spend more time with other, perhaps less prestigious company. In these alternate groups, you will be more likely to network with people who can help you along in your trilingual journey. For a hopeless introvert like myself, this doesn't really matter, but if you are a social butterfly, you might want to ponder it just a little.

Neighbors and extended family members might pose a similar problem. The neighborhood watch committee organizer across the street might take notice of the fact that you are regularly bringing foreigners into your home, and maybe Grandpa will raise a similar eyebrow. Not too many decades ago, people commonly believed that multilingual children were intellectually inferior, and some of your older relatives may still cling to this fallacy. Think just a little bit about how you might address these matters before they arise. I hesitate to say "xenophobia," but you may see a little of it from time to time, particularly if you allow your children to speak other languages in public. By the way, unless you feel it's patently dangerous, you absolutely should allow your children to speak all their languages outside the home. And you should probably allow your babysitters to take your children to the park, to the ice cream shop, and to the baseball diamond. Some days you might feel like an immigrant yourself, and that can be edifying.

But concerned relatives and nosy neighbors usually cannot match the opposition that can come from your children themselves. Kids usually like to take the path of least resistance, and it's a little extra work to speak a less familiar language. If they can, they will often try to get themselves excused from this task. I think this is one of the reasons you have to keep the trilingual process as fun as you can. Still, there may be times when you just have to dig in and stand your ground. There are just certain battles that a parent should always try to win: drugs, underage drinking, and homework. As far as I'm concerned, a multilingual upbringing belongs on this list too. When they're 18, they can decide if they want to continue with all their languages. Until then, don't let it be just an optional part of their education.

Particularly early on in the process, multilingual children sometimes go through what experts commonly call a silent period, in which they resist using a new language. This is not necessarily rebellion; it's just that they are processing the information without giving you any audible feedback.

When they do start talking, they will probably still have a small vocabulary in that language. In this setting, children often substitute words in their stronger language (the "mixing" phenomenon we discussed). Many impatient parents fret about this, but most experts believe that you should be tolerant of it, particularly early on. If you waste your time correcting this mixing, you'll end up frustrated, and your children will lose interest.

In truth, all of us are guilty of mixing. If English is your dominant language, how many of the words you regularly speak are actually of Spanish derivation, of German, French, or Greek origin? Mixing is how cultures merge and languages evolve. In our new era of global communication, we have probably entered an era of intense language mixing, and no one knows for sure what the ultimate result will be. Already, we are seeing the emergence of Spanglish, Chinglish, Hinglish, Benglish, Taglish, and Franglais, each with its own unique, sophisticated grammatical rules. As many languages die, new ones are being born, and it's not necessarily clear that they are merging together.

There is perhaps one battle that will not be winnable. Almost without exception, siblings will speak to one another in their first language. I don't know of anyone who has figured out a way to get around that. If you find one, let me know, and I will include it in the 2nd edition of this book. This could be a bit of an issue if you have one babysitter caring for two or more children at the same time. It's probably better to have a one-to-one situation, but that's just not always practical or affordable.

As your children move closer to starting school, you need to think more about classroom readiness. Wanting you to understand the relative importance of preschool, I spent a lot of time on this in previous chapters. You have to understand that children who regularly use three languages will probably have a slightly reduced vocabulary in each of them. In most circumstances, this won't matter a bit, and by the time your children have their 10th birthday, they will very likely have just as broad a vocabulary in the school language as all their classmates—maybe even broader. However, if you're considering a highly competitive college-preparatory preschool with waiting lists, high tuition, and entrance exams, your children could be at a bit of a disadvantage. Some elite preschools implicitly frown on multilingualism, and your poor 2-year-old might do slightly less well on the exams. I've already frowned on this for you, so check it out with the school and with other parents as early in the game as you can, if this is your monolingual dream. You'll need to satisfy yourself that a trilingual program would not rain on your parade.

Maybe your children are already a little bit older, and you are wondering if it might be too late to start a trilingual program. I would say start anyway, but consider making some modifications. Maybe it would be better to expand your family repertoire by just one language, rather than two, and hope that you could find a school immersion program in your area. At home, you could intensify the exposure to one additional language rather than splitting it into two parts. But if you're seriously committed to a trilingual program with your slightly older children, go ahead. There's no law that says you cannot continue the process into the school years. Start early if you can, but if it's already later than that, do not be deterred, if it's what you really want. For the most part, I'm leaving discussions of what you should be doing after the start of school for a second book, but suffice it to say that this "language babysitter" technique will work for many years beyond kindergarten.

CHAPTER 20

Limited Proficiency

● ● ●

ACROSS THE GLOBE, MOST IMMIGRANTS pay taxes that help fund their host countries' retirement systems, health plans, public roads, bridges, and schools. They also remit an incredible amount of money back home to countries that might otherwise destabilize. Most politicians understand this, and that is why they often take a public stance on immigration that seems a little hypocritical on the surface. No developed country wants to see its retirement system go bankrupt, and no struggling nation wants to be under the thumb of a more powerful one that sends it official foreign aid. And there are limitations to the amount of foreign aid that taxpayers in prosperous countries will tolerate. You have to understand that the amount of money being sent home by immigrants is much, much larger than the world's combined amount of official foreign aid; about a half trillion dollars are remitted annually. If all the world's immigrants decided to go home, we would probably see immediate financial calamities of all kinds. Even if only the world's undocumented immigrants were suddenly deported, we would probably still be confronted with a huge financial crisis.

Even if you don't realize it, you're probably supporting world stability by the money you pay to immigrants. Who processed the chicken that you just bought at the grocery store? Who picked the lettuce? Who did the contractor hire to roof your house when it was built? Some of that money you spent is probably being used to prevent a faraway country from going into economic collapse. Some of it is finding its way to support your grandfather in the nursing home. Some of it is probably helping your local school system buy new textbooks.

But no matter where you are in the world, some immigrants, both legal and undocumented, are being paid in cash under the table, without reporting it to the taxation authorities. If you regularly pay a fellow to mow your grass or weed your garden or pay a nice woman to mop your floors and fold your clothes once a week, you are probably required to report that activity to your country's taxation authorities if it exceeds a certain amount. Though you might be tempted to tell yourself that "everybody's doing it" and just offer cash, hoping that nobody will say anything, that's risky, not to mention illegal. The same goes for babysitters.

In our own situation, we've met fascinating people who seemed like they would be really excellent language babysitters, only to find that they mysteriously lost interest after we made it known that we preferred to pay by check rather than cash or when we asked for a Social Security number for tax-reporting purposes. Honestly, we felt the temptation just to pay the seemingly enthusiastic people in cash and have them be a part of our children's lives, but we decided it was better to obey the law. You can always ask an accountant for more information.

In most places, you need to request a Social Security number (or your country's equivalent) and a work authorization document, such as a permanent residence card ("green card") or work visa. That's how you know that an immigrant has a legal right to work in your country. Throughout the entire world, however, there is a vast underground network that supplies fake versions of these documents. I can't know for sure, but I get the idea that fake green cards and fake Social Security numbers are fairly easy to obtain—for a price. I have no idea what that price might be. In the modern technological era, it seems to me that it would be relatively easy for governments to crack down on the distribution of fake work documents, but it doesn't really seem to happen very much. I'm speculating here, but I think this must have something to do with the fact that politicians recognize the importance of immigrant labor sources to their economies, not to mention their reelection campaigns.

In this world of widely available fake work documents, how can you as an ordinary citizen know which are genuine and which are not? I think the answer is…you can't. But as an employer, you have to do your due diligence and request copies of the documentation that your country requires. If you don't do what your local laws demand, you could probably get away with it. It happens all the time, but you could also get into a horrible amount of trouble. I suggest you obey your local laws.

Most governments prefer to have immigrants who obey the laws as well. An immigrant who commits a crime that attracts the attention of the local police and gets arrested has an excellent chance of getting deported, after paying fines and serving jail time. That can send a family back home into economic ruin in a big hurry. Most of the time, the local police do not seem terribly interested in basically law-abiding immigrants who fail to report their otherwise legal cash transactions to the tax authorities. Police officers prefer to give speeding tickets, investigate burglaries, chase after drug dealers, and hunt down murderers. Income-tax crimes tend to be matters for the federal authorities, who always seem to be understaffed. But the majority of immigrants opt for a low profile and just pay their taxes even if they do not have legal status. More often than not, they have children in the public schools too, and the money they pay to the government helps educate them.

In public schools, many of these children face language obstacles. In the United States, one in five children comes from a family that speaks a language other than English. About a third of them will not complete high school.[82] Some attribute this to "language barrier." Others say it's a phenomenon euphemistically called "low socioeconomic status." Just about all immigrants are starting their lives over, and many have financial difficulties.

Imagine that you are an immigrant child. Not speaking a word of the local language, you arrive with your parents in a strange new land and get thrust into the local school system. The teacher doesn't speak your language, and most of the other students probably don't either. Unlike you, they've already mastered the local language. They're ready to begin the process of learning to read, count, do math, and everything else. When you receive homework assignments, which you do not understand, your parents at home have no ability to help you. With each passing month, you fall further and further behind your classmates as you struggle to learn the basics of everyday communication that everyone else already takes for granted. Math lessons grow increasingly sophisticated, but you can't follow along because you can't process the verbal concepts that the teacher is introducing.

You are ostracized. You have trouble making friends on the playground. Children have a nasty habit of being cruel sometimes, and maybe you are the target of their ridicule. Your self-esteem suffers, and you grow to hate school. Eventually, maybe, some older kids of your same ethnic background befriend you. They accept you into their ranks and make you feel a part of their group. Unfortunately, they once had the same bad experience in school that you are having. They have dropped out and taken to a life on the streets. At all too young an age, you find that you are gravitating toward increasingly dangerous gang activity. Even if you manage to avoid this particular trap, you're probably not terribly interested in staying in school through graduation. You're more interested in finding a job as soon as you can. That would seem to be a better pathway to self-worth and a good way to help your family.

How can this problem be avoided? How can societies be more successful at integrating children who do not speak the school language into classroom activities? You can imagine that many experts have given it an incredible amount of thought, and they have tried many different approaches. Before the 1960s, scientists who studied immigrant groups observed that they always seemed to score lower on IQ tests. They assumed that these lower scores were related to the fact that the immigrants spoke more than one language.[83] We now know that was incorrect. To remedy the matter, schools used a teaching methodology that has been called "sink-or-swim." Immigrant children were tossed into mainstream classrooms and expected to make the transition to a new language on their own—total immersion to the extreme.

The results were predictably unfavorable. Many of these immigrant children drowned. They had the trajectories of their native languages irreversibly disrupted, and they failed to learn the dominant school language well enough to survive in the classroom environment. Many ended up joining the local unskilled labor pool at an all-too-early age without much prospect of a better life. Maybe they weren't even literate in any language.

Here in the United States, in the mid-1970s, a Supreme Court case ended the practice of sink-or-swim: *Lau v. Nichols*. School systems were thereafter required to provide support for children who did not speak the classroom language. In some areas where a single large immigrant group predominated, the schools could meet this mandate relatively comfortably. In other areas where small pockets of multiple immigrant groups existed, this was a huge problem. Take the case of a city like New York, where various immigrant groups speak hundreds of different languages. How can the school system find the resources to meet the special language needs of every child in a setting like that? To a great extent, the question remains unanswered.

What emerged was a tendency on the part of school systems to create mirror programs, in which teachers instructed minority-language students in their native tongue. For the most part, these programs continue to this day, and they have not been all that successful. Children who do not speak the mainstream school language end up being quarantined in their own classes conducted in their own languages. There is a serious attempt to move these children toward satisfactory performance in a mainstream classroom, but it is not always successful. Perhaps there is not a lot of social intermingling going on in a setting like this, and in many instances the dropout rates remain very high.

In the early days after *Lau v. Nichols*, the preponderance of scientific opinion held that children who lost their home language had their linguistic "trajectory" disrupted, and they underperformed in school as a result. Many immigrant children, as they approached school age, were not encouraged by anyone (their parents included) to continue learning their home language. School entry was to be a sink-or-swim affair. Many immigrant parents did their best to speak the future school language at home, but they often had limited ability to do this. As a result, a lot of the immigrant children heard rudimentary language—perhaps broken, not fluent, and quite restricted. These children entered school speaking a watered-down version of the community language after they had virtually lost their native language. This was viewed as a major disruption of the language trajectory. These children never developed the degree of linguistic sophistication necessary to function well in the school setting, in either language. The results included school underperformance and high dropout rates.

The new scientific paradigm became an encouragement of parents to continue speaking their native language with their immigrant children at home. As these children entered school, they spoke at least one language well, but they didn't necessarily have usable skills in the dominant school language. They were "quarantined" in special sections of the school system called "bilingual programs." Most of the instruction occurred in the children's home language, and there were various attempts to gradually introduce the dominant school language over a period of years. Unfortunately, many of these children continued to drop out at an unacceptable rate. Largely, this particular method of assimilation continues to this day in the United States. The results may be marginally better than the old sink-or-swim model, but there is still a big problem. Many of these children seem to develop enough community-language skills to function in a conversational setting, but they don't necessarily acquire the ability to succeed in a mainstream classroom. It's probably very fair to say that it requires much more language skill to survive in a classroom than it does to conduct a basic conversation.

Why this particular model of education for minority-language immigrant children has not been more successful is a matter of some speculation. You might very well imagine that it's an extremely politically charged topic. Some people feel that these school programs unnecessarily shelter immigrant children from learning the community language that they will need in their world one day. Such people believe that there is not enough pressure to motivate these children to learn the dominant language. Others say that the programs are underfunded and that the children do not have enough time to make the adjustment into the dominant-language classroom. Many experts feel that children need an adjustment of at least 4 to 7 years to make this transition. If you consider the idea that nonimmigrant children spend the first 6 years of their lives getting ready to enter the 1st grade, then perhaps it really does take a long time. Consider that immigrant children who might enter the 1st grade not having any skills in the dominant language will, after 6 years, have to enter the dominant-language classroom at the 6th-grade level, and face an even more daunting task.

Still others point to the home environment. They feel that immigrant parents should assume a larger role in their children's education. Some immigrant parents are not themselves highly educated, and perhaps they place less emphasis upon education as a pathway to a successful life. Since a large percentage of immigrant families are engaged in labor-related trades, maybe they would rather instill a value of hard work than of high education, or, very possibly, many immigrant parents are so busy working just to put food on the table that they don't have a lot of time to be more involved in their children's school activities.

Most of the scientific research available on the topic of language acquisition and school success has focused on children of low socioeconomic status. Of course, growing up in poverty is without a doubt a risk factor for school failure, totally independent of language deficiency. Since most immigrants don't earn large amounts of money, their children not only have to overcome their language barriers but also must face the barriers to a good education posed by living in or near poverty. It's not really possible to determine how much of the problem is poverty and how much is language. In any case, without question, children who fail to succeed in the school system are at risk of remaining in poverty.

If you know the solution to world poverty, you should publish it and win the Nobel Prize! Probably, your plan would have something to do with education. Interestingly, it has been found that immigrant children who do not come from impoverished socioeconomic backgrounds have a much easier time learning the school language. Some are capable of entering 1st grade not understanding the school language at all and emerging as high school valedictorians bound for Ivy League schools 12 years later. What key factor separates our valedictorian from the kid living in poverty who drops out of a bilingual school program to join a street gang? Who knows? Maybe the valedictorian just went to a weekend school where she got calculus help and SAT prep. If you're like most people, you probably already have some pretty strong opinions about this topic, and they're most likely interwoven with your basic political beliefs. That's probably a very deep rabbit hole. Suffice it to say that children in a classroom setting must be able, from the very start, to understand the sophisticated level of speech that the teacher is directing their way. If they are not yet able to do this, they probably need a lot of support. Without some swimming lessons or life preservers, they cannot be expected to make it on their own. Again, it's one thing to be able to converse with your playmates on the monkey bars, but it's quite another to be able to follow the teacher as she explains how to solve a long division problem. If it takes an ordinary child from a middle-class background 6 years to get ready for that, how long does it take a child who has language barriers and comes from a relatively impoverished setting to get to the same point? What's the best way to help such a child? Are there any new ideas?

I believe there are. In a recent scientific article that I think is nothing short of groundbreaking, a team of researchers reported that immigrant children who begin learning their future school language from reasonably skilled adults before the age of *3 years* do not eventually struggle in school the way their friends who begin learning the language later in life do.[84] Furthermore, it is these early bilinguals who eventually read the best in both languages. Additional work in functional brain imaging has shown that children who begin learning a language after the age of 3 process that language in their brains very differently than children who begin learning it at an earlier age.[85] Something about learning a language early— and learning it from a reasonably sophisticated source—makes a huge difference. Probably, the dialect does not matter too much, as long as the underlying grammatical sophistication exists.

Of course, some immigrant children do not have the luxury of beginning a new language before this age. Maybe they're older than 3 when they arrive in a new country, or maybe they don't have unlimited access to reasonably sophisticated adult conversation partners. In the last decade or so, a new form of bilingual education has gained popularity. As we saw in Chapter 4, it's usually called two-way immersion, in which disadvantaged, minority-language immigrant children are placed into a classroom with an approximately equal number of mainstream children who speak the dominant community language. Each group learns the other's language, and the bilingual teacher divides instructional time between both. These programs are not all exactly the same, but many of their published results have been attention grabbing. Interestingly, their benefits do not stop at language: children in these programs are also outperforming in math and other subjects.[86] Apparently, immigrant children in these programs are dropping out of school far less.

But we may have to face a painful reality. Very possibly, we can't continue to support over 800 unique immigrant languages in our public schools and expect to have a healthy economy. Perhaps we should be doing more to ensure that all our children are acceptably proficient in the school language *before* they enter 1st grade, but these are very sensitive political issues without easy solutions.[87] As we just discovered, the ultimate solution may lie in beginning the process well before age 3, and not many of the world's educational systems are prepared to handle that.

While we grapple with these problems, the two-way immersion model has begun to trickle down into the preschool environment. Native English-speaking preschoolers are invited into playrooms with native Spanish, Mandarin, Korean, or Vietnamese speakers. Perhaps you could find one of these if you want. But if you can't, just turn your living room into one!

If yours is an immigrant family with very little in the way of skills in the local language, and particularly if you meet the local definition of "low socioeconomic status," perhaps you understand the dilemma of language barriers all too well. If your family speaks the community language quite well, and you are more comfortable economically, perhaps you feel more shielded from this issue, but let me offer a few illustrations of how it might affect your life.

Suppose you have just adopted a 4-year-old girl from a country with a different language. If the available research can be trusted, you should probably not allow her to lose her native language. How will you see to that? Additionally, how will you prepare her to succeed in your local public schools in 2 years? Suppose you have a preschool-age son and your employer transfers you to an overseas job. What impact will that have on his education? What happens when your employer relocates you once again in 5 years? Suppose you live in a developed country with a low birth rate and a prosperous economy that, like it or not, has retirement, healthcare, and infrastructure systems that all depend upon migrant labor to keep the wheels turning. How do you keep the children of those laborers from dropping out of high school and establishing a new cycle of poverty? And finally, suppose you decide to get really aggressive with a trilingual program for your children. Is it possible to go too far, neglecting the school language?

Sometimes, the best questions are the ones left unanswered. I had a professor in college who used to do that to me. It drove me crazy.

CHAPTER 21

Learning Disabilities

● ● ●

THE OTHER DAY, I MET a boy who had been brought into our clinic with an ear infection—a delightfully energetic 2-year-old. His dad spoke respectable English, but his mom did not. It didn't take much inquiry to learn that the family language was Mandarin Chinese. The couple was a little worried about making sure their child learned English so he would be ready for school. As quickly as I possibly could, I invited the little boy to come and play at our house. I promised his parents that our girls would speak to him in English if the mom would agree to speak to our girls in Mandarin. I really hope to hear from them, because our current babysitter has accepted a better job in another city, a job more appropriate for someone of her educational background.

With one look at the child, I could tell that he would probably learn English quickly; he was attentive, interactive, highly social, and interested in everything going on around him. It got me to thinking how incredibly lucky I am to have two children who are the same way. Neither of them has major obstacles thrown in her path, as of yet, and both are learning all the ordinary things that ordinary children learn.

But many children are not so fortunate. They must bravely face the likes of attention deficit disorder, autism, Down syndrome, dyslexia, and a long list of other conditions that make the process of childhood learning more of a challenge. For these children, the traditional classroom will be an immense challenge one day. But perhaps a program of early childhood multiple-language learning could create a more level playing field for them. I hope I've shown you that the ability to function well in a tra-ditional classroom setting is not a prerequisite for becoming trilingual. Children really only need a desire to play. Most children have this instinct, and it is a gift that has been passed out more broadly, and fairly. As far as I'm concerned, any child who can learn to speak one language can just about as easily learn to speak one or two more. That is the consensus in the scientific community.

If there is a child with a developmental condition or a learning disabil-ity in your life, then you probably know much more about it than I ever will. Like so many other human endeavors, experience is the best teacher, and I just don't have very much. I'm lumping all of these conditions into a single category here, but of course that's not the actual case. Each is dif-ferent from the others, and each poses a unique set of obstacles and oppor-tunities. Where multiple languages are concerned, however, viewing them all together is simpler, because they all share one commonality: without exception, none of them is a reason for a child to remain monolingual.

Any child who can learn to communicate in one language can just as readily learn to communicate in one or two more. I use the word *com-municate* rather than *speak* because, where the brain is concerned, there is really not a difference between speaking one and signing one. The brain processes both forms of communication the same way.[88] As an interesting aside, I think it's fair to assume that sign languages are best learned early in life, just as spoken ones are.

Research has shown that bilingual children with speech difficulties, including language delay, are not helped at all if they are forced to give up their second language and become monolingual. In fact, forced mono-lingualism can actually make the condition worse. Much in the way that school officials used to encourage bilingual immigrant children to give up their home language and focus on the school language, many school advi-sors—and even speech pathologists lacking specialized bilingual train-ing—still recommend that a bilingual child with any form of speech or learning disorder abandon one of the languages and focus more intently on the other.

I can tell you that if you suspect your child has a language delay for any reason, you should definitely seek professional guidance. However, if the professional recommends that your child give up one or more languages, you should be very careful about accepting that advice. You would probably do better to seek the guidance of a professional specifically trained to help multilingual children. Almost certainly, such a professional will not give that advice. Not only would giving up one language fail to solve the speech problem and potentially make it worse, but it could mean that the child would lose the ability to communicate with loved ones at home and in the community—definitely not a good thing for a child needing as much emotional and psychological support as possible.[89]

Similarly, if one of the children in your life is found to have any of these impairments, you should feel perfectly comfortable in raising that child to be multilingual if you choose. Multilingualism will not worsen the condition in any way.[90] Children with language and learning impairment are usually steered toward monolingual school options. However, early scientific data on the subject strongly suggests that they do just as well in bilingual settings as children with similar impairments do in monolingual ones.[91] So you do not need to avoid a language-immersion program just because your child has a language or learning challenge. In fact, I'm certain that immersion programs are prohibited by US law from discriminating against these children. The National Association for Hearing and Speech Action (NAHSA) would probably be a great resource. A section of their website is dedicated to helping parents.

Can a child with a language or learning difficulty benefit from being multilingual? The best answer is a qualified yes. Though there's nothing really to suggest that being multilingual would lead to any sort of magical cure, and the general cognitive benefits of being multilingual are not necessarily gigantic, multilingualism is beneficial in its own right. This advantage extends to all children—of course, speaking multiple languages allows you to speak with more people. Being multilingual seems to help children focus better, and they seem to have better attention skills. It's therefore reasonable to suppose that children with attention deficit spectrum conditions might improve if they learn an additional language. There is no scientific data on that yet, but some ongoing research projects are looking at it. There are some new intriguing findings with respect to dyslexia, a condition that is usually not diagnosed until after school begins. It appears that dyslexia in an alphabetic language does not necessarily imply dyslexia in a character-based language such as Mandarin Chinese.[92]

But as I see it, the real advantage of teaching languages to small children with speech and learning disorders remains the simple fact that they do not have to be able to function well in a classroom setting in order to learn. Say you are the parent of a young child who you are fairly certain is destined to struggle in the classroom because of a learning disability. Learning to read will pose a major challenge; perhaps sitting still for an hour at a time and staying focused on the lesson may be an even greater one. These challenges simply do not apply to a playful youngster on the living room floor. These children can learn languages in that environment just as easily as other children. It would seem to me that being multilingual could be a great advantage, helping to offset the many disadvantages they will have to overcome in the classroom. A genuine head start, if you will. The advantage could easily become life long, life altering, and life enriching.

Thanks to the new technology of functional brain imaging, it's becoming possible to diagnose many speech and learning disorders at an earlier and earlier age. With that capability, it would be fascinating to know if early childhood multiple-language acquisition could make the adult lives of people with these conditions better. A fascinating question, but the answer is probably still many decades away.

No doubt, having a learning disability is stigmatized. In many cases, it's not even a disability; it's just an alternate skill set that modern society does not recognize as valuable. We all want perfect children, and we put a lot of pressure on ourselves in that respect. Society has a way of increasing that pressure, and all of it seems to fall on the backs of our children. But, ultimately, they will follow their own paths and chase their own rainbows.

Their lives and their decisions belong to them, and as parents, we can only help them to play the hand that has been dealt them. Ensuring that the game is always fair is something we cannot do.

Though we might wish it for them, maybe our children do not have the capacity to grow up to be beautiful, famous, powerful, or rich. Lacking these often predetermined avenues to conventional prestige, what can we offer our children to help them become happy adults one day? What worthwhile challenge can we put before them in which success is virtually assured? Though it is certainly not the only pathway, I think that adults who have been given special language talents have better self-images and find it easier to avoid feeling inadequate in our highly competitive society overrun with unattainable iconic imagery. But even if your children are destined to be perfect, center-of-attention superstars, no matter how many high cards they are dealt, none of them will have perfect lives. Each will face unique obstacles.

Unfortunately, as they gain independence, many if not all of our children will make bad choices along the way, with potentially disastrous results. Maybe our children will become pregnant in high school, fall under the spell of addictive drugs, or just decide to drop out and go surf on a beach somewhere. Maybe they will choose the wrong companion and end up brokenhearted or choose the wrong career and end up unfulfilled. If this happens (be realistic about your capacity to prevent it), they are going to need some irrevocable adaptation skills to get their lives back on track. Being trilingual could be an excellent resource in the emergency toolbox of life. This resource could help them more readily climb out of whatever trap they recklessly jump into. We can give this skill to them at a time in their lives when we as parents have significantly more influence and control. We want to give them as many of those tools as we can, while we can.

In that interest, consider an extra language or two.

CHAPTER 22

After Six

● ● ●

I NEED TO QUALIFY THOSE "irrevocable adaptation skills." Even if your children are speaking three languages really well when they reach school age, you're not done. In fact, if you stop at that point, you risk losing everything.

If you end the trilingual journey at age 6, your children will become monolingual again in a big hurry. I don't want to excessively alarm you, but some experts from the adoption community note that, after only 6 months, a child's preadoption language can already have vanished.[93] Generally speaking, somewhere around puberty, say age 12, a spoken language, even if neglected, seems to become a more permanent part of a child's brain architecture, and it's less vulnerable to complete loss.[94] As we have seen, the youngest children seem to have almost magical language-learning abilities. Unfortunately, their talents do not stop at that; the younger their age, the more amazingly children can completely *forget* a language if they do not have regular exposure to it.[95] Conversely, post-pubescent children find it more difficult to learn new languages, but they seem to be more able to retain the ones they already have. It's as if the teenage brain becomes more resistant to change, like a bowl of concrete that hardens and can no longer be molded into a different form! It might also be fair to say that the puberty hormones have something of a pickling effect on the brain, preserving its content but halting its growth.

Of course, the best possible advice is: Do not stop at 6! If you were satisfied with your children's linguistic abilities at the start of school, maybe you could avoid this loss by adopting some sort of low level life-support program, but most likely, you would prefer to have them progress to speaking all those languages like adults by the time they become adults. And just as likely, you'd be happy for them to read and write them as well. In any event, the school years will add some new twists to the process. As children learn to read and write at school, the line between literacy and fluency gets blurred. Older children who understand the printed word can use that new ability to advance their spoken-language skills—if they choose. (Hopefully, you'll still have some say in the matter.) While grade schoolers can still learn a language through conversation alone, they will have a new opportunity to advance the cause of literacy at the same time.

The online world and all its craziness can assume a larger role in pursuit of this goal. If you haven't already done so, brace yourself, and begin to explore the Internet resources available for school-age language learners. Personally, I would put Skype language buddies and online tutoring sessions at the top of this list. Though I develop a faint gluteal ache as I have this thought, maybe you could even allow a little texting with a friend in a foreign country.

But while you're celebrating the fact that you'll have more resources, understand that your children will probably have less time available with each passing year. Baseball practice, class parties, swimming lessons, homework, and eventually boyfriends or girlfriends, broken hearts, driver's licenses, summer jobs, and later-into-the-night class parties will take a bigger bite out of your trilingual program. Under this progressively severe time crunch, I think you'll need to become a little more efficient.

A useful trick might be to seek out activities that accomplish two goals at once. Weekend language schools become increasingly valuable, and maybe you could even find one that has tutoring sessions in calculus, biology, or physics. Some music instructors are willing to teach in an alternate language, and, if you are so inclined, you might find minority-language worship services. If you decide you want a math tutor for your children, find one who can do the job in your target language—it's amazing to watch and an incredibly efficient use of educational time. Similarly, consider installing Skype on your cell phone and letting your children do a little video chatting while you're driving to that weekend soccer tournament. If you're lucky, you might find a sports team practicing in your target language. If you're really lucky and have time for a family vacation, consider choosing one that's more substantial than a beach, geographical monument, or theme park flowing with cotton candy and little plastic souvenirs. Instead, choose a destination where some language learning might actually take place. As we saw before, Workaway and other related travel sites might give you some ideas here. But if you insist on being a common tourist, consider doing it in a target language: see the Grand Canyon, Disney World, or Hawaii from a Chinese tour bus, or find a Spanish-speaking guide to show you the Statue of Liberty.

Though your teenagers might prefer to sit on the couch and watch local television, you might consider paying the extra bucks to get some stations in another language. With a little persistence, you could probably manage to keep the remote control set on one of these. You can watch NFL games or weekly drama shows in foreign languages. If your budding linguists need gas money and want a part-time job, see if you might steer them toward another type of language opportunity. Give some consideration to a predominantly Hispanic work crew or a Mexican or Chinese restaurant. Perhaps a Hindi-speaking motel owner is looking for an extra housekeeper in your town. If your teenagers really have some respectable language abilities, consider networking with an aid agency and seeing if they might be able to work as language tutors for new immigrants and refugees. Perhaps they could offer affordable tutoring services to some of their classmates off to a later start on their own language-learning journeys.

If you manage to enroll your children in a school-based language-immersion program beginning in kindergarten or 1st grade, the school principal will be responsible for hiring and training at least some of your babysitters for you! If your children have already had several years of language babysitters, you just might see them enjoy at least a period of academic stardom in the school immersion world, as their monolingual friends struggle with the basic concepts of the new language that your children mastered years before. If your children have grown up with language babysitters, YouTube cartoons, and weekend schools, I think you'll find that they're light-years ahead of the other kids in the class. But that's OK—believing that they're smarter than everyone else (even when they're not) will boost their self-esteem.

My secret hope is, after an early taste of being academic stars in the immersion world, my children will become addicted to that feeling and be willing to work extra hard to remain in this particular limelight. And don't worry too much about your little language prodigies getting bored. Though they might be very advanced in fluency, the literacy playing field will be more level, and they'll be learning to read, write, add, and subtract right along with all their friends.

Remember that many school immersion programs have waiting lists, and even lottery systems. Many districts don't have immersion programs at all. So, to the greatest extent possible, begin investigating what your local schools have to offer. While you're at it, go ahead and look into what traditional language courses are offered in high school and maybe middle school. By the time your children reach that age, these courses will probably be far too basic for them, but the classes still might have some minimal utility on the literacy front if you have no other local options. Of course, if you find out early enough that the schools in your neighborhood don't have anything helpful to offer, you might just move somewhere else.

No doubt, parental involvement is crucial in all aspects of a grade-schooler's education. Where a trilingual education is concerned, you'll probably have to be more involved than you were in the preschool years. Your language babysitters have no question about who writes their paychecks, but teachers and administrators sometimes get confused. Too easily, they forget that you, as a taxpaying parent, are their employer. To help remind them of this, I suggest getting involved, attending some school board meetings, and voicing some opinions from time to time when you see your employees drifting off course. They might not always appreciate your leadership qualities, but in an important way, it's your job as a concerned citizen. Ultimately, though, even under the best of circumstances, no school is going to assume all responsibility for all aspects of a trilingual learning program. There are a few Luxembourgian exceptions, but very few. Your school system might do OK in terms of social studies, football, and sex education, but the multiple-language end of it will probably remain your job.

As you take the helm of this aspect of your children's educational voyage, approach the responsibility with enthusiasm. However, temper your zeal a little bit, and don't let your family's language activities have a negative impact on your children's school performance. This might not be too much of a problem in the early grade-school years, when the academic workload is typically light, but as courses become more advanced, your children will need more and more time to devote to them. Home language learning is important, but not as important as formal schooling. Where to draw this line is difficult to say. Only you as the parent can decide.

This brings us to a very important question: To what degree will additional language learning affect your children's ability to perform as well as possible in school? Where immersion programs are concerned, I wouldn't worry. The available research has shown that children in immersion programs do at least as well if not better in all subjects, including math, science, and the local community language.[96] Were that not the case, they probably would've been outlawed long ago. On the other hand, if you choose to be more ambitious and increase your children's linguistic load to a total of three languages, you have to give this some thought. If all this additional language learning is occurring outside the classroom, you might be asking your children to learn a lot more new material than their friends will be learning. Since I'm a big fan of breadth of knowledge rather than depth, I feel that the possible small reduction in traditional subject proficiency, allowing children to have additional abilities that most of their peers will not have, is an acceptable trade-off. However, each situation is different, and I think it would be worth keeping this potential concern on a back burner somewhere. Whatever course of action you choose, I think you have to let your children's school language dominate, and you need to keep home language activities from interfering with classroom activities. I guess what I'm hoping to say here is, give classroom activities the top priority they deserve, let your children be children, and don't go overboard.

I think you can best accomplish this by trying to keep home language learning as fun as it was when your little toddler was playing patty-cake with the language babysitter on the living room floor. For a number of reasons, I believe that simple, low-stress conversational activities should remain the bedrock, foundation, and cornerstone of your home language program. While this might have the effect of nurturing fluency more than literacy, I'd ask you to remember that a person can develop literacy equally well at just about any age. The same can't be said for fluency.

I also think it would be helpful to discuss the concept of transfer a little more, where multiple-language learning is concerned. Suppose your children's primary language is Italian. At school they have learned to read and write this language. If they have also learned to speak Spanish at home, how difficult do you suppose it would be for them to learn to read and write in Spanish? The answer, of course, is not very. Not only are the languages closely related, but they use the same alphabet. In this particular instance, you might find that your children would learn to read in Spanish as if by magic.

With languages that use the same alphabet, there is an incredible amount of transfer. Once your children learn to read in one of them, learning to read in the others is a virtual snap. Perhaps that is a bit of an overstatement, but I really wouldn't worry excessively about literacy under these circumstances.

As you can imagine, however, the situation gets more complicated if all your children's languages do not utilize the same alphabetic structure. Where character-based languages such as Mandarin Chinese and Korean are concerned, there is even less transfer. This is probably one of the reasons why a majority of Chinese and Korean weekend schools begin introducing literacy instruction at an early age: it takes a while to master these characters, and being able to read English or Spanish is not terribly helpful. On the spectrum of difficulty, languages like Arabic or Russian that use alternate alphabetic structures fall somewhere between these two extremes.

Where school immersion programs are concerned, experts have concluded that it doesn't matter very much when reading and writing in the dominant school language are introduced.[97] These multilingual children seem to end up reading and writing at least as well in the dominant school language as their cohorts in the traditional monolingual classroom. If you consider it important that your children read and write as well as kids in the monolingual classroom from the very start, though, you might like to know that, with as little as 1 hour per day of instruction in the dominant community language, these kids progress on par with their cohorts in the monolingual classroom.[98] Though Laura and I have chosen, to the greatest extent possible, to allow our children to learn to read and write in one language before introducing others, the research says that there is no harm in introducing reading and writing in multiple languages at the same time, from the very start.

This last point, however, assumes that all the children in the classroom are doing the same thing—reading and writing in several languages. It's more likely that your children will read and write in one language at school and potentially read and write in others elsewhere. I don't think there's much data on that, but I wonder if that might be a little confusing for a child. That's basically why we have chosen to delay the introduction of writing in multiple languages with our own children. Having said that, I'd point out (very proudly) that our children have begun to read and write in their additional languages on their own. That's so amazing that it's even a little scary. As it happens, these additional languages both use the roman alphabet. Their spelling is still a little funky, but that only adds to the fun.

For now, you'll be on your own to decide how and when to introduce literacy in your children's second and third languages. As soon as I can, I'll be along with Book 2 to help you out.

CHAPTER 23

The Recipe Card

● ● ●

THAT'S IT. YOU'RE DONE. Now you know about as much as anyone else. You just need enough courage to make it happen. As an extremely concise review, I want to summarize this trilingual plan in no more space than one side of a standard index card:

Beginning as early in life as you possibly can, find language baby-sitters or other live humans to play and converse with your children in your chosen languages for about 10 hours per week, each. More hours are fine, but let your children's future school language dominate if at all possible. Make sure that these conversation partners speak only in the desired language. Also make sure that they are sufficiently talkative to keep a running dialogue. Once your children begin to speak the desired language, make sure that their conversation partners are good listeners in addition to good talkers. Once your children are old enough to enjoy animation, introduce cartoons and other videos in the desired language. Keep all language activities fun and entertaining. Avoid workbooks, flashcards, and other more structured resources that your children find uninteresting. In order to maximize proficiency in the primary language, you as a parent should probably speak to your children only in your native language. Prepare them for future literacy by reading storybooks every evening. Encourage your children's babysitters to do the same in their native language. Always remember that this process is a marathon, not a 100-yard dash.

And let's just say goodbye with a final, even more concise epilogue:

Start early.
Children learn best through play.
Find those enclaves.

Good luck!

● ● ●

www.trilingualbysix.com
Facebook: Trilingual by Six

About the Author

● ● ●

A VICTIM OF HIS OWN restive curiosity, Dr. Lennis Dippel has always refused to fully appreciate the finer things in life, and avoided the limitations of a mainstream expert. With a degree in General Studies from Texas Tech University, he attended Southwestern Medical School. Intending return to his small-town roots, he completed a residency in Family Medicine; but, an ill-fated romantic interest detoured him through Europe, where he made an equally doomed attempt to learn German. He eventually married a native Spanish speaker who had no better luck at teaching him her language.

Resolved to give his children the opportunities he missed, Dr. Dippel exposed them to multiple languages from the very start, while he researched the world's database on childhood language acquisition. Based on this investigation, and findings from his highly successful home laboratory, he concludes that, without a doubt, there is an easier way to become multilingual...for kids at least.

BIBLIOGRAPHY

Ahmad, F. and K. Hamm. 2013. *The School-Readiness Gap and Preschool Benefits for Children of Color.* Washington, DC: Center for American Progress. http://www.americanprogress.org/wp-content/uploads/2013/11/PreschoolBenefits-brief-2.pdf.

The Albert Shanker Institute. 2008. *Preschool curriculum: What's in it for children and teachers?* December. Retrieved November 25, 2013. http://www.shankerinstitute.org/Downloads/Early%20Childhood%20 12-11-08.pdf.

American Academy of Pediatrics. 1999. "Helping your child learn to read." http://www.healthychildren.org/English/ages-stages/preschool/pages/Helping-Your-Child-Learn-to-Read.aspx.

American Academy of Pediatrics. 2012. "Media and Children." http://www.aap.org/en-us/advocacy-and-policy/aap-health-initiatives/pages/media-and-children.aspx.

Anderson, J. 2011. "Suit faults test preparation at preschool." *The New York Times,* March 14. http://www.nytimes.com/2011/03/15/nyregion/15suit.html.

"Arab immigration to the United States." n.d. *Wikipedia.* http://en.wikipedia.org/wiki/Arab_immigration_to_the_United_States.

Bates, K. G. 2012. "Nailing the American dream, with polish." In *American Dreams: Then and Now,* produced by A. Fehling, June 14. Washington, DC: National Public Radio. http://www.npr.org/2012/06/14/154852394/with-polish-vietnamese-immigrant-community-thrives.

Bialystok, E. 2001. *Bilingualism in development: Language, literacy, and cognition.* Cambridge, England: Cambridge University Press.

Bickerton, D. 1984. "The language bioprogram hypothesis." *Behavioral and brain sciences* 7 (02): 173–188.

Bird, E. K. R., P. Cleave, N. Trudeau, E. Thordardottir, A. Sutton, and A. Thorpe. 2005. "The language abilities of bilingual children with Down syndrome." *American Journal of Speech-Language Pathology* 14 (3): 187–199. http://dx.doi.org/10.1044/1058-0360(2005/019).

Boocock, S. S. 1995. "Early childhood programs in other nations: goals and outcomes." *The Future of Children* 5 (3): 94–114. http://dx.doi.org/10.2307/1602369. http://www.futureofchildren.org/futureofchildren/publications/docs/05_03_04.pdf

Bridges, M., B. Fuller, R. Rumberger, and L. Tran. 2004. "Preschool for California's children: Promising benefits, unequal access." Policy Brief 04-3. *Policy Analysis for California Education (PACE)*, September. http://files.eric.ed.gov/fulltext/ED491703.pdf.

Bruer, J. T. 1999. *The myth of the first three years: A new understanding of early brain development and lifelong learning.* New York, NY: Simon and Schuster.

Bruer, J. T. 2002. "Avoiding the pediatrician's error: how neuroscientists can help educators (and themselves)." *Nature Neuroscience* [supplement] 5 (October): 1031–1033. doi:10.1038/nn934.

Burke, L., and R. Sheffield. 2013. "Universal preschool's empty promises." *Heritage Foundation*, March 12. http://www.heritage.org/research/reports/2013/03/universal-preschools-empty-promises#_ftn21.

Bylund, E. 2009. "Maturational constraints and first language attrition." *Language Learning* 59 (3): 687–715.

Caccavale, T. 2007. "The correlation between early second language learning and native language skill development." *Learning Languages* 13 (1): 30–32.

Calvin, W. H., and D. Bickerton. 2001. *Lingua ex machina: Reconciling Darwin and Chomsky with the human brain.* Cambridge, MA: MIT Press.

Center in International Education Benchmarking. n.d. "South Korea." http://www.ncee.org/programs-affiliates/center-on-international-education-benchmarking/top-performing-countries/south-korea-overview/.

Chakrabarti, R. 2013. "South Korea's schools: Long days, high results." *BBC News*, December 2. http://www.bbc.com/news/education-25187993.

Chia, A. 2013. "In Seoul, tuition for pre-schoolers is a norm." *Today Magazine*, November 21. http://www.todayonline.com/world/asia/seoul-tuition-pre-schoolers-norm.

Chomsky, N. 1967. "Recent contributions to the theory of innate ideas: Summary of oral presentation." *Synthese (Including A Symposium on Innate Ideas)* 17 (1). http://isites.harvard.edu/fs/docs/icb.topic1327223.files/Recent%20Contributions.pdf.

"Critical Period Hypothesis." n.d. *Wikipedia.* http://en.wikipedia.org/wiki/Critical_Period_Hypothesis.

Cummins, J. 1979. "Linguistic interdependence and the educational development of bilingual children." *Review of educational research* 49 (2): 222–251. http://dx.doi.org/10.3102/00346543049002222.

Dalporto, D. n.d. "South Korea's school success." *We Are Teachers.* http://www.weareteachers.com/hot-topics/special-reports/teaching-around-the-world/south-koreas-school-success.

Dixon, L. Q., J. Zhao, J. Y. Shin, S. Wu, J. H. Su, R. Burgess-Brigham and C. Snow. 2012. "What We Know about Second Language Acquisition: A Synthesis from Four Perspectives." *Review of Educational Research* 82 (1): 5–60. http://dx.doi.org/10.3102/0034654311433587.

"Education in Finland." n.d. *Wikipedia.* http://en.wikipedia.org/wiki/Education_in_Finland.

Elkind, D. 1987. *Miseducation: Preschoolers at risk.* New York, NY: Random House.

Genesee, F. H. 2008. "Early dual language learning." *Zero to Three* 29 (1): 17–23.

Genesee, F. H. 2009. "Early childhood bilingualism: Perils and possibilities." *Journal of Applied Research on Learning* 2 (2): 1–21. http://www.ccl-cca.ca/pdfs/JARL/Jarl-Vol2Art2-Genesse_EN.pdf.

Gladwell, M. 2008. *Outliers: The Story of Success.* New York, NY: Little, Brown, and Company.

Guddemi, M. 2013. "Important new findings: Linking self-regulation, pretend play and learning in young children." *SEEN Magazine*, August 21. http://seenmagazine.us/articles/article-detail/articleid/3237/important-new-findings.aspx.

Gutierrez-Clellen, V. F., G. Simon-Cereijido, and C. Wagner. 2008. "Bilingual children with language impairment: A comparison with monolinguals and second language learners." *Applied Psycholinguistics* 29 (1): 3–19. http://dx.doi.org/10.1017/S0142716408080016.

Hackney, R. n.d. "Is preschool necessary?" Video file. http://www.mon-keysee.com/play/4260-is-preschool-necessary.

Hakuta, K., and D. August, eds. 1997. *Improving Schooling for Language-Minority Children: A Research Agenda.* Washington, DC: National Academies Press. Retrieved September 21, 2014. http://202.118.84.143:85/dmtzy/yy/7/wwdzs/Education/index98.pdf.

Hart, B., and T. R. Risley. 1999. *The Social World of Children: Learning To Talk.* Baltimore, MD: Paul H. Brookes Publishing Co.

Hathaway, J. 2014. "Brazilian kids learn English by talking to lonely Chicago seniors." *Gawker,* May 7. http://gawker.com/brazilian-kids-learn-english-by-talking-to-lonely-chica-1573138921.

Hermanto, N., S. Moreno, and E. Bialystok. 2012. "Linguistic and meta-linguistic outcomes of intense immersion education: How bilingual?" *International Journal of Bilingual Education and Bilingualism* 15 (2): 131–145. http://dx.doi.org/10.1080/13670050.2011.652591.

Hernandez, A. E., and E. Bates. 1999. "Bilingualism and the brain." *MIT encyclopedia of cognitive science,* 80–81.

Hernandez, A. E., and P. Li. 2007. "Age of acquisition: Its neural and computational mechanisms." *Psychological Bulletin* 133 (4): 638–650. doi:10.1037/0033-2909.133.4.638.

Hernandez, J. C. 2013. "Private schools are expected to drop a dreaded entrance test." *The New York Times,* September 19. http://www.nytimes.com/2013/09/20/nyregion/private-schools-are-expected-to-drop-dreaded-erb-entrance-test.html?pagewanted=all.

Hill, C., W. Gormley, and S. Adelstein. 2012. "Do the short-term effects of a strong preschool program persist." Working paper.

Washington, DC: Center for Research on Children in the United States, Georgetown University. http://fcd-us.org/sites/default/files/CROCUSWorkingPaper18%20%281%29.pdf.

Hirsh-Pasek, K., and R. M. Golinkoff. 2003. *Einstein never used flash cards: How our children really learn—and why they need to play more and memorize less.* Emmaus, PA: Rodale.

Hoff, E. 2009. *Language Development,* 4th ed. Belmont, CA: Cengage Learning.

Hoff, E. 2013a. "Interpreting the early language trajectories of children from low-SES and language minority homes: Implications for closing achievement gaps." *Developmental Psychology* 49 (1): 4. http://dx.doi.org/10.1037/a0027238. http://media.eurekalert.org/aaas-newsroom/MCM/FIL_000000000046/2013_Hoff_Interpreting_trajectories.pdf.

Hoff, E. 2013b. *Language Development,* 5th ed. Belmont, CA: Cengage Learning.

Holman, J. R. 1998. Learning a language. *Better Homes and Gardens,* January: 40–42. http://www.languageworkshopforchildren.com/lwfc/docs/BetterHomes.pdf.

Howard, E. R., J. Sugarman, and D. Christian. 2003. "Trends in Two-Way Immersion Education. A Review of the Research (Report 63)." Baltimore, MD: Center for Research on the Education of Students Placed At Risk (CRESPAR)/Johns Hopkins University. http://www.csos.jhu.edu/crespar/techReports/Report63.pdf.

Hyltenstram, K., and N. Abrahamson. 2000. "Who can become native-like in a second language? All, some or none?" *Studia Linguistica* 54 (2): 150–166.

Jia, G., and D. Aaronson, D. 1998. "Age differences in second language acquisition: The dominant language switch and maintenance hypothesis." *Boston University Conference on Language Development*, November. Paper presented at Boston University, Boston, MA.

Johnson, J. S., and E. L. Newport. 1989. "Critical period effects in second language learning: The influence of maturational state on the acquisition of English as a second language." *Cognitive Psychology* 21 (1): 60–99. http://www.psy.cmu.edu/~siegler/423jhnsn-n89.pdf.

Karoly, L. A., and J. H. Bigelow. 2005. *The economics of investing in universal preschool education in California*. Santa Monica, CA: Rand Corporation. http://www.rand.org/content/dam/rand/pubs/monographs/2005/RAND_MG349.pdf.

Kim, S. Y., Y. Wang, D. Orozco-Lapray, Y. Shen, and M. Murtuza. 2013. "Does 'tiger parenting' exist? Parenting profiles of Chinese Americans and adolescent developmental outcomes." *Asian American Journal of Psychology* 4 (1): 7–18. doi:10.1037/a0030612.

Kovelman, I., S. A. Baker, and L. A. Petitto. 2008. "Age of first bilingual language exposure as a new window into bilingual reading development." *Bilingualism: Language and Cognition* 11 (2): 203–223. http://dx.doi.org/10.1017/S1366728908003386.

Kuhl, P. K., F. M. Tsao, and H. M. Liu. 2003. "Foreign-language experience in infancy: Effects of short-term exposure and social interaction on phonetic learning." *Proceedings of the National Academy of Sciences* 100 (15): 9096–9101. http://dx.doi.org/10.1073/pnas.1532872100.

Larsen, J. M., and C. C. Robinson. 1989. "Later effects of preschool on low-risk children." *Early Childhood Research Quarterly* 4 (1): 133–144. http://dx.doi.org/10.1016/S0885-2006(89)90142-7.

Le, C. N. n.d. "School of education at Johns Hopkins University: A closer look at Asian Americans and education." Johns Hopkins University School of Education. http://education.jhu.edu/PD/newhorizons/strategies/topics/multicultural-education/A%20closer%20look%20at%20asian%20americans%20and%20education.

Leak, J., G. J. Duncan, W. Li, K. Magnuson, H. Schindler, and H. Yoshikawa. 2010. "Is timing everything? How early childhood education program impacts vary by starting age, program duration and time since the end of the program." In *Biennial Meeting for the Society for Research on Child Development, Montreal, Quebec, Canada*, November. http://www.education.uci.edu/docs/Leak_Duncan_Li_Timing_Paper_APPAM_102810.pdf.

Lien Foundation Project. 2013a. "An Introduction to Shanghai's Preschool System." *Today Online*, October 15. http://youtu.be/7-Xz-xsB-_M.

Lien Foundation Project. 2013b. "Play-based learning in Shanghai's pre-schools." *Today Online*, October 15. http://youtu.be/fw29nV4obww.

Lien Foundation Project. 2013c. "Challenges faced by Shanghai's pre-schools." *Today Online*, October 15. http://youtu.be/Sth87zw2h8M.

Lindholm-Leary, K. J. 2004. "Two-Way Immersion." *Educational Leadership*, 56–59. http://www.glchouston.com/pdfs/Two%20Way%20Immersion.pdf.

"List of languages by number of native speakers." n.d. *Wikipedia*. http://en.wikipedia.org/wiki/List_of_languages_by_number_of_native_speakers.

Loeb, S., M. Bridges, D. Bassok, B. Fuller, and R. W. Rumberger. 2007. "How much is too much? The influence of preschool centers on children's social and cognitive development." *Economics of Education Review* 26 (1): 52–66. http://dx.doi.org/10.1016/j.econedurev.2005.11.005.

Long, M. H. 1990. "Maturational constraints on language development." *Studies in second language acquisition* 12 (03): 251–285. http://dx.doi. org/10.1017/S0272263100009165.

Lopata, C., N. V. Wallace, and K. V. Finn. 2005. "Comparison of academic achievement between Montessori and traditional education programs." *Journal of Research in Childhood Education* 20 (1): 5–13. http://dx.doi. org/10.1080/02568540509594546. http://www.pearweb.org/teaching/ pdfs/Schools/Cambridge%20Montessori%20Elementary-Middle%20 School/Articles/Montessori%20article.PDF.

Lowry, L. n.d. "Bilingualism in Young Children: Separating Fact from Fiction." http://www.hanen.org/Helpful-Info/Articles/Bilingualism-in-Young-Children--Separating-Fact-fr.aspx.

MacSwan, J., and L. Pray. 2005. "Learning English bilingually: Age of onset of exposure and rate of acquisition among English language learners in a bilingual education program." *Bilingual Research Journal* 29 (3): 653–678. http://dx.doi.org/10.1080/15235882.2005.10 162857. http://bama.ua.edu/~jpetrovi/bef585/readings/macswanan-dpray.pdf.

Magnusun, K. A., C. J. Ruhm, and J. Waldfogel. 2004. "Does pre-kindergarten improve school preparation and performance?" Working paper No. 10452, April. Cambridge, MA: National Bureau of Economic Research. http://www.nber.org/papers/w10452. pdf?new_window=1.

Marinova-Todd, S. H., D. B. Marshall, and C. E. Snow. 2000. "Three misconceptions about age and L2 learning." *TESOL Quarterly* 34 (1): 9–34. doi:10.2307/3588095.

Massey, D. S., ed. 2008. *New faces in new places: The changing geography of American immigration.* New York, NY: Russell Sage Foundation.

McCabe, A., C. S. Tamis-LeMonda, M. H. Bornstein, C. B. Cates, R. Golinkoff, A. W. Guerra and L. Song. 2013. "Multilingual children: Beyond myths and toward best practices." *Social Policy Report* 27 (4). http://www.srcd.org/sites/default/files/documents/E-News/spr_27_4.pdf.

McDaniel, T. n.d. "An overview of the Korean education system (additional notes)." http://www.greenriver.edu/Documents/about-grcc/teaching-and-learning-center/Teaching-international-students/korea-education-system.pdf.

Mechelli, A., J. T. Crinion, U. Noppeney, J. O'Doherty, J. Ashburner, R. S. Frackowiak, and C. J. Price. 2004. "Neurolinguistics: Structural plasticity in the bilingual brain." *Nature* 431 (7010): 757–757. http://dx.doi.org/10.1038/431757a.

Met, M. n.d. *When should foreign language learning begin?* College Park, MD: National Foreign Languages Center. http://www.celebratelanguages.com/PDFEduDocuments/EarlyLanguageLearning.pdf.

Nash, J. M. 1997. "Special report: Fertile minds." *Time* 149 (5).

Olsen, D., and L. Snell. 2006. "Assessing proposals for preschool and kindergarten: Essential information for parents, taxpayers and policymakers." Reason Foundation, May 1. http://reason.org/news/show/assessing-proposals-for-presch.

Paradis, J. 2010. "The interface between bilingual development and specific language impairment." *Applied Psycholinguistics* 31 (2): 227–252. http://dx.doi.org/10.1017/S0142716409990373.

Paradis, J., M. Crago, F. Genesee, and M. Rice. 2003. "French-English bilingual children with SLI: How do they compare with their monolingual peers?" *Journal of Speech, Language, and Hearing Research* 46 (1): 113–127.

Paradis, J., F. Genesee, and M. Crago. 2011. *Dual language development and disorders: A handbook on bilingualism and second language learning.* Baltimore, Maryland: Paul H. Brookes Publishing Co.

Pearson, B. Z. 2009. "What parents need to know about being and becoming bilingual (And what their child care center needs to help them know)." Lecture conducted February 19 at the Yeled v'Yalda Research Institute, Brooklyn NY. http://www.umass.edu/aae/YeledvYalda0219.pdf.

Pearson, B. Z., S. C. Fernandez, and D. K. Oller. 1993. "Lexical development in bilingual infants and toddlers: Comparison to monolingual norms." *Language Learning* 43 (1): 93–120. http://dx.doi.org/10.1111/j.1467-1770.1993.tb00174.x.

Pearson, B. Z., S. C. Fernández, V. Lewedeg, and D. K. Oller. 1997. "The relation of input factors to lexical learning by bilingual infants." *Applied Psycholinguistics* 18 (01): 41–58. http://dx.doi.org/10.1017/S0142716400009863.

Petersen, J., S. Marinova-Todd, and P. Mirenda. 2012. "Brief report: An exploratory study of lexical skills in bilingual children with autism spectrum disorder." *Journal of Autism and Developmental Disorders* 42 (7): 1499–1503. http://dx.doi.org/10.1007/s10803-011-1366-y.

Pinker, S. 1994. *The language instinct: The new science of language and mind.* London, England: Penguin UK.

Polk, A. 2012. "Paving the way for groundbreaking research in bilingualism." *Gallaudet Today*, Spring. http://oes.gallaudet.edu/bl2/.

Potowski, K. 2013. "No child left monolingual." *TEDx*. Lecture conducted in May at University of Illinois-Chicago, Chicago, IL. http://www.youtube.com/watch?v=pSs1uCnLbaQ.

Protzko, J., J. Aronson, and C. Blair. 2013. "How to Make a Young Child Smarter: Evidence From the Database of Raising Intelligence." *Perspectives on Psychological Science* 8 (1): 25–40. http://dx.doi.org/10.1177/1745691612462585.

R. B. 2014. "Dyslexia in Chinese: Disability of a different character." *The Economist*, September 8. http://www.economist.com/blogs/analects/2014/09/dyslexia-chinese.

Ruuskanen, D., and A. Gupta. n.d. "Ask a linguist FAQ." *The Linguist List*. http://linguistlist.org/ask-ling/biling.cfm.

Schiff-Myers, N. 1988. "Hearing children of deaf parents." In *Language development in exceptional circumstances*, edited by D. Bishop and K. Mogford, 47–61. Edinburgh, Scotland: Churchill Livingstone.

Seal, K. 2010. "Asian-American parenting and academic success." *Pacific Standard*, December 13. http://www.psmag.com/navigation/books-and-culture/asian-american-parenting-and-academic-success-26053/.

"Second-language acquisition." n.d. *Wikipedia*. http://en.wikipedia.org/wiki/Second-language_acquisition.

Sharma, Y. 2013. "Asia's parents suffering 'education fever.'" *BBC News*, October 22. http://www.bbc.com/news/business-24537487.

Singleton, D. M., and L. Ryan. 2004. *Language acquisition: The age factor*, 2nd ed. Bristol, England: Multilingual Matters.

Singleton, J., and M. Tittle. 2000. "Deaf parents and their hearing children." *Journal of Deaf Studies and Deaf Education* 5 (3): 225. http://dx.doi.org/10.1093/deafed/5.3.221.

Spinks, S. 2002. "The first years fallacy." In *Inside the Teenage Brain*, produced by S. Spinks, January 31. Washington, DC: PBS Frontline. http://www.pbs.org/wgbh/pages/frontline/shows/teenbrain/science/firstyears.html.

Steiner, N. 2008. *7 Steps to Raising a Bilingual Child.* New York, NY: Amacom.

Stipek, D., R. Feiler, D. Daniels, and S. Milburn. 1995. "Effects of different instructional approaches on young children's achievement and motivation." *Child Development* 66 (1): 209–223. http://dx.doi.org/10.2307/1131201.

Suggate, S. P., E. A. Schaughency, and E. Reese. 2013. "Children learning to read later catch up to children reading earlier." *Early Childhood Research Quarterly* 28 (1): 33–48. http://dx.doi.org/10.1016/j.ecresq.2012.04.004.

Teeter, C. 1998. "Language Acquisition and Subtractive Bilingualism." Eastern European Adoption Coalition, Inc. http://www.eeadopt.org/articles-mainmenu-76/76-schooling/98-language-acquisition-and-subtractive-bilingualism.html.

Tillis, P. 2013. "Poor little tiger cub." *Slate*, May 8. http://www.slate.com/articles/double_x/doublex/2013/05/_tiger_mom_study_shows_the_parenting_method_doesn_t_work.html.

Ventureyra, V. A., C. Pallier, and H. Y. Yoo. 2004. "The loss of first language phonetic perception in adopted Koreans." *Journal of Neurolinguistics* 17 (1): 79–91. http://dx.doi.org/10.1016/S0911-6044(03)00053-8.

Vos, J. n.d. "Can preschool children be taught a second language?" *Earlychildhood NEWS*. http://www.earlychildhoodnews.com/early-childhood/article_view.aspx?ArticleId=60.

Werker, J., and K. Byers-Heinlein. 2008. "Bilingualism in infancy: First steps in perception and comprehension." *Trends in Cognitive Science* 12: 144–151. http://dx.doi.org/10.1016/j.tics.2008.01.008.

Westman, M., M. Korkman, A. Mickos, and R. Byring. 2008. "Language profiles of monolingual and bilingual Finnish preschool children at risk for language impairment." *International Journal of Language & Communication Disorders* 43: 699–711. http://dx.doi.org/10.1080/13682820701839200.

Whitehurst, G. J. 2013. "Can We Be Hard-Headed About Preschool? A Look at Head Start." Brookings Institution/The Brown Center Chalkboard, January 16. http://www.brookings.edu/blogs/brown-center-chalkboard/posts/2013/01/16-preschool-whitehurst.

"World Languages for Toddlers, Preschool and Beyond..." 2012. *InlyInsights*, May 25. http://inlyinsights.org/2012/05/25/world-languages-for-toddlers-preschool-and-beyond/.

Yoshikawa, H., C. Weiland, J. Brooks-Gunn, M. R. Burchinal, L. M. Espinosa, W. T. Gormley and M. J. Zaslow. 2013. *Investing in our future: The evidence base on preschool education*. Ann Arbor, MI: Society for Research in Child Development and Foundation for Child Development. http://fcd-us.org/sites/default/files/Evidence%20Base%20on%20Preschool%20Education%20FINAL.pdf.

Zigler, E. F. 1987. "Formal schooling for four-year-olds? No." *American Psychologist* 42 (3): 254. http://dx.doi.org/10.1037//0003-066X.42.3.254.

CITATIONS

1. Hirsh-Pasek and Golinkoff, 2003, p. 67

2. Olsen and Snell, 2006

3. Whitehurst, 2013

4. Hill, Gormley, and Adelstein, 2012

5. Magnusun, Ruhm, and Waldfogel, 2004

6. Boocock, 1995

7. Magnusun et al., 2004; Yoshikawa et al., 2013; Karoly and Bigelow, 2005; Loeb, Bridges, Bassok, Fuller, and Rumberger, 2007; Olsen and Snell, 2006; Zigler, 1987

8. Bridges, Fuller, Rumberger, and Tran, 2004

9. Magnusun et al., 2004

10. Leak et al., 2010

11. Stipek, Feiler, Daniels, and Milburn, 1995

12. Hernandez, 2013

13. Anderson, 2011

14. Larsen and Robinson, 1989

15. Suggate, Schaughency, and Reese, 2013

16. Suggate, Schaughency, and Reese, 2013

17. Boocock, 1995

18. Lopata, Wallace, and Finn, 2005

19. Ahmad and Hamm, 2013

20. Guddemi, 2013

21. Loeb et al., 2007

22. Leak et al., 2010

23. Yoshikawa et al., 2013

24. Protzko et al., 2013

25. Loeb et al., 2007

26. Karoly and Bigelow, 2005

27. Elkind, 1987

28. Burke and Sheffield, 2013; Hackney, n.d.

29. Hoff, 2013a

30. Suggate et al., 2013

31. "Education," n.d.

32. Dalporto, n.d.

33. Chia, 2013

34. Dalporto, n.d.

35. Center in International Education Benchmarking, n.d.; McDaniel, n.d.

36. Sharma, 2013; Chakrabarti, 2013

37. Lien Foundation Project, 2013a; 2013b; 2013c

38. Sharma, 2013

39. Seal, 2010; Le, n.d.

40. Tillis, 2013; Kim, Wang, Orozco-Lapray, Shen, and Murtuza, 2013

41. Spinks, 2002

42. Pinker, 1994

43. Chomsky, 1967, p. 1

44. Bickerton, 1984; Calvin and Bickerton, 2001

45. Genesee, 2009; Werker and Byers-Heinlein, 2008

46. Kovelman, Baker, and Petitto, 2008

47. Kovelman et al., 2008

48. Hoff, 2009, p. 65; Johnson and Newport, 1989

49. Hoff, 2013b, p. 274

50. Abrahamsson and Hyltenstam, 2009

51. Hoff, 2013b, p. 274

52. Bialystok, 2001, p. 58; Caccavale, 2007; Dixon et al., 2012; Elkind, 1987, p. 148; Genesee, 2008, p. 20; Hermanto, Moreno, and Bialystok, 2012; Hernandez and Bates, 1999, p. 80; Hoff, 2013b, p. 286; Holman, 1998; L. Wang, personal communication, December 6, 2013; Long, 1990, p. 251; McCabe et al., 2013; Met, n.d.; Nash, 1997; Paradis, Genesee, and Crago, 2011; Ruuskanen and Gupta, n.d.; Singleton and Ryan, 2004, p. 62, 201; Ventureyra, Pallier, and Yoo, 2004, p. 90; Vos, n.d.; "World Languages," 2012

53. S. Curtiss, personal communication, December 2, 2013

54. Hernandez and Li, 2007; Hoff, 2009, p. 66; Hyltenstram and Abrahamson, 2000, p. 161; Long, 1990, p. 251; Marinova-Todd, Marshall, and Snow, 2000; Mechelli et al., 2004; Nash, 1997; "Second-language," n.d.; Steiner, 2008, p. 9

55. Hoff, 2013b, p. 286

56. Jia and Aaronson, 1998 ADD

57. Steiner, 2008, p. 9

58. Bruer, 2002, p. 142; Potowski, 2013; Vos, n.d.

59. "Critical Period Hypothesis," n.d.; Hoff, 2009, p. 67

60. MacSwan and Pray, 2005

61. Spinks, 2002

62. Kuhl et al., 2003

63. Hart and Risley, 1995

64. Moyer, 2013

65. Hoff, 2013

66. McCabe et al., 2013

67. Hoff, 2013a

68. Pearson et al., 1993

69. Schiff-Myers, 1988, p. 60; Singleton and Tittle, 2000

70. Hoff, 2013b

71. Kuhl et al., 2003

72. American Academy of Pediatrics, 2012

73. American Academy of Pediatrics, 2012

74. Massey, 2008, p. 144

75. Bates, 2012

76. McCabe et al., 2013

77. Pearson, 2009

78. Hoff, 2013a

79. List of languages, n.d.

80. Arab immigration, n.d.

81. Hathaway, 2014

82. Hoff, 2013a

83. Hoff, 2009

84. Kovelman, Baker, and Petitto, 2008

85. Kovelman, Baker, and Petitto, 2008

86. Lindholm-Leary, 2004; Kovelman, Baker, and Petitto, 2008; Thomas and Collier, 2002

87. Hoff, 2013

88. Polk, 2012, 6:28

89. Steiner, 2008

90. Bird et al., 2005; Gutierrez-Clellen, Simon-Cereijido, and Wagner, 2008; Paradis, 2010; Paradis, Genesee, and Crago, 2011; Paradis, Crago, Genesee, and Rice, 2003; Petersen, Marinova-Todd, and Mirenda, 2012; Westman, Korkman, Mickos, and Byring, 2008

91. Lowry, n.d.

92. R. B., 2014

93. Teeter, 1998

94. Bylund, 2009; Hoff, 2009, p. 311

95. Ventureyra, Pallier, and Yoo, 2004

96. Hakuta and August, 1997; Howard, Sugarman, and Christian, 2003

97. Cummins, 1979

98. Genesee, 2009

ACKNOWLEDGEMENTS

Many thanks to Helen San, my first and most insightful editor, who helped me connect some very important but overlooked dots, and to my family who put up with my many obsessive disappearances. Thanks also to Ling-Chi Wang, Jeannette Vos, Naomi Steiner, Hallie Stebbins, Steven Pinker, Erika Hoff, Kathy Hirsh-Pasek, Anthea Gupta, Marcy Guddemi, Roberta Golinkoff, Susan Curtiss, John Bruer, and Ellen Bialystok.

Printed in Great Britain
by Amazon